D1067277

FIELD GUIDE TO

# MYSTERIOUS PLACES

## OF EASTERN NORTH AMERICA

### SALVATORE M. TRENTO

AN OWL BOOK    HENRY HOLT AND COMPANY    NEW YORK

Henry Holt and Company, Inc.
*Publishers since 1866*
115 West 18th Street
New York, New York 10011

Henry Holt ® is a registered
trademark of Henry Holt and Company, Inc.

Copyright © 1997 by Salvatore Michael Trento
All rights reserved.
Published in Canada by Fitzhenry & Whiteside Ltd.,
195 Allstate Parkway, Markham, Ontario L3R 4T8.

Library of Congress Cataloging-in-Publication Data
Trento, Salvatore Michael.
Field guide to mysterious places of eastern North America /
Salvatore M. Trento.—1st ed.
p.   cm.
"An owl book."
Includes bibliographical references and index.
1. Northeastern States—Guidebooks.   2. Canada, Eastern—
Guidebooks.   3. Curiosities and wonders—Northeastern States—
Guidebooks. 4. Curiosities and wonders—Canada, Eastern—
Guidebooks. 5. Northeastern States—Antiquities—Guidebooks.
6. Canada, Eastern—Antiquities—Guidebooks.   I. Title.
F106.T83   1997                                          96–44299
917.4—dc21                                                CIP

ISBN 0–8050–4449–3

Henry Holt books are available for special promotions and
premiums. For details contact: Director, Special Markets.

First Edition—1997

Designed by Kate Nichols

Printed in the United States of America
All first editions are printed on acid-free paper. ∞

10   9   8   7   6   5   4   3   2   1

*Reason, or the ratio of all we have already
known, is not the same that it shall be when
we know more.*

*He who sees the Infinite in all things sees God.
He who sees the Ratio only sees himself only.*

—William Blake
*There is No Natural Religion* (1788)

# Contents

# A Note to the Reader

This collection of mysterious places is not a definitive atlas. There are far too many sites to list in one volume, so consider this book to be a sampling of the best that's out there. Due to the astonishing input from readers who have contacted me recently about weird sites in their vicinities, I've added a section called Further Investigations in Area for *some* areas of the east that details as much information about a site as possible. This listing means either that I have not yet visited the site or have not thoroughly examined a site in detail, so I can't be completely sure of its nature. In some cases I've gotten the lead in the field or while searching through historical archives, such as the ones in Yarmouth, Nova Scotia. Other times, someone sent a letter with a great photo of a ruin. I've listed the information because the lead seemed intriguing and full of tantalizing potential. But aside from the things that you actually can touch on a consistent basis, no guarantee is given for UFO sightings, ball lightening, or other events of seemingly altered perception.

Get out there and look at as much as you can! If you come across anything, send me a letter:

Sal Trento/Mysterious Places
c/o Henry Holt and Company, Inc.
115 West 18th Street
New York, New York 10011

# Acknowledgments

**M**y first and biggest thank you goes to James P. Whittall of the Early Sites Research Society. Ever since I bumped into Jim over twenty years ago in the woods of northern Westchester County, he's been a constant source of inspiration, awe, and knowledge. Jim is one of those rare individuals who questions everything. A dedicated field and archival researcher, he has surveyed, excavated, and catalogued more archeological sites than anyone in North America. He is the Source.

I send a collective thank you to all those people over the years who have written, faxed, and telephoned me about strange stone ruins in their backyards. Your kindness allowed me to enter a strange world of mystery.

Grateful acknowledgment is due to: the Java Hut in Cherry Creek, Denver, for those languid, late spring mornings of strong coffee, table space, and the chance to write for hours undisturbed; James Hatfield of Pleasant River, Nova Scotia, for interrupting his haying to chat all afternoon about weird sites in that province; Anne Marie White at *The Chronicle-Herald*, in Halifax, Nova Scotia, for making the acquisition of hard-to-find prints a breeze; Laura Bradley, archivist of the Yarmouth County Historical Society, for pulling out all those strange files from the back room; Walter Elliot, for detailed information on that intriguing "burial tomb" up in northeastern Maine and for his careful use of my photographic equipment. I owe you!; Rabbi Mark Lipson of Norwalk, Connecticut, and his brother Kevin Lipson of the Washington, D.C., firm Hogan and Hartson, for realizing my lack-of-planning plight one glorious July afternoon in Port Clyde, Maine. Their twenty-five-foot Proline got me to Monhegan Island in around forty minutes! Such graciousness is far too infrequent these days. A 1,001 thanks for the trip, the laughs, and the experience, guys. May Neptune keep watch over the two of you and your boat; Bob and Dennis Stone, and the gang at Mystery Hill— America's Stonehenge—for opening doors there and allowing me to take a host of measurements. Dennis was kind enough to share the preliminary results of several intriguing excavations at the Hill. Keep up the good work, guys!; David and Pat Barron, for extending hospitality on short notice and for taking me on a mysteriously intriguing tour of the Gungywamp, as they had so many years before. And for planting the idea of writing another book one boozy evening. How can I repay you for that one?; Joyce, Henry, and Sam Dane, my longtime friends who live and breathe Cape Cod every moment of their lives. Joyce, your interest in this project and your tireless efforts to get me sources makes me giddy. Henry and Sam, may the gods give your sails good wind and another silver trophy!; my old friend Pat Clyne, for those early leads on mysterious places; Kathy O'Neil, for access to her strange stone chamber and for that great literature on it; Jay Mahoney, for helping in so many ways with his vast knowledge of mystery minerals. And to Meg Phillpot, for providing stability and clarity during those wonderful autumn days; Phil Hickey, Tony Gerlicz, and Jeanie Hoover, for taking the time to read and comment on an early draft of this book; Hayden Hirschfeld, for listening, commenting, and photographing ancient sites during those early days of exploration, and for participating in the Bermudan ritual of Wilde Hogg quaffing; Buzz, Nancy, and Katy Neusteter, for information about and access to their wonderful mud concretion collection; Michelle Davis, Jonathan Jerald, Lindsey Paddor, Steve Abramson, and Steve Feld of Paramount Studios, for arranging early video shoots of the sites; Jim Pruett of Pruett Publishing in Boulder, Colorado, for initially taking a chance on an odd project, and for all his expert advice and suggestions thereafter; *The Chronicle-Herald* and *The Mail-Star*, Halifax, for permission to reprint their photograph of the Mount Hanley stone; Cassandra Leoncini, my agent, friend, and sounding board. You never give up!; Bryan Oettel, editor, and the rest of the gang at Henry Holt who made this project a breeze; my wonderful mom and dad, who know no limits in their love and understanding; Reane and Sarah: It was a summer without Daddy, but one that you can read about over and over as you grow up; and, finally, to my wife, Leslie, who supported this project over the years with her editorial, managerial, and loving help. This series of field guides could not have been done without you.

# FIELD GUIDE TO
# MYSTERIOUS PLACES OF
# EASTERN NORTH AMERICA

# Introduction

This book is the second in a series dedicated to mapping out mysterious places. The first, *A Field Guide to Mysterious Places of the West*, focused on strange archeological and geological sites of the Rocky Mountain region.

*A Field Guide to Mysterious Places of Eastern North America* takes a broader view and examines anomalies in northeastern America and along the coast where unusual sites abound.

The goals of this book remain the same: to detail why a site is peculiar, to map out how to get to it, and to describe all available information concerning it.

Unusual sites exist throughout the world. On the island of Minorca, in the western Mediterranean, for example, there exists a carved stairwell that spirals down 150 feet into the limestone bedrock. Archeologists are at a loss to say anything about the origins of this unusual structure, as it's the only known example in the world. Local farmers, however, tell a different story: They claim it was carved by flesh-eating giants. Popular legend described the site as an enormous cavern carved into the bare rock face by giants. The well water supposedly was used for religious services. At midnight a servant girl would descend the stairs, returning with a basin of water to quench the blood thirst of the feasting creatures. The water also insured immortality, it was claimed.

In China's Xinjiang Uygur Autonomous Region is the notorious "Devil Valley," a lush, sixty-mile-long valley, that peasants in the region have feared for centuries. People who entered the valley and survived reported freak lightning storms that caused trees and even people to burst into flames. The area, the subject of great myth, seemingly was cursed. Why? In the last few years,

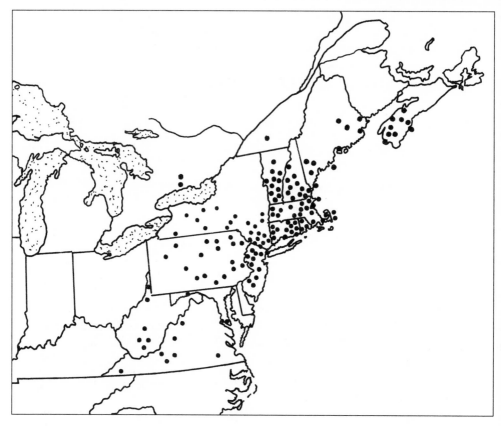

*Mysterious Sites in the eastern North America (unless otherwise noted all maps are drawn with north at the top of the page)*

geologists from Qinghai Province have conducted a survey of the valley and have provided some of the answers. The valley contains vast quantities of magnetized basalt that erupted from ancient volcanoes over 240 million years ago. Electrical charges in clouds passing over the valley are attracted to the basalt's magnetic fields, hence the frequent storms. People who get in the way are zapped out of existence.

Along the eastern coast of the United States, scattered throughout the hills and valleys of this densely populated area are stone ruins unlike anything ever found anywhere else. The existence of these ancient constructions has confounded and delighted people for centuries.

In the early seventeenth century a settler from western Massachusetts wrote asking the governor of Connecticut for more information about a "strange stone fort" in the region of southern Connecticut. The governor never responded. In the 1970s, amateur archeologists were convinced that structures found near Long Island Sound were evidence of ancient Old World contact in pre-Columbian America. Professional archeologists laughed all the way to the conference hall, for it was assumed the ruins were built sometime in the 1700s, merely the handiwork of ingenious Yankee settlers. Of course, the *purpose* of these stone ruins was never adequately explained, and the amateurs kept coming up with some pretty amazing prehistoric radiocarbon dates for organic material associated with the ruins.

It is not the purpose of this field guide to promote arguments over who did what. I'm not interested in garnering academic points or stroking egos. While there seem to be echoes of pre-Columbian contact with the Americas, this book will not champion one group of possibilities to the exclusion of another, be they Phoenicians, Egyptians, extraterrestials, or Colonial farmers.

There are several possible explanations for the origins of the enormous number of stone structures to be found throughout the Northeast and elsewhere.

- The ruins are the product of an ancient native American people.
- The ruins are the handiwork of a people who sailed to the New World many years before Columbus.
- The ruins are the product of the first ingenious Colonial-period settlers who utilized large blocks of stone for reasons as yet unknown.

Any one of these theories provokes controversy and mystery. That's what makes the stonework so intriguing. It evokes passionate responses from visitors.

When one travels the primary roads of America, it is astonishing how similar everything looks. The advent of strip malls has homogenized much of the landscape, creating a look that is unique to the latter part of the twentieth century.

While it may seem incongruous that antiquity could exist within a softball's throw of any densely populated area, the fact is that it does. Not everything has been paved over . . . yet. What is even more astonishing is how few people know what's in their backyards. People today have a relationship with the land that is completely different from that of earlier times. Most city dwellers either have difficulty finding opportunities to truly engage nature, or they simply prefer to avoid it. Aside from the dedicated nature walker, adventurous teenager, or the occasional autumn hunter, people rarely venture off the marked trail; some never walk into the woods at all, preferring to view nature from a towering, air-conditioned four-wheel drive vehicle.

This peculiar behavior has allowed the landscape to maintain its unusual collection of weird places. Avoidance of the unpaved road or trail, coupled with the fact that America is still a relatively young country, makes it possible to seek out, detail, and experience strange sites untrammeled by many people.

Recent research into geomagnetic energy provides some intriguing clues as to why some of these mysterious places in America and elsewhere provoke unsettling feelings.

Our planet is surrounded by a gigantic electromagnetic field that emanates from its core. This geomagnetic field is what makes a compass needle point north, and it's also the vast "belt" that deflects radiation from space. This energy field, however, is not uniform across the planet. There are variations across land masses due to the conductivity of the soil, the amount of magnetized rock in the crust, deep faults within the earth, the density of mountain ranges, and the relative thinness of the ocean floor. Solar radiation bursts, the type that peak every eleven years or so producing sunspots can also affect the power and distribution of this massive magnetic field.

For years scientists have known that many animals—from birds to bacteria—can sense tiny variations in the earth's geomagnetism. Migratory birds navigate by means of subtle clues in the sun's position and by detecting minor changes in the earth's magnetic pull. It is possible that people can also detect these slight variations. The anecdotes abound, particularly with respect to dowsing, or "water witching." A dowser walks over a tract of ground and "senses" where to dig a well. Although the technique has aroused controversy, could it be that these people, however small in number, have the ability to detect slight geomagnetic aberrations—discrepancies where water or underground fault systems cause the field to deviate? Perhaps.

We are electrical beings living on a vast magnetic sphere. We have electrochemical energy coursing through every cell in our bodies. As health researcher Ross Adley has stated: "Everything on earth has evolved in weak natural electromagnetic fields that oscillate at very low frequencies . . . We are bathed in them from conception to death. The fields come from some very esoteric sources such as a belt of continuous electrical thunderstorms in Central Africa and the Amazon basin, or sunspot cycles."[1]

It is possible that our pineal gland (a cone-shaped organ, located deep within the brain's cerebrum, near the thalamus), ". . . which regulates behavioral cycles by producing tides of neurochemicals in response to light signals, can also detect changes in electromagnetic fields."[2] It has been shown "that applying a magnetic field . . . , oriented so as to add or subtract from the earth's normal field, will increase or decrease production of pineal melatonin and serotonin."[3] These two hormones affect not only the body's cycles, like sleeping and waking, but also one's mood. For example, it has been found that darkness produces increased melatonin secretion, and calm, relaxed, introspective behavior; light produces a decrease in melatonin and increased alertness. Changes in the total magnetic field can also create this effect. The problem with geomagnetism, however, is that the data is not consistent for the *specific* type of aberration and the effect on neurotransmitter secretion. Does a high to low total magnetic field produce lower secretion rates or higher secretion rates? At the moment, all we can say is that geomagnetism definitely affects the metabolism and production level of a variety of human brain neurotransmitters.

Over the last thirty years, a host of scientific papers have reported on the connection between geomagnetic aberrations and their effects on the human body. A Czechoslovakian study in 1962, for instance, first showed that during periods of geomagnetic disturbances (due to periodic solar flares interacting with the earth's magnetic field) fewer women than usual menstruate. Conversely, during those periods of geomagnetic calm, more women than usual menstruate.[4] A Montreal hospital noted a significant association between violent, excited behavior in a psychiatric ward and disorder in the earth's magnetic field.[5] A German study of 40,000 patients found a similar pattern between emotional disturbances, suicide attempts, and geomagnetic fluctuations.[6] A follow-up study of approximately 29,000 patients in New York State over a four-year period showed that same relationship.[7] These and other detailed studies clearly show that geomagnetic aberrations affect people's behavior and hormonal rhythms in astonishing ways.[8]

In the mid 1980s, Dr. Robert Becker, a pioneer in the field of research on bone regeneration, astonished the scientific community with his provocative book *The Body Electric*. Among the many detailed studies of the effects of electrical currents on living things, Dr. Becker cited dozens of peer-reviewed studies on magnetic field aberrations affecting humans and animals. It was also found that over twenty-seven different species of birds and other animals had body tissue that ". . . contained yellow crystals of the iron-storage protein ferritin . . ."[9] Translation? These creatures were synthesizing their own cellular magnets!

When scientists examined human tissue, they found the same type of ". . . magnetic deposits close to the pineal and pituitary glands in the sinuses of the . . . ethmoid bone, the spongy bone in the center of the head behind the nose and between the eyes."[10]

The pineal gland in conjunction with tiny "magnetic crystals" found in all of us may be partly responsible for detecting the electromagnetic fluctuations that often are found at mysterious sites.

Perhaps the ancients were more attuned to the emissions from mysterious places—be they electrogeomagnetical anomalies or otherwise—than we are today. If recent findings on the pineal gland and other neurological input experiments are correct, there's good reason to believe they probably built sacred places in areas of extreme fluctuation. Consider the fact that from the very start of life on our planet over 3.5 billion years ago, ". . . the earth's average magnetic field had a frequency of one to twenty hertz. [A hertz is a unit of frequency of one cycle or vibration per second. When a wave goes by, from peak to peak, it has gone through one cycle.] Today, America's electrical-power delivery system has a sixty-hertz frequency—something that never existed on the planet until this century."[11]

Is there any wonder why most of us who live in or near cities never experience the subtler energy fields produced by nature when we are awash in an enormous, artificially induced electrical barrier of our own design? We've become callused to the earth's call.

But many people, when they step out into those natural fields, away from the pulse of the city, come alive with emotion and sensation. Some even feel altered levels of perception. Perhaps this interplay of our biology and the earth is a partial explanation for the lore of mysterious sites.

Come along with me on an adventure into strange, weird, and unusual places, some of which are far removed from the masking effects of our civilization. I can almost guarantee you will find much that is fascinating. You may even experience their magic in ways that will affect you forever.

# ONE

# History and Background

S ome of the mysterious sites detailed in this book and in my earlier *A Field
Guide to Mysterious Places of the West* hint that in ancient times people were
sailing all over the world—how else to explain a stone with Hebraic script
from the second century A.D. found at the base of an Indian mound in
Tennessee? Or four hundred stones found in the Delaware River inscribed
with an early version of Punic, the writing of the Phoenicians? Or the strange
events leading up to Columbus's westerly voyage? Without getting too
wrapped up in this three-hundred-year-old controversy, I offer the following
brief sketch of a possible worldwide maritime tradition that could reach back
many thousands of years.

## ANCIENT SAILORS?

The further back in time we go the less sure archeologists are about cultural
origins. But there is a paradigm implicit to twentieth-century thought on such
matters: that civilizations slowly arose through time in a linear progression,
from a "primitive" to a more advanced state. This mental construct was radically challenged a few years ago in Egypt, where one of the most sophisticated
ancient cultures ever to exist came to light along the Upper Nile valley.

In the late 1980s, two researchers expertly pointed out that the Sphinx,
long thought to be a monument built around 2565 B.C., was much more ancient. The scientists claimed that the erosion patterns in the Sphinx base were
caused by heavy rainfall—not by desert wind and blowing sand. The last time
there was rainfall of any significance in Egypt was close to ten thousand years

ago! If these researchers are correct in their geological analysis, then the evidence could suggest the Sphinx was built by some unknown and unrecognized culture at a time when our ancestors, based on traditional dogma, should not have known how to cut and transport massive blocks of stone. Presently, Egyptologists scoff at this mysterious civilization idea, while some geologists look at the rocks and say it must be so.

In much the same way, there is a curious void in our knowledge about prehistoric seagoing peoples. For instance, we know that crafts must have been used to reach the island of Malta in the central Mediterranean, because we find some of the oldest megalithic (large stone) monuments there (close to six thousand years old). However, no such vessels have survived the centuries, no doubt due to their perishable wood construction. Similarly, along the coast of western Europe we find five-thousand-year-old megalithic communal tombs that are indicative of very old communication and trade via the sea; yet we find no boats.

An examination of a number of ancient Greek and Roman writers, from Herodotus in 480 B.C. to Plutarch in 70 A.D. to Proclus in 440 A.D. points out two remarkably consistent themes:

1. An early group of sailors discovered islands somewhere beyond the Straits of Gibraltar in the western Mediterranean

and

2. The islands had navigable rivers.

These astonishing themes suggest to some that a sophisticated maritime tradition existed *years* before the classical geographers recorded their stories. This *could* be the case, for west of Africa no islands with navigable rivers are encountered until Haiti, Cuba, and the Americas. This important point takes on additional significance when we learn that Christopher Columbus guided his ships, with the aid of sea charts depicting islands, into this very part of the Caribbean. Could Columbus have known, in fact, where he was going?

## ANCIENT KNOWLEDGE?

On Friday, October 12, 1492, seventy days after leaving the port of Palos, Spain, Admiral Christopher Columbus and a crew of ninety men landed on San Salvador Island in the Bahamas and said hello to India. Traditional history tells us that the Genoese mariner at first thought the sandy beach was India, land of silk, spices, dazzling palaces, and bejeweled maharajas. And what did he present to the wealthy Asians to gain their respect? Worthless glass trinkets and colored cloth. He dipped into his ship's coffers and produced beads, bells, and bangles—awfully strange currency to bring to the relatively sophisticated people of the Far East, known to European merchants since the thirteenth century. Glass beads were a perfect choice to dazzle the natives on San Salvador Island, but it would seem that an intriguing sense of resourcefulness was responsible for taking these trinkets on board "to charm into Christian ways the simple heathen."

Columbus was a visionary who worked in mysterious ways. Ever since his logbook became available for public reading almost four hundred years ago, controversy has raged over whether he knew where he was going. Throughout the years, skeptical scholars have poured over the admiral's notes, searching for telltale scribblings in book margins and on supply sheets that might support this theory. But only recently have certain details of the mariner's entries become meaningful. Similarly, his prevoyage conversations, travels, and sailings all suggest that Christopher Columbus may have obtained information, by way of maps and eyewitness accounts, of a land mass west of the Portuguese Azores. It was land he might have known was neither India nor the China of Marco Polo. In fact, it is possible that Columbus was only the most recent practitioner of a maritime tradition that may have extended back thousands of years.

Interestingly, for centuries, both in Europe and Central America there were stories relating to "white gods" and "sailing saints." It told of a Great White God who came among the Indians' forefathers, ministered for a while, and then left vowing to return. The legend had been preserved down through generations of Indians from Chile to Alaska, and had likewise been persistent especially among the Polynesians from Hawaii to New Zealand. Although the traditions differed in name and minor details from island to island and from country to country, the overall outline remained essentially the same.

This god was known as Quetzalcoatl in parts of Mexico, primarily in the Cholula area. He was Votan in Cipas and Wixepechocha in Caxas, Gucumatz in Guatemala, Viracocha and Hyustus in Peru, Sume in Brazil, and Bochica in Colombia. To the Peruvians, he was also known as Contici or Illa-Tici, tici meaning both "creator" and "the light." To the Mayans he was principally known as Kukulcan. In the Polynesian Islands he was Lono, Kana, Kane, or Kon, and sometimes Kanaloa, the Great Light or Great Brightness. He also was known as Kane-Akea, the Great Progenitor, or Tongaroa, the God of the Ocean Sun.

The enormous geographical range of the white god legend should give us pause. To believe, as some scholars do, that the legend is merely the result of an initial story being diffused upriver via the wanderings of Indian tribes repeating the mythical tale to other tribes over generations is stretching a rational explanation. Would this one legend have the greatest distribution of all American Indian myths if there were not some truth to it? Of course it is possible that all the various traditions reflect an ancient memory of the intrepid sailor(s) blown off course.

It seems that *if* Christopher Columbus, during his twenty-year search, had found the documents on charts that pointed the way to the Western Hemisphere and elsewhere, then the admiral, although a great sailor and exquisite navigator in his own right, was merely a pupil of a skilled sailing people thousands of years removed from us. If so, could we be looking at the remains of some of their mysteries? If not, we are still vexed with the problems of *who* built these structures and for what purpose. And the question of whether there were special factors that determined where some of them were erected.

# T W O

# Mysterious Places:
# Overview

When we speak of mysterious sites, what exactly do we mean? Mysterious places come in many forms. Some locales have a strange feeling associated with them, and unusual events happen there. Other places have tangible rocks and ruins to look at and touch that might be the remnants of a long gone culture, of a people from another time. As you search for and find these peculiar sites, always remember to look beyond the present and into the past.

If geomagnetic flux actually had more of an influence on behavior in ancient times due to the lack of artificial masking electromagnetic patterns, then it is important to begin measuring the total magnetic field associated with specific sites and the surrounding region. We can pose the questions rather simply: Is there a geomagnetic aberration or radical change associated with mysterious sites compared to the surrounding vicinity? And, if so, did this change in geomagnetism influence the placement of the sites? The first question can be answered with actual field measurements—climb around the sites and take readings. The second question necessitates rigorous laboratory studies under controlled circumstances. But the little research conducted so far by endocrinologists, physiologists, and others suggests this may be an interesting area of inquiry.

Most of us are aware that the earth has its own magnetic field. A compass needle, for example, is itself a magnet and when placed in the earth's magnetic field it points toward the north magnetic pole, which presently nearly coincides very nicely with the north geographical pole. The compass needle points north because of the effect of the earth's field on the needle. It pushes, or aligns the needle along the magnetic field pathway in which the needle rotates.

A compass, however, provides only directional information. A magnetometer, a sophisticated, highly accurate instrument that can detect a wide range of milligauss (a unit of magnetism measurement), can measure both direction and magnitude of the earth's magnetic field. Out in the field I took readings with a handheld digital magnetometer.

Measurements were taken by finding the horizontal (H) and vertical (V) fields in and around a site with the magnetometer. From these measurements the total magnetic field (TMF) for a particular place was determined. The inclination angle (IA) that the total magnetic field makes with the surface of the earth also was calculated. The inclination angle refers to the actual angle the magnetic field makes with the earth's surface as the field radiates up from the crust.[1]

I've listed some preliminary measurements and their possible meanings under the section category of Total Magnetic Field/Inclination Angle. I make no claims to have done a comprehensive analysis of all sites. I'm merely providing hints that might help explain the currently unexplainable.

Nonetheless, results indicate that there are some geomagnetic fluctuations at key sites. In other words, in most cases an area surrounding a site had standard total magnetic field readings and inclination angles. Measuring progressively closer to a given site led to radical changes in the total magnetic field and inclination angle! Clearly there was a difference, no doubt due to deep rock fissures within the crust. Now, was that difference responsible for the placement of the inscription, stone pile, chamber, or ruin? Did the change in the earth's geomagnetic field make people feel special at certain places? Did it make those places sacred?

The suspicion is that some areas of the planet are geomagnetic hotspots. That is, the geomagnetic vectors emanating from the earth's interior, for whatever geological reason, are in disarray. The ancients made these places sacred no doubt because they *felt* differently there.

How one reacts to a geomagnetic hotspot or a sacred site depends on what cultural trappings the feeling is filtered through. If you grew up in a culture that sees spirits in all things, then the unusual sensations experienced in some chamber or mountaintop could be interpreted as spiritual enlightenment. If you are convinced that Satan is out to get you and your Puritan neighbors, then you experience demons at these places. Throughout this book there are sites that appear to be located on specific spots of extreme geomagnetic fluctuation. I suspect that they were placed there deliberately to take advantage of an altered state of mind. How you experience these sites will depend on your own particular sensitivities and cultural perceptions.

The following summarizes a few categories of strange archeological and geological sites.

## STONE PILES

Stone piles (also called cairns, heaps, and stone mounds) were recorded by the earliest white settlers. The first surveyors used them as reference stations, while Colonial farmers found the piles very convenient as a source of building stone. The heaps have been reported throughout North America.

Stone piles come in many shapes and sizes. Some are as large as 60 feet in diameter and 8 feet in height, while others are little more than 2 feet by 2 feet. There is good indication that smaller American cairns are merely the result of Colonial field clearance. In the early 1700s, farmers used ox-driven wooden platforms to collect and stack miscellaneous rocks; these stones were dumped at the edges of their properties so that they could be used later to build property walls. Many of the smaller heaps are found near such boundaries. The larger piles, however, are more difficult to explain.

There is endless speculation over the origin and function of these large piles. James Adair, whose *History of the American Indians* appeared in 1775, felt that the Indians "raised those heaps merely to do honor to their dead, and incite the living to the pursuit of virtue."[2] Earlier books all mentioned passing Indians throwing rocks onto existing piles. And even Washington Irving, high above the Hudson River at his dreamy Sunnyside Estate, told a similar story in a fanciful essay entitled "Traits of the Indian Character."

Inevitably, as more people took to the forest, other explanations arose. Richard Smith, writing of the New Jersey Indians in the eighteenth century, noted that "to know their walks again, in infrequent woods, they heaped stones or marked trees."[3]

Explanations changed with time. A newspaper account from the 1920s spoke of Indians crouching behind the piles to site various horizon points where water was to be found. Property owners often assured early investigators that the piles were of recent origin, reciting family stories that told of country doctors erecting the stones as animal lookouts and band platforms. Aging mountain men spoke of mentally challenged neighbors who repeatedly heaped stones, knocked them down, and piled them up again. Deer hunters said the old loggers piled them up, while rangers claimed the charcoal burners of the last century erected them. That some piles were revered and were added to by Indian tribes has been confirmed finally by modern anthropological work, but the ethnographic data still has not explained the origin and meaning of the custom.

One of the more striking features about stone piles is the great amount of care that went into their construction. Specific stones were selected, chinked, and laid into place at an angle sloping toward the center. Evidently, in many cases, the builders took great pains to keep the piles from toppling, for they frequently placed them on top of flat boulders, regardless of the soil condition. (A base rock acts as a platform that prevents piled stones from sinking into the ground and falling over.)

In the late 1880s, the Smithsonian Institution excavated a mound on a farm near Patterson, North Carolina, and was surprised to discover several skeletons and stone piles that had been simultaneously buried. The cairns accompanying the skeletons seemed to confirm age-old legends about the sites being repositories for the dead. One might assume that archeologists would have flocked to other stone pile sites en masse since such obvious burial markers were rarely found. Yet more than fifty years elapsed before any professional team took on the problem; when they did, they discovered that only the odd cairn was a burial site. Almost all the others were simply heaps of stone, totally mysterious and without explanation. Archeological interest rapidly faded as the problem was brushed aside and efforts were invested in sites with a far grander allure, like the cliff dwelling cities of the Southwest.

Stone piles can be categorized into three rather simple schemes:

1. **Small.** Size varies from 3-by-10 foot *conical piles* to randomly placed 2-by-3-foot *heaps of stone*. They are found most often on old Indian trails. Conical Piles:
   - Are usually erected on large-surface boulders.
   - Occur in clusters, ranging from ten to several dozen.
   - Are located so water source—stream, river, swamp or lake—is always nearby.
   - Are usually found at the upward slope, on the east side of hills and small mountains.
2. **Medium.** Oval in shape with heights ranging from 2 to 4 feet. Inexplicably, the long axis of the mounds runs east-west in the New England states and north-south in the southern New York region. Length varies from 10 to 30 feet, and width ranges from 10 to 20 feet.
3. **Large.** Usually great circles of rocks and small boulders of varying sizes. Diameters range from 20 to 60 feet, with heights varying from 3 to 8 feet at the center. Usually found on top of high ridges.

Stone piles very often have mysteriously large stone walls nearby. Researchers from Illinois, Tennessee, and West Virginia report that some of these walls are 30 feet wide, 6 feet high and, sometimes, miles in length! These cairn-wall sites also share common characteristics: They are of dry stone construction, and they're usually situated on high bluffs.

It seems clear that different types of stone piles served different purposes. And yet, no one has adequately explained exactly who erected the North American stone piles and what they mean.

## TUNNELS/SHAFTS/CAVES

There are many complex underground tunnels, shafts, and mining pits found throughout North America and elsewhere. Locations range from central Massachusetts to the Ohio Valley and beyond. Some are long tunnels constructed into the base of hillsides, while others were built sixteen feet below ground level.

Many of the islands flanking the eastern coast of America are associated with tales of hidden treasure, dating to the pirate threats of the sixteenth century. Could pirates have constructed them? On Oak Island just off Nova Scotia is one of the most bizarre shaft and tunnel systems ever found. For well over two hundred years researchers have been trying to figure out who built it, when and how it was dug, and why. The sophistication and complexity of this very mysterious site lead some to conclude that untold riches lie somewhere in the labyrinth of shafts.

In northern Michigan and on Isle Royale in Lake Superior are thousands of worked copper mines that were discovered in the early 1500s by French Jesuit missionaries who reported that the local Indians knew nothing of their origin. We now know there was good reason for the tribes people not to have known anything about the miners. Recent carbon dating of the mine debris places their excavation back almost 4,000 years.

Coupled to this incredible date is the astonishing amount of copper excavated. Metallurigical engineers estimate that over 500,000 tons of copper were removed from the region! To the present that quantity of almost pure ore has never been found in the Americas.

The remnants of copper-ore mining can be found in other parts of the Americas. Along a trail skirting the western slope of a mountain ridge in northern New Jersey and southern New York State, for example, are a series of exploratory tunnels. A low-grade conglomerate of copper ore permeates the ridgeway. Scientists are at a loss to say who cut the tunnels, but all indications are that they were carved in prehistoric times.

These mining pits continue to plague rationally minded people who trek up to Isle Royale and elsewhere to see them. Who dug out the copper, and where did it go? Some scholars have argued that New World copper was mined thousands of years ago by Phoenicians for extensive shipment to various Mediterranean civilizations such as Egypt, a country that required a lot of copper saws and tools for cutting, shaping and building with limestone blocks. Other scientists claim that the mined copper ore merely has not been excavated yet in America. They believe it lies underground somewhere in this country.

No matter what, the antiquity of the mines is real, and we haven't a clue as to who scooped out the ore. The many unanswered questions regarding these strange places spark the imagination.

## STANDING STONES / PERCHED ROCKS

On cliffs high above the rivers of many western and eastern states are arrangements of standing stones and curious configurations of boulders balanced on top of smaller stones. The standing stones are the remnants of a concerted effort by people to position stones in a particular way. Some of the tall stones are isolated markers of some type, while others appear in clusters, usually in the form of circles.

The perched or balanced rocks present a problem when it comes to origin. While some clearly were placed by people, most can be traced back to the end of the last Ice Age some 12,000 years ago, when large melting glaciers released assorted debris. Some of the rocks that tumbled from the ice plopped on top of other rocks and were covered with mud. Years of wind and water erosion removed the soil and revealed, in some cases, precariously balanced boulders. But it's not the origin of these stones that is important here; it's *how* they were used by the early cultures of America. There are countless stories and tales about how some balanced rock or boulder was considered sacred by an indigenous group. As you travel the country and seek out these odd geological formations, the story is always the same: The site was revered by Indians. Why?

The axes of many balanced boulders and stone circle sites are sometimes oriented toward the position on the local horizon where the sun sets at key times of the year. Careful observation of the stones' features hint at possible astronomical functions. The positions of nearby cairns and curiously marked rock slabs give one the distinct feeling that something more than nature's playful hand has been at work. In fact, some of these sites give the impression of being the vestiges of an ancient solar calendar system, that is, the sun rises or sets in alignment with these stones. Such stone markers that track the sun's yearly position, for example, are well known at ancient Anazazi Indian sites in the American Southwest.

In southern New York, western Connecticut, and central Vermont there are reports of similar arrangements of placed boulders: stones protruding out of the ground with a clear view of the equinox sunrises and sunsets; perched rocks lying in conjunction with stone semicircles on high bluffs above waterways; and massive dry stone walls running due north-south toward solstice sunrises and sunsets. Moreover, in Woodstock, Vermont, the late Byron Dix, a former aerospace engineer specializing in the design of sophisticated, high-altitude instruments, uncovered impressive stone ruins that hinted at a sophisticated astro-alignment observatory.

These formations clearly are not the result of glacial debris since some of them appear to be reworked. This begs the question: Who tampered with these rocks?

## SLAB-ROOFED CHAMBERS

With slab-roofed, drystone (mortarless) chambers, we are out of the category of glacial happenstance and into the domain of man-made certainty. These dirt-covered chambers have gone by many names and are attributed to many different peoples and a variety of purposes ranging from simple geological formations to Colonial root cellars to Indian huts to solar temples built by Celtic mariners in 800 B.C.!

In recent years, few of the theories and speculations put forth by researchers have adequately explained these mysterious, slab-roofed structures. Unfortunately, there are not many firsthand accounts from the Colonial period. Only a few documents speak of chambers at all, and those are buried deep within musty archives and filled with only the vaguest references to "man-works."[4] And oddest of all, after months of searching I found only a handful of definite notations. If the structures are provisional storage, animal, or slave shelters from the Colonial period, then the vast number of similarly built chambers found in a geographical area ranging from New York to Canada suggests a widespread use of a very popular construction design. That in two to three hundred years of American growth absolutely no recollection of this technique, either written or oral, has come down to us is extremely puzzling. Is it likely that we suffer from such cultural amnesia that nothing has been passed down over the last four centuries?

On the other hand, if the colonists did not erect the slab-roofed chambers, but simply took advantage of their presence, why didn't more people write about them? Perhaps they just didn't merit introspection. Since generations of settlers regarded them as always having been there, could they have easily been forgotten? The chambers were ordinary, common, and as unworthy of detailed descriptions as the side of a barn. Add to this the massive emigration to the Midwest following the poor crop yields of the early 1800s, and we have the perfect social conditions for lost knowledge and unexplained places.

They also don't seem to represent cultural transplantation. For the first Colonial settlements in New England, all sorts of English vernacular architecture was emulated and duplicated in the New World—including thatch on the first settlements before wood shingles proved easier and longer lasting. These settlers tried to make their strange and forbidding surroundings into a little piece of England.

When we get to stone chambers, however, we are faced with a peculiar anomaly: Stone-chambered root cellars don't exist in England. So, indeed, if there were root cellars in American Colonial times, then the idea did *not* come from Britain. Is it possible that they could have been something devised by settlers once they got to the New World? Why then don't we have any history of their development? In Bermuda, for example, a country as old as the English settlement of America, we can trace accurately the architectural changes in outbuildings as the first Bermudans began to cope with the local environment of rain, hurricanes, heat, and humidity. We can see the slow adaptations to the local topography and climate. But this is not so with eastern "root cellars." The scant records left by the settlers indicate that the chambers preceeded their arrival.

So who built them? Many are located deep in the woods away from the nearest farm or barn site. Almost all of the remote chambers seen had no trace of mortar or any other insulating material. The walls are bare, cold stone—better to preserve dead bodies than to preserve delicate produce.

There may be an astronomical association connected with the structures. Some of the chambers are oriented toward the winter solstice sunrise and sunset—the points on the local horizon where the sun rises and sets on December 21, the shortest day of the year. Others are aligned toward the spring equinox sunrise on March 21. Clearly a lot of thought went into constructing these stone rooms.


## UNUSUAL PLACES

There are many places throughout the world that create neurological havoc on people. At some sites, people claim altered perception—either a feeling of ultimate bliss or chaotic fear. Is this the pineal gland picking up some aberra-

*Making an earth-and-straw-covered root cellar* (*Stewart*, The Shepherd's Manual).

*Early photo, circa late 1800s, of stone chambers somewhere in New England. (Photo found at a yard sale in Concord, Massachusetts, by James Whittall. Reprint courtesy of Malcolm Pearson).*

tion in the geomagnetism and translating that into a flood of neurotransmitter secretions? Or is the brain/body picking up some other, unrecognized energy source? Difficult to say, as researchers now are just beginning to look into this phenomenon.

There are many places where unusual events have happened for centuries. The shore area north of Boston Harbor has been the center of strange activities for a long time. Over the years, people in the Cape Ann region have reported seeing everything from sea monsters to devil spirits. In fact, if one believes the late seventeenth century court records of Salem, the region was once a hot zone for Satan worshippers—the infamous witch trials were held there in the late 1600s.

This area also is privy to interesting flashes of light. Many residents in the coastal town of Essex have reported even seeing gaseous balls of light floating around their homes. Similar reports of spheres of light floating about are well ensconced in rural America's consciousness. When the data is compiled and analyzed two consistent features become evident: The sightings are usually made around swamps or a wetland-like environment, and the balls appear to hover a bit before they vanish. The few scientists who have looked into this phenomenon now state that it's possible for plant/animal life decomposing in the marshes to create the gas methane that ignites as it is rising and floats in a ball-like plasma.

There also are areas of the country where people see lots of unusual things in the air—particularly late at night. For years people around Pine Bush, New York, and in the lower Hudson Valley have reported seeing the classic cylindrical-shaped UFO, complete with lights and whirring sounds. Why there? What's so special about southern New York State? The answer may have to do with the many faults permeating the region, as well as the bedrock below the Hudson River itself—the rock was scored, cut, and deformed during the last Ice Age when a gigantic valley glacier, estimated to be over 2,000 feet high, worked its way south through the juvenile river.

Is it possible that the weight of the glacier so depressed the lower Hudson Valley region that today the earth's crust periodically presses against "base-ment" rock faults far below the earth and generates electrostatic charges that may result in the strange luminosities seen by local residents? Then again, there may be other explanations.

There also are mysterious sites where people exhibit strange behavior. Once such spot is along a road in central New Jersey. For reasons that perplex transit officials, far too many people driving along one particular stretch of road fall asleep. This happens during daylight hours and not during the usual late-night road ventures. Why there?

There are many different types of intriguing sites to visit. All of these lo-cales share a common theme: They are difficult to explain, and many people feel odd while visiting them. Some are mere ghosts of what once was: sites that were sacred to indigenous tribes or to settlers for one reason or another. Other sites are clearly visible constructions of questionable antiquity. But who built them, when, and for what purpose? Perhaps the real mystery is in the place itself.

# THREE

# Nova Scotia/Quebec/ Ontario

## NOVA SCOTIA

For thousands of years the native Mi'kmaq (Micmac) Indians hunted and fished the lands and waters off Nova Scotia. Soon after John Cabot's exploration of the region in 1497, European fishermen sailed to the new land to harvest the seemingly endless amount of codfish. In 1605 the French established Port Royal, the first permanent settlement here, and named the lands around their small settlement, Acadie. By 1713 part of this land was under British control, and they gave it the name Nova Scotia, which is Latin for New Scotland.

Germans and Swiss arrived as many French-speaking Acadians were being expelled. The American Revolution saw thousands more arrive as Colonial loyalists fled to Nova Scotia to start a new life. Much later, great numbers would trek to Nova Scotia to mine gold. The peninsula's multicultural mosaic, however, may reach back in time much further than anyone could have imagined.

There is evidence of non-Indian settlement on Nova Scotia *much* earlier than the 1600s. Since the first record of European contact with the native Micmac, there have been tantalizing clues as to an earlier people wandering throughout the peninsula. The very symbols used by the Micmacs on birch bark pads to record their legends and stories suggested to early Jesuit priests that there had been contact with an ancient European culture. Indeed, even some of the words, games, and mythical figures recounted by these Nova Scotian tribes suggested some borrowing from a radically different people.

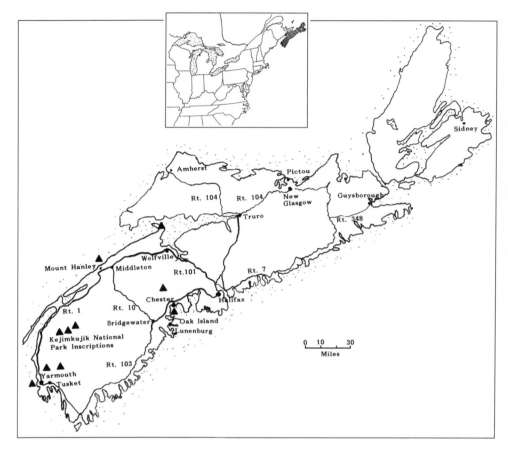

*Mysterious sites in Nova Scotia*

But it's the ruins scattered about the island that are most telling. Who built the stone mounds and "cellar-holes" referred to by scholars at the turn of the century? Who carved the strange symbols on stones scattered around the peninsula? What engineering crew held back the tide and constructed an ingenious pit complete with water traps, false leads, and a maze of tunnels more than 230 feet deep into island limestone? Who left the ruins of a hilltop "castle" tucked into the middle of the peninsula? What is the origin of the Glooscap man-god legend? The province is ripe for new discoveries.

## SOUTHWEST NOVA SCOTIA

Nova Scotia is one of three Maritime Provinces of Canada. There are four distinct geological regions on the peninsula, one of which, the southern section, consists of resistant rock covered by glacial debris. The many coves, inlets, hills, and ponds, the products of melting ice and tidal-wave action, have been home to countless numbers of people for an undetermined amount of time.

## INSCRIBED STONE
Yarmouth County Museum, Yarmouth, Nova Scotia, Canada

### Site Synopsis
In 1812 a Dr. Richard Fletcher took a shoreline stroll along his property. Across from Yarmouth, a little way from a place called Salt Pond, he found a stone inscribed with strange symbols. From that moment on, a strange controversy has been brewing over the nature of those markings.

### Location
The so-called Runic Stone is presently housed in the Yarmouth County Museum and Historical Research Library. A detailed study of all revelant archives places its original location across the harbor near Sandy Pond.

### Considerations
U.S. citizens do not need passports to visit Canada, but they should carry some identification papers showing their citizenship. I recommend that you take along your passport anyway—it's much easier to carry around.

The Yarmouth County Museum is a fascinating place, so plan on spending hours roaming around it. But if your interest is limited to the inscribed stone, you will not be disappointed. The museum employs an archivist who cares for a wonderful collection of documents concerning the stone and other sites scattered throughout Nova Scotia. Some of the files contain personal letters written a hundred years ago by Canadian residents. Other items include original printings of limited-edition pamphlets detailing some weird sites. In other words, you can't pull this information off the Internet—you have to *go* to Yarmouth to see what's there to read. And there is no general index!

*Note*: For consistency in map format throughout this guide, I've listed distances in miles. In Canada, however, the metric system is used. While I give distance in both miles and kilometers in the location text, you may want to convert map distances into kilometers. It's easy. To convert miles to kilometers, multiply the number of miles by 1.62. For example, 40 miles = 40 x 1.62 = 64.8 kilometers. To convert kilometers to miles, multiply the number of kilometers by 0.62. For example, 20 kilometers = 20 x 0.62 = 12.4 miles.

### History / Background
This inscribed stone goes by many names. Sometimes it's referred to as the Yarmouth Stone, other times it's called the Runic Stone. The original reference to it was the Fletcher Stone, after its discoverer. There was much confu-

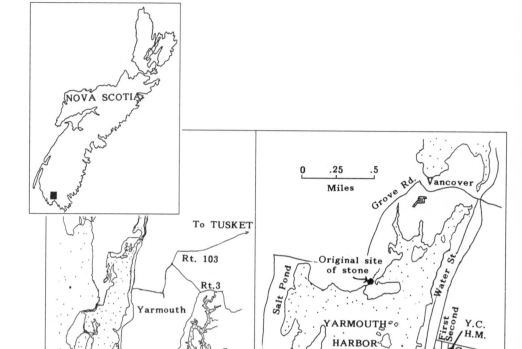

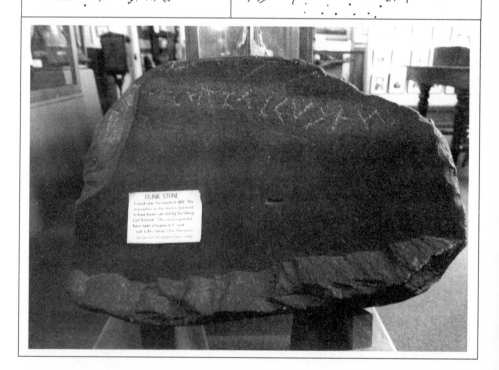

sion over the exact location of the find, but an 1892 article cleared up the matter:

> It was on the west side of Yarmouth Harbor; at the foot of a hill on the east side of a small cove, into which runs a stream from a marsh about a mile long, called the Chegoggin Flats or Salt Pond. An old road, traces of which may yet be seen, used to run around the foot of this hill and cross the bar at the mouth of the stream. The stone lay a few steps to the east of the road, on the northwest slope of the hill.[1]

The stone weighs about 400 pounds and is common quartzite. It measures about 31 x 20 x 13 inches. The inscription is rather smooth, while the reverse is somewhat jagged. There are thirteen characters carved almost across the entire flat section of the stone. According to a scientist who examined the stone in the 1800s, the etchings were fainter and less deep at one end of the stone.

Soon after the discovery, a report stated that "on an island near the mouth of the Tusket River there are also two very large stones with inscriptions" that are similar to the Fletcher Stone. The Tusket River is about six and a half miles east of the Salt Pond area. Intriguingly, an article in a popular magazine from the 1930s mentions "old stone cellars"—stone chambers—near this very region:

> Or can it be mere coincidence that here, on this very basin, the Loyalist settlers . . . came upon certain mysterious ancient cellars which they hastily, but . . . erroneously ascribed to the Acadians? And but a short distance away, at the head of the tidewaters . . . several other ancient cellars are still plainly discernible, clustered upon the slopes of Robbins' Hill—a lofty elevation commanding the terrain for miles around. . . . [2]

As usual, the markings on the Yarmouth Stone have been attributed to everyone from Phoenicians to Micmac Indians. Henry Phillips, Jr., writing in the May 2, 1884, edition of the *American Philosophical Society Proceedings* stated quite firmly that the markings were actually glyphs called runes, a type of writing system used by ancient Scandinavians—Vikings. In fact, Phillips offered a translation: "Harko's Son Addressed the Men."

Other scholars of the 1800s offered different kinds of "proof" that the Vikings made it to North America before Columbus. Detailed Norse narratives of sailing expeditions still exist today for scholars to examine. While fascinating, they are short on exact locales, as one would expect from 800-year-old texts. The voyages of Leif Eriksson are depicted, as well as those of other sailing warriors. Phillips found the name Harko in the 1007 A.D. expedition account of the Viking Thorfinn Karlsefne.

The fascinating thing about North American inscriptions, however, is that

*Viking rune stone found along the southwestern coast of Sweden. The many inscribed stones found in America during the 1800s with markings similar to these and others led scholars to assume Viking contact with the New World before Columbus (Montelius,* The Civilization of Sweden).

every decade or so their interpretation changes. By 1934 the eminent rune-ologist Olaf Strandwold also thought the stone's carvings were runes. But his translation differed from Phillips's. Strandwold wrote that he was "convinced that the inscription on the rock was carved by Leif Eriksson himself or at his direction by some member of his party." According to Strandwold the stone says, "Leif to Erik Raises (This Monument)." Scholars of the time jumped on the idea noting that it was a custom to erect monuments to distinguished people. It was therefore quite in tradition that Leif should raise a memorial to his father, Erik the Red who ruled Greenland—the place from which the expedition took place.

Interesting, but it gets better. Some modern Scandinavian scholars who have examined the glyphs state quite emphatically that the markings look nothing like the ancient Norse runes that they have studied. By the mid 1970s, the markings miraculously changed cultures. The late Dr. Barry Fell, a noted marine biologist from Harvard and a pretty good epigrapher (one who studies ancient writings), wrote that the stone was carved in a form of early Basque, the language of a people who live in the extreme northwestern section of Spain. Fell's translation: "Basque people have subdued this land."

It didn't end there. One researcher was convinced that the glyphs were ancient Mycenean! The translation of this early Mediterranean civilization's etchings? "Exalted Throne: The pure lions of the royal household sent into the sunset to protect, to seize, and to make a hole in the mighty waters at the summit have been sacrificed—the whole corporate body."

The Yarmouth County Museum has an extensive file filled with other interpretations. As they write in their handout, "Other theories have included Japanese, fourteenth-century Scandinavian and even tree roots. Some descendants of Richard Fletcher, who found the stone in 1812, feel that the doctor himself carved the runes as a practical joke."

So what do we make of all this? The Dr. Fletcher practical joke theory doesn't make sense. Eighteen-twelve was the wrong time period for someone to forge a runic inscription, since the evidence for and popular notion of Vikings in America were at least a few decades away.

In the 1970s, a researcher for the Nova Scotia Museum noted that some of the rock drawings of the Micmac Indians resemble a few of the glyphs on the Yarmouth stone.[3] (See illustration on following page.) These Micmac ideograms—symbols that convey entire concepts or ideas rather than individual letters—were found scattered throughout the rocks and boulders of the Kejimkujik National Park. These ideograms also were being connected to ancient writing forms in other ways. Jesuit priests in the seventeenth century had used these symbols to teach the natives Christian prayers and church services—the better to convert them from their pagan ways. By the mid 1800s, the entire Roman Catholic catechism was "translated" into Micmac glyphs. Around the same time the Nova Scotia researcher was uncovering similarities between the Micmac ideograms and the Yarmouth stone glyphs, Barry Fell used the nineteenth-century catechism to claim that the symbols used in the Micmac ideograms were the *same* symbols used by certain ancient Mediterranean peoples!

Fell also saw a staggering number of similarities between the Micmac symbols and an Egyptian hieroglyphic writing system used throughout North Africa in the ancient world. The similarities are astonishing. Key symbols for religion, mountains, animals, I, and so on are almost exact duplicates of each other. Furthermore, the Micmac's symbol for metals—three small circles in a vertical row—is the very symbol used by the ancient Egyptians. Until the fifteenth century, the Micmac Indians used stone as their cutting tool and had not mined or used metal in any form prior to this time.

If Dr. Fell's work is correct, then the only explanation for this amazing coincidence between the Micmac and Egyptian glyphs is that someone or some group from ancient North Africa or thereabouts visited Nova Scotia and hung around for a while—people don't learn a complex writing system in a day. Are there any Micmac oral legends that mention someone suddenly stopping by and sharing wisdom? Absolutely. There may be more to the Glooscap story than mere myth.

It is intriguing to think that North African Egyptians possibly were roam-

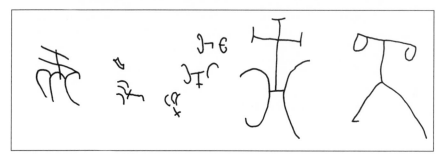

*Yarmouth Stone inscription. Micmac glyphs, from
Kejimkujik National Park, Nova Scotia.*

ing around Nova Scotia centuries ago. Is there any truth to this idea? Hard to
say, though the faint notion leaves one's pulse racing.

With respect to the Yarmouth Inscribed Stone, which is the correct interpretation? The stone was a mystery in 1812, and it remains one today. You can
go see and touch it. You can walk to the original site. You can drive to Tusket
Falls to look for the "ancient cellars." You can visit Kejimkujik National Park
and compare the symbols there with the Yarmouth Stone. You can even compare this stone to several in Maine, Massachusetts, and Rhode Island that we
will be visiting in a few chapters.

### Contact Person(s) / Organization

Yarmouth County Museum and Historical Research Library
22 Collins Street
Yarmouth, Nova Scotia
Canada B5A 3C8
(902) 742–5539

Yarmouth County Tourist Association
PO Box 477
Yarmouth, Nova Scotia
Canada B5A 4B4
Tel: (902) 742–5355
Fax: (902) 742–8391

Kejimkujik National Park is a 147-square-mile wilderness preserve of forests,
lakes, streams, and rock petroglyphs. Camping, picnicking, swimming, hiking,

canoeing, cycling, and scenic views are offered. The hamlet of Maitland Bridge is the entranceway to the Park. Jeremy's Bay Campground, near Maitland Bridge, is a great place to camp out to see the rock drawings. It's open all year.

(902) 682–2722

For general inquiries into Nova Scotia's park system:

Department of Natural Resources
Parks and Recreation Division
RR #1 Belmont, Nova Scotia
Canada B0M 1C0
(902) 662–3030

### Total Magnetic Field / Inclination Angle
None taken at this site.

### Further Investigations in Area
A thorough investigation of the Salt Pond area is in order. James Hatfield, a longtime resident of Pleasant Lake, a town a few miles east of Yarmouth and west of Tusket, was given a stone with a hole carved in it. Uncovered near where the Yarmouth Stone was found in 1812, this stone might be an ancient anchor since it is exactly the type that Viking long ships used. (See illustration below.)

Another site that demands rediscovery and investigation is the hilltop stone cellars. I came across this reference while reading through the archives in the Yarmouth County Museum. The 1935 article mentions that some are on a Robbin's Hill near Tusket Falls. Local archivists as well as older residents

*Anchor-style stone uncovered in the 1980s near Salt Pond, where the Yarmouth Inscribed Stone was found. This type of stone was used by the Vikings to secure their long boats.*

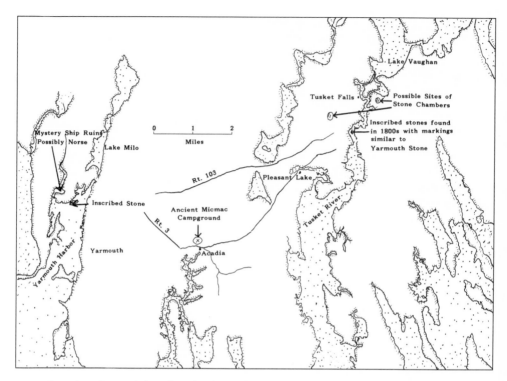

*Overview of potential ancient sites in southwest Nova Scotia.*

were perplexed by the name of the hill, although I did manage to locate the general region where a Robbins family lived over sixty years ago. A nearby hill-top that fits the article's description is just northwest of the Route 103 bridge over the Tusket River. Just south of this bridge is the Canadian National Railroad bridge. The only other possibility is just east of the village of Tusket Falls, across the Tusket River. There's a radio tower on this 200-foot-high hill-top. Go find those "ancient cellars!"

## BAY OF FUNDY COAST /
## SOUTH CENTRAL NOVA SCOTIA

The Bay of Fundy along the northern coastline is perhaps the most dramatic of all coastal regions in Nova Scotia. There's a mixture of vertical sandstone, red conglomerates, and assorted glacial sand and gravel. Dinosaur tracks, fossils, and other assorted geological wonders—such as semiprecious stones—are common finds along the beaches and cliffs.

Twice daily, over 115 billion tons of water move in and out of the funnel shaped bay causing, in some cases, a tide differential of 52 feet. Tidal action has eroded some of the cliffsides into strange formations.

The South Central region of Nova Scotia is a completely different geological story. While heavily scarred by the last glaciation, the bedrock here is made up of black slate and granite that have been folded and twisted. Wave action broke up gold-strewn white quartzite veins and deposited the pieces along the sandy beaches. The many offshore islands found along the southern shore are drumlins—sandhills—that were partially submerged when sea level rose worldwide after the last glaciers melted over 12,000 years ago.

## GLOOSCAP
Cape Blomidon, Scots Bay, Nova Scotia

### Site Synopsis
Along the northern central shore of Nova Scotia, a reddish prong of land juts into the Bay of Fundy. Ancient Micmac legend states that this region was the abode of the man-god, Glooscap. Why here?

### Location
From Halifax take Route 101 north. Turn off at Exit 10, near Wolfville. You'll now be traveling on Route 1. Go through Wolfville turning north onto Route 358. Go 11 kilometers (6.8 miles) through the town of Canning and the stop area Look Off. Turn right (east) onto Stewart Mountain Road. Travel down this dirt/gravel road for 3.1 kilometers (1.9 miles). Turn left (north) at the intersection and continue driving up into Blomidon Provincial Park. Walk down to the coastline and examine the beach pebbles.

To get to the end of the peninsula, get back to the Stewart Mountain Road / Route 358 intersection. Turn right (north) toward Cape Split. Before that, however, stop off at Scots Bay, where the rocks are even prettier and more valuable. On a clear day you can see the southwestern tip of the cape. After Scots Bay, continue on the road to the end. You'll need to park here and hike four miles to the rocky tip. The view from Cape Split is breathtaking. You'll feel the presence of Glooscap everywhere. This is sacred ground.

### Considerations
Give yourself plenty of time to take in all of these sites. Walking along a beach in search of semiprecious stones can eat up an entire day. You'll want to spend lots of time at Blomidon's red cliffs and Scots Bay. Each tide brings in marvelous wonders to the beach.

If you are not used to hiking, forget about the walk out to Cape Split.

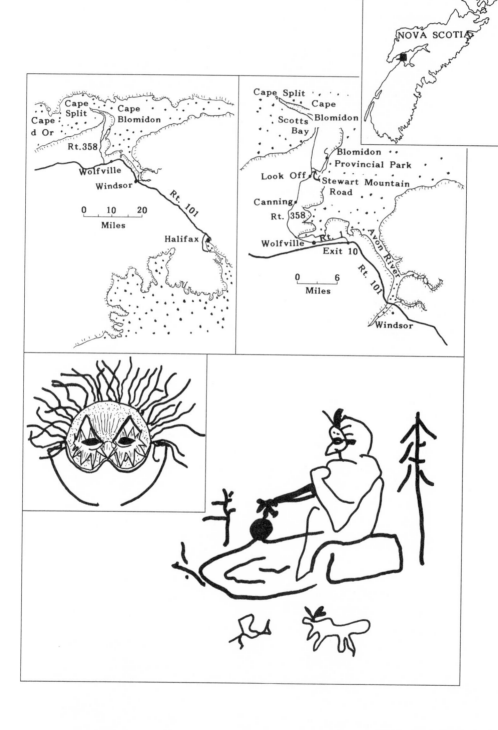

While not a difficult hike, it does take time—most people can leisurely cover the four miles in less than two hours. Once at the tip, you'll want to relax, meditate, and take in the view. Bring along some food, but always remember to take out what you bring in.

### History / Background

Blomidon has had several names. Micmac Indians called it Owbogegechk, meaning "abounding with *owbok*," or dogwood. Samuel de Champlain called the cape Cap Poutrincourt, after his friend who successfully scaled the cliffs.

It was also called Cape Porcupine, due to the abundance of that creature. The French Acadian settlers called it Cap Baptiste, from the Norman word *baptisterie*, meaning the place where sailors get baptized by the waters.

The common term for Cape Porcupine was Blow Me Down, from the gusts that blow from it when the wind is from the west and southwest. The contracted form of this is Blomidon. It is thought that the term was adopted by New England planters when they began their settlement in the late eighteenth century.

The geology of this entire region is spectacular and ancient. The Blomidon area, composed predominantly of red sandstone, siltstone, conglomerate, and shale dates to the late Triassic period—some 240 millions years ago. The Scots Bay region, made up of volcanic basalt, sandstone chert *and* limestone dates to the Jurassic period—some 200 millions ago. Indeed, this area is quite special. The volcanic origins included the deposition of gemstones like agate, chalcedony, jasper, and amethyst.

The story of Glooscap, like all legends and myths, is filled with mystical, magical, and remarkable events. In some cases, the story helped the Micmacs to explain the unexplainable, like the spectacular tides or the strange geology of the Fundy Bay. A careful reading of the legend will point to obvious embellishments. But one thing is certain: Something momentous happened a very long time ago to an early group of Micmac Indians. Somebody so impressed these people that they preserved that initial contact and and the events surrounding it in a series of oral legends that have survived to this day thanks to the work of a scholar and a missionary in the 1800s who recorded the ancient tales.

The Glooscap tales were shared by many northeastern Atlantic seaboard tribes, such as the Penobscots, the Passamaquoddies, the Malecites, and, of course, the Micmacs. These tribes represent an enormous geographical area that extends from Massachusetts all the way up to northern Nova Scotia. Depending on the region, he was known as Gluskap, Kulo-scap, Kul-skap, or Klotescarp.[4]

Glooscap, a man-god with special powers, was a kind, powerful person who was a savior to his followers and a ruthless warrior to his enemies. He taught the Micmacs how to fish with nets, how to better their chances in the hunt, how to cultivate crops, and how to cure food for long-distance travel. He showed up in Nova Scotia one day claiming to have traveled from a great land in the East. His timing could not have been better according to Micmac legend, for the locals were having trouble with their traditional methods of hunting and fishing. On top of that, there were hideous animals and evil sorcerers creating havoc among the people.

Glooscap never married, but he lived on Cape Blomidon with Noogumee, an adopted grandmother, and a young boy named Marten. He stayed for a long time helping out in ways known only to man-gods, and then one year he told his followers that it was time to leave. There was a great feast on Blomidon, and many people came by to pay their respects. The last thing he told the group was to forgo being evil and to live a kind and just life: refrain from cheating and stealing, and make sure you plant your crops and feed the children. If they followed this sage advice, they would one day live forever with him. With that he got into a stone canoe and paddled west, never to be seen again.

On the one hand, this story sounds a lot like the white-god legends found throughout the Americas (see Chapter 1: History and Background). The eternal-life concept after leading a good earthly existence has overtones of early Christian teachings. On the other hand, Glooscap's doings have a remarkable similarity to the Viking gods Thor and Odin, particularly in the areas of making mountains and taming animals.

Over the years, many scholars have tried to explain the Glooscap legend. In the 1970s, American author and historian Frederick Pohl made an intriguing case for the myth being based on the travels of the fourteenth-century Scottish Prince Henry Sinclair.[5] According to Pohl's analysis of a fourteenth-century narrative, Sinclair stopped off in Nova Scotia sometime in 1398. He explored the countryside while wintering in a bay not too far from Cape Blomidon. Apparently, he greatly impressed the natives with his wit, his good looks, and social graces. Pohl puts forth an impressive selection of place names, legend, and geography that makes a pretty convincing argument. Of all the material listed, however, the most interesting is from archeological excavation.

Fishing nets need stones to hold the net down in the water. Excavation of Indian sites closely affiliated with the Micmacs and with the Glooscap legend have shown that these stone weights came into use around 1400.[6] Prior to that date, there's a decided absence of them, suggesting that the Indians at the time fished in other ways. Then, suddenly, they appear. Micmac legend makes it very clear that Glooscap taught them how to fish with nets.

There are two ways to look at all of this. Either the legend is a corrupted/enhanced version of a visit by someone from another culture, or the legend is pure fantasy based on people's need for a "father" figure or a god of some type. Either way the Blomidon/Cape Split region is filled with drama. It's also a setting of peculiar geomagnetic flux.

### Contact Person (s) / Organization

If you're interested in the European-contact basis of the Glooscap legend, then get a copy of Frederick Pohl's *Prince Henry Sinclair*. Take it along with you on a visit to this part of Nova Scotia.

Cape Blomidon is a provincial park that offers camping for a nominal fee. There are a host of the usual rules and regulations that go along with camping in places like this, including:

- All campers must be registered (do so at the gate)
- Only one vehicle per site
- A total of six (6) people per site and only three (3) tents allowed per site (so make sure you go with someone you can be around for a while).
- Visitors permitted in the park until 10:30 P.M. Quiet time after 10:30 P.M. That means no loud music, operating generators, or generally running amuck and shouting obscenities at the trees.

Contact the following for information on camping at Blomidon:

The Department of Natural Resources
PO Box 130
Lawrencetown, Nova Scotia
Canada B0S 1M0
(902) 584–2229

### Total Magnetic Field / Inclination Angle

There were a few unusual magnetic fields associated with Blomidon. In general, the total magnetic field (TMF) increased from the beach area to the cape's highest point. Along with this, the beach area had inclination angle (IA) of 74 degrees; while at the cape's high point, it dropped to 60 degrees. I noticed the same differences at Scots Bay and along the Cape Split trail.

The result of all this? The electrophysiology work of Dr. Robert Becker (see Introduction) indicated that only a *slight* change in total magnetic field was enough to change the secretion levels of various brain neurotransmitters. The implication is that the levels of magnetic flux recorded here would probably affect the secretion rates of melatonin, serotonin, and other brain chemicals, thereby affecting mood and perception.

The Cape Blomidon region is a prime candidate for a spiritually enhanced site. Perhaps it was a combination of factors that led Micmacs to place their man-god Glooscap here. If there was a visitor from across the ocean who stopped by this spectacular setting, a visitor who was so different from anything anyone on Nova Scotia had seen before, then one could understand the lasting impression. But maybe it was the cape itself that reinforced this impression. Perhaps the varying geomagnetic field that one hikes through on the way to the top of the cape made the early Micmacs more pensive, more introspective, more willing to watch and listen for a god. Hike from the beach to the top of Blomidon. Then walk out to Cape Split and try to feel this place's special nature. No doubt, it is a powerful place.

### Further Investigations in Area

### Site Synopsis
Nova Scotia author Michael Bradley, whose must-read book, *Holy Grail Across the Atlantic*, believes Sinclair wintered in the Cape d'Or region, which is across the Minas Channel from Cape Split. If so, then definitely spend time scouting out the remarkable terrain there. It's well worth the effort.

## INSCRIBED STONE
Mount Hanley, Nova Scotia, Canada

### Site Synopsis
In 1984 while plowing his field, a farmer uncovered a slab of rock with strange markings on it. Controversy has raged ever since as to their meaning.

### Location
From Yarmouth take Route 101 north. Take Exit 19 going *away* from Lawrencetown. At the first major intersection, turn right. Stay on this road until it meets Mount Hanley Road. Turn left and continue for about 3.2 kilometers (2 miles) The stone is at 2327 Mount Hanley Road.

### Considerations
Before you go rushing into the yard where the stone is located, please ask permission from the homeowner. Also, the stone is presently being used as an outside doorstop. Years of banging doors have taken their toll on this fascinating rock. The marks have worn down somewhat.

### History / Background
Joe Banks was eighty years old when he and his grandson Eddie Hare uncovered a large rock with strange markings while clearing a field in this town not far from the fertile Annapolis Valley of southwestern Nova Scotia. The stone lay around his yard for a few years before a local amateur epigrapher claimed the scratchings were a form of Celtic ogam—a writing system used thousands of years ago in ancient Britain.

There is a great controversy about ogam, with amateur epigraphers claim-

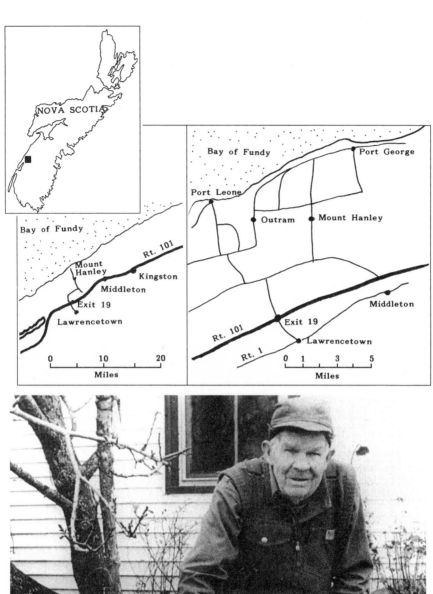

ing it was much more widespread and much older than the academics believe. In fact, the amateurs insist that many fine examples of ogam can be found in North America, suggesting, of course, pre-Columbian transatlantic crossings.

Another amateur epigrapher examined the Banks stone and thought the markings were indeed Celtic ogam. He attempted to "read" the stone's symbols by using a document known as the *Book of Ballymote*. The Ballymote reference is a medieval document that has passages in both Ogam and Latin, a sort of Rosetta Stone for this ancient writing system. According to the epigrapher, the stone's markings translate into: "To the son of Mui from the green, grassy place." He believed it was a memorial stone dating to a fifth-century Irish landing in Nova Scotia.

Not surprisingly, traditional archeologists begged to differ with such interpretations. A scientist from the Nova Scotia Museum in Halifax examined the stone soon after it was uncovered in 1984. His analysis: If the stone is turned on its end it has a striking resemblance to an eighteenth-century British ordinance marker. And the supposed ogam slashes? Plow marks from the last 200 years of farming.

Who's right? Could this stone and others like it simply be reflecting the scraping of metal plows? It seems entirely possible until one scans the stone horizon for other plow-scraped stones with similar slashes. Scattered throughout North America are many marked stones that superficially look like the Mount Hanley stone. Those could be evidence of farming as well. Except that the same type of markings also appear in *caves and rock shelters* ranging from West Virginia to Colorado! Researchers who have taken the time to carefully examine these markings and others found on field stones conclude that they have a regularity and precision to them. It would certainly appear that either they are some type of Native American tally system, or else they represent some form of ogam writing. We need to carefully study and rethink the inscribed stone found in Mount Hanley, Nova Scotia.

### Contact Person(s) / Organization

Anna-Maria Galante of the *Chronicle-Herald* in Halifax first reported on this stone in 1992. She collected a good amount of information concerning the stone, and no doubt has material that did not appear in her article due to space constraints.

The Chronicle-Herald and the Mail Star
1650 Argyle Street
PO Box 610
Halifax, Nova Scotia
Canada B3J 2T2
(902) 426–3080

Isabell Hare (owner of stone)
2327 Mount Hanley Road
Mount Hanley, Nova Scotia
Canada

### Total Magnetic Field / Inclination Angle
None taken at this site.

### Further Investigations in Area
If this stone really indicates early Irish exploration into Nova Scotia, then there must be more tangible remains left in the vicinity of Mount Hanley. Farming families dot the landscape here, and they would be the people most like to have found any similarly marked stones.

Whatever this stone represents, similar stones may exist in the vicinity. A careful scouting of the terrain along the coastline at Mount Hanley and over in the very fertile Annapolis Valley might uncover a host of other items.

## SHAFT / TUNNELS
Oak Island, Mahone Bay, Nova Scotia

### Site Synopsis
For over two hundred years, thousands of people have spent close to ten million dollars digging into a manmade shaft that descends deep into island bedrock. Whoever built this intricate pit took great pains to foil anyone trying to uncover it, for there are many cleverly designed water traps throughout. All indications point to something very important, like a king's treasure, lying at the bottom of this weird complex. An old legend states that when all the oak trees are gone from the island and seven men have died, an amazing treasure will be found. Most of the island oaks are gone, and six men are dead.

### Location
From Halifax take Route 102 leading out of the city. Turn off onto Route 103 West. Stay on this road for about 49 kilometers (30 miles). Take Exit 9 (Gold River, Western Shore, Oak Island) going south for .8 kilometers (about half a mile) before turning onto Route 3. Stay on Route 3 for around 6.5 kilometers (around four miles) before turning left onto Crandell Road. This leads directly to Oak Island via the causeway.

### Considerations
While the Oak Island Field Museum is open all year, (10 A.M.–6 P.M.), it's a good idea to write prior to driving to Mahone Bay. There's a causeway constructed in the 1960s that allows visitors to drive to this privately owned island.

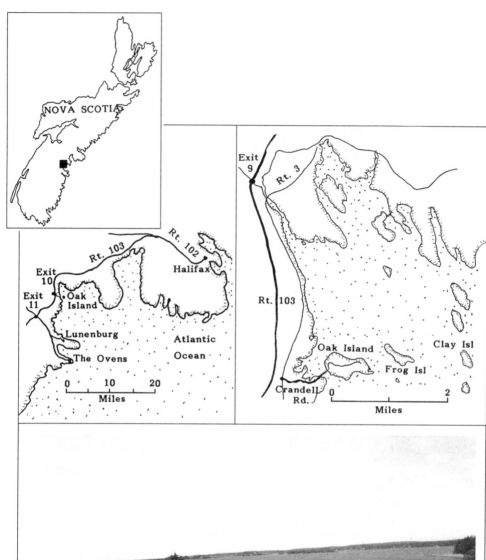

Plan on spending a good amount of time at the field museum. There's a short audio presentation and quite a number of artifacts brought up from the shaft. There's a small fee charged for access to the site.

While it is tempting to photograph the artifacts, leave your camera in its case, because they don't allow photos or videotaping inside the museum. You can, however, shoot everything else on the island.

Buy the pamphlet that explains key sites along the walk. It will orient you to the general scheme of the island. Bring along some water, and wear comfortable walking shoes. You'll need to walk about a mile in and a mile back.

Once you've seen the original hole, which has been greatly enlarged over the years, walk over to Bore Hole 10X and Smith's Cove.

### History / Background

There's an enormous amount of written material about this tiny, peanut-shaped island about 65 kilometers (40 miles) south of Halifax. Oak Island is one of over 300 islands strewn throughout Mahone Bay.

Some of the islands off Mahone Bay were formed during the end of the last glacial period, when giant chunks of ice deposited small, oval-shaped hills of sand as they melted. The other islands, including Oak Island, are composed of sand and limestone and were deposited in small tropical seas about 340 million years ago when the climate of this area was completely different from what it is today.

Mahone Bay, on Nova Scotia's Atlantic side, was named after a type of shallow draft boat long favored by pirates in the region. These waters were infamous throughout the 1600s and 1700s (and probably before that) as the home port of buccaneers, pirates, and privateers who prowled the open sea in search of silver, gold, and jewels. The large bay, easy beach access, and numerous coves protected from the fierce Atlantic allowed these predators to rest, drink, recaulk their ships, and bury their stolen treasure.

Oak Island had always been a peculiar place for the settlers around Mahone Bay. Many eighteenth-century residents spoke of seeing "strange lights" late at night on the island. Some even said the place was haunted. It was in this context that the mystery of Oak Island began.

During the summer of 1795, three farmboys rowed out from mainland Nova Scotia to Oak Island to discover a filled-in shaft at the top of a small hill near the eastern end of the island. The boys spent the next several months excavating. Over the years, as word got out, other people formed organizations to continue the excavation.

The results of those early years in the 1800s were intriguing. As the digging continued downwards, log platforms were found about every 10 feet. A type of putty and coconut fiber sealed a few of the oak platforms—this on an island 1,500 miles north of the nearest coconut! At 90 feet a large slab of rock bearing some type of incomprehensible hieroglyphic inscription was uncovered. It was very clear that someone or some group of people had gone to a great deal of trouble to lay out this shaft. Then, after the 90-foot platform was removed, something strange happened. Seawater began to percolate slowly into the pit. Soon it rose to within 35 feet of the surface! A thorough search of the island, and even more digging, eventually solved this puzzle. Someone had constructed two stone-lined, one-by-one-foot tunnels that snaked out to the coastline. At the eastern end, the tunnel fanned out into five box-style drains. At the southern end, the tunnel merely stopped at the beach splash zone. The result of all this: At high tide the main shaft filled in to the high-tide level, a clever booby trap to inhibit further digging.

Bore-hole drilling through the water level turned up clues that got even more people interested in this weird site. The drill auger went through metal, wood, empty space, then more metal, and so on, which suggested a series of chests. The auger brought up more coconut fiber and three golden links of a chain!

The flood tunnel discovery led to 100 years of excavation that has completely obliterated the original layout of the shaft found in 1795. Many holes were sunk in and around the original site in an attempt to bypass the flood tunnels and drill *into* the shaft. All failed. A part of the eastern flood tunnel was blown up to stop tide water from entering. It too failed. In the 1860s a worker burned to death when a water pump exploded over the shaft. About thirty years later another man was killed at the tunnel site. And in the mid

*Section view of the Oak Island shaft / tunnel system and bore hole.*

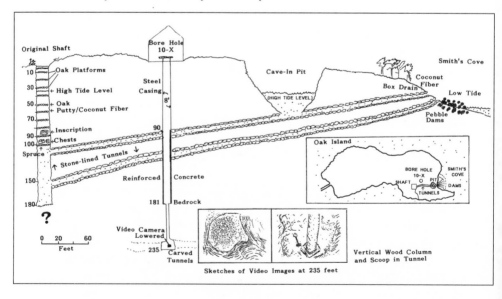

1960s, four people fell into a water-filled tunnel near the beach cove and died. The place has been hexed with tragedy and a lot of money lost.

The late 1960s brought a more focused, technologically based team to the island—Triton Alliance, Ltd., a holding company of Canadian and American businessmen, interested in sophisticated treasure hunting. In 1990 the Oak Island Exploration Company was spun off from the original Triton Alliance syndicate to continue the search.

Triton Alliance brought in divers, deep-drilling machinery, and underwater video equipment, and the results were astonishing. A short distance east of the original shaft, test drilling initially revealed an ancient type of metal that was made well before the mid-eighteenth century. Steel casing was laid out along the enlarged 144-foot-deep hole, giving it a diameter of about 27 inches. From that level, small-bore drilling took the tunnel down to 235 feet. In 1971 a video camera was lowered into this tiny opening, but the original images were blurry and fluttered ferociously. Not much could be seen in the snowy, poor quality black-and-white video.

In 1994, armed with newer and more sophisticated imaging technology, the Oak Island treasure hunters isolated and printed hard-copy scenes from the old video. Incredibly, a complex series of clearly carved, wood-cribbed tunnels can be seen at a depth of over 235 feet. In the ice-cold seawater, there's also a series of chest-like images, a spade, and, amazingly, a flesh-covered human face and hand, no doubt preserved by the frigid water.

Triton Alliance has opened up an entirely new dimension to this 200-year-old mystery. And, like all good mysterious places, new information yields more questions than answers. There are some hints, however, of the activities of the ancient people who did this. The clues come from two spruce platforms found below the 100-foot level of the original pit. Carbon dating of the other *oak* platforms lining the shaft date from 1550 to 1600—the pirate era. But the two spruce platforms found below the 100-foot level of the original pit dated from between 860 and 1135.[7]

The carved tunnels at the bottom of a 235-foot shaft indicate either a time period of much lower sea level—such as during the end of the last glaciation some 12,000 years ago—or else a people with an intimate knowledge of blocking tidewater. Early on in the Oak Island treasure hunt, researchers uncovered the ancient dams that were constructed to do just that. Today at Smith's Cove, you can examine these artificial coffer dams—rows of stones built up to hold back the water. Furthermore, whoever constructed the Oak Island shaft and tunnels was very familiar with limestone geology. So what do we make of this mystery?

I suspect we are dealing with *several* mysteries on Oak Island from vastly different time periods. For example, part of the pit and flood tunnels suggests

*Peering down into Bore Hole 10–X on Oak Island. This steel-encased, 8-foot-in-diameter hole drops down over 180 feet. At that level a smaller diameter hole drilled down to 235 feet. A video camera lowered into the water-filled hole captured images of carved tunnels, wooden columns, a shovel and, most incredibly, a human face! Someone is buried deep within Oak Island! But who could have drilled down that far and when?*

pirate involvement; the much deeper tunnels suggest antiquity that boggles the mind! Nevertheless, until more work is done at Borehole 10X, we need to confine ourselves to the surface finds scattered around the island.

If you can, get permission to walk *around* Smith's Cove Point back toward the main road, following the beach path. Watch for small remnants of survey stone, inscriptions, and other pieces of this intriguing puzzle. If you are very observant, you'll notice a variety of strange things: stones with drilled holes; split rocks; cone-shaped base boulders; rectangular, sandstone "spikes" (sandstone is not native to Oak Island), and so on strewn across the rocky shore. Everything on the island speaks of strange doings. There are signs and symbols everywhere.

Fred Nolan, a long-time treasure hunter on the island, as well as a landowner there, believes the answer to the Oak Island mystery lies in the odd arrangements of stones, boulders, and such gracing his property and elsewhere. Nolan, a professional surveyor, has spent thirty years mapping out curiously placed rocks on the island. He talks of a giant cross made up of conical

*Sandstone "spike" found along the rocky south shore cove of Oak Island. Some believe this carved implement, and others like it, served as ancient survey markers. The artifact was definitely brought to the island, as there is no local source of sandstone. Other spikes scattered throughout the island have been found by land surveyor Frederick G. Nolan.*

*One of dozens of granite boulders found throughout the island with strange chiseled holes. One theory is that these boulders represent a marker in a survey system that points to buried treasure. This boulder, found along Oak Island's south shore cove, first was carefully sliced and then a hole was carved into the middle section. Dozens of unusual stones, alignments, and markings appear along this cove, a few hundred yards from the original money pit.*

boulders; he sites the stone triangle, found along the south shore in the 1930s. The triangular arrangement of stones seems to point northwards toward the original shaft. Nolan also believes the sandstone spikes and the swamp on the island hold clues to a great treasure. His work is intriguing and thought-provoking.

It would be interesting to systematically examine the other islands in Mahone Bay for traces of depressions, tunnels, sandstone stakes, rock triangles, and the like. There's every reason to believe that something will turn up.

### Contact Person(s) / Organization

Oak Island Exploration Company
Oak Island, Mahone Bay
Nova Scotia, Canada B0J 2E0

Mahone Bay, Tourist Bureau
(902) 624–6151

An excellent way to start an exploratory trip to Nova Scotia's mysterious ruins is to stop in at a government bookstore for some detailed topographic map information. Phone or fax for their superb catalog of materials.

In Halifax:

Government Bookstore
One Government Place
1700 Granville Street
PO Box 637
Halifax, Nova Scotia, Canada B3J 2T3
(902) 424–7580
Fax: (902) 424–8425

### Total Magnetic Field / Inclination Angle

None taken at this site due to the extensive digging, prodding, and blasting over the past two hundred years.

### Further Investigations in Area

The Oak Island Exploration team should thoroughly investigate *all* of the islands in Mahone Bay and elsewhere for curious depressions. They also should perform a detailed underwater scan in and around the eastern and southern shores. Now, it's very possible that the group has already done this. As a private company they are under no obligation to report their findings. My guess is they've found some real clues to treasure, or even the treasure itself, but are keeping the information close to their breast. Twenty-plus years for one group to continue looking with all the expense, equipment, and so on is a very long time for even the most long-term-minded investor. Walk around the island, talk to the locals, even try talking with the principal characters. They've no doubt found something important there.

For the time being, it would be fun to get a skiff and explore some of the surrounding islands in Mahone Bay. You'll probably have as much fun as the first farmboy discoverers did in 1795. But do watch our for Private Property signs and gold fever.

About 28 kilometers (17 miles) north of the village of Chester (a few kilometers north of Oak Island), there's a report of strange stone ruins on a hilltop. The ruins are reputedly the remains of an ancient castle constructed by a crusading Templar knight. An excellent book on the subject (*Holy Grail Across the Atlantic* by Michael Bradley) mentions this site without detailing *where* it is! The photos and line drawings in the book make some intriguing connections between the Oak Island mystery and this strange hilltop ruin in the central woods of Nova Scotia.

# QUEBEC / ONTARIO

Located in the east are Quebec and Ontario, two of the ten provinces making up the vast country of Canada. Filled with huge glacial lakes and mountains and valleys, this region has been home to Native Americans for thousands of years.

## STONE INSCRIPTIONS
Sherbrooke Seminary Museum, Sherbrooke, Quebec

### Site Synopsis
Two flat slabs found over 100 years ago in a farmer's field are etched with a strangely controversial set of markings. Some scholars claim it is ancient, non-Indian script.

### Location
From Montreal take Route 10 east for about 146 kilometers (90 miles). Get off at the Sherbrooke exit. Continue for a few miles. Take Belvedere Street to Marquette Street. The Museum is at 195 Marquette Street.

### Considerations
The museum is open in June, July, and August from 10 A.M.–5 P.M. From September through May, the hours are 12:30 P.M.–4:30 P.M.

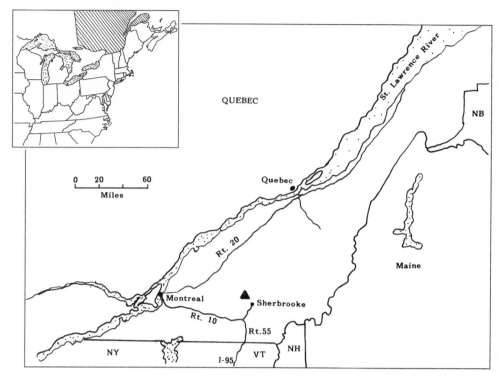

*Mysterious sites in southern Quebec.*

### History / Background

In the nineteenth century, a Canadian farmer was working his land near Bromptonville, Quebec, a small town about 130 kilometers (80 miles) southeast of Montreal, when he uncovered two flat-faced stones in a field beside the Saint Francois River. The stones remained in the puzzled farmer's possession until the early 1900s, when they were acquired by the Sherbrooke Seminary in Sherbrooke, a community about 8 kilometers (5 miles) south of Bromptonville. Turn-of-the-century scholars believed the V-shaped incisions cut into the stones were Norse runes. By the 1920s, however, as American interest in antiquities shifted to the Lower Nile and the spectacular discoveries of Lord Carnarvon and Howard Carter at the Tomb of the Egyptian Kings, the Sherbrooke stones, as well as other New World inscriptions, faded into oblivion.

However, in the fall of 1966, Dr. Thomas E. Lee, professor of archeology at the University of Laval in Quebec, strolled into the Museum of the Sherbrooke Seminary and peered into a glass display case. Inside the case were two 800-pound slabs of limestone measuring about 3 feet long by one-half to one-and-a-half feet in width and breadth. A quick analysis of the four rows of

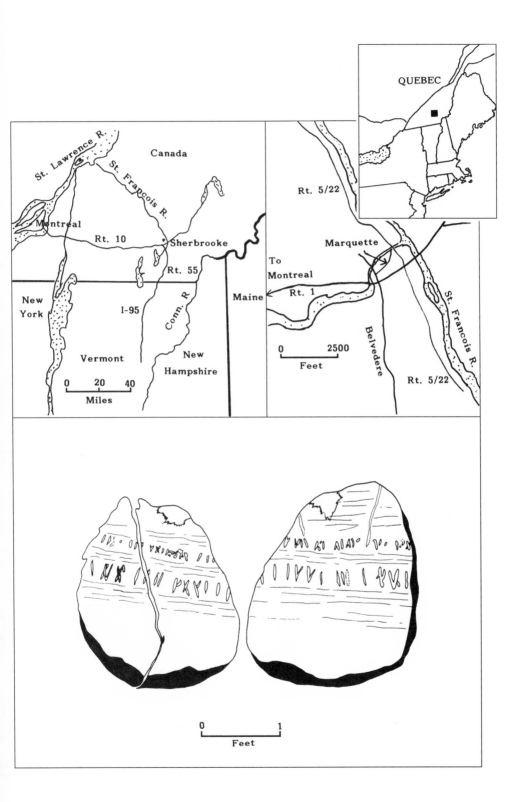

markings cut deeply into both stones told Dr. Lee that the script was in no way related to Norse runes, as the yellowing display placard insinuated. Since then, the stones have been subjected to intensive study and have generated bitter disagreement over their meaning.

Then Dr. Barry Fell entered the scene, the same man who made such a splash with his theories on Micmac ideograms in Nova Scotia. Upon analysis of photographs and rubber mold copies (latex peels) of the markings, Dr. Fell issued a report in the *Bulletin of the Early Sites Research Society* stating that the writing style was Libyan, with a tentative date of 500 B.C. With the aid of tombstones of Roman soldiers found in North Africa and inscribed in both Latin and Libyan, Professor Fell made the following translation: Top line: "Thus far our expedition traveled in the service of Lord Hiram, to conquer land." Lower line: "This is the record of Hanta, who attained the great-river. And these words cut on stone." The great-river reference was presumably to the St. Lawrence.

Thus, according to Fell, the Sherbrooke stones represented the written records of ancient Mediterranean explorers in America. With this introduction, two University of Laval professors spent the next several months analyzing the markings. They concluded that the Sherbrooke inscription was *not* in any way related to Libyan, since, according to one of the scientists, Libyan contains certain elements that are not found on the Sherbrooke inscription. Instead, the markings seemed to match an obscure style of writing found on a cave wall in southern Bulgaria! Even more remarkable, the two Canadian scholars postulated that if the markings on the Quebec stone were genuine, they could mean that an as yet unknown Old World people preceded a Carthaginian-Libyan exploration of North America by at least a millennium; according to their studies, the Bulgarian script appears to predate the development of the Phoenician alphabet in the Mediterranean by at least 500 years!

Libyans, Carthaginians, Bulgarians? What do we make of all this? It seems as though some scholars in the 1970s and 1980s had Mediterranean North Africans on the brain. It will take many decades of study before we know the provenance of the people who carved the Sherbrooke inscriptions. Assuming the markings are genuine, future scholarly disputes over exact translations are inevitable. What is important is to recognize that two incised rock slabs housed in a seminary museum in southern Quebec have mysterious markings that have provoked some researchers to make the most outlandish interpretations. But inscriptions do that to people. Especially ones with script markings that are indecipherable.

Then again, there is the possibility that someone "recently" carved and left the stones in the farmer's field. Wouldn't that be interesting?

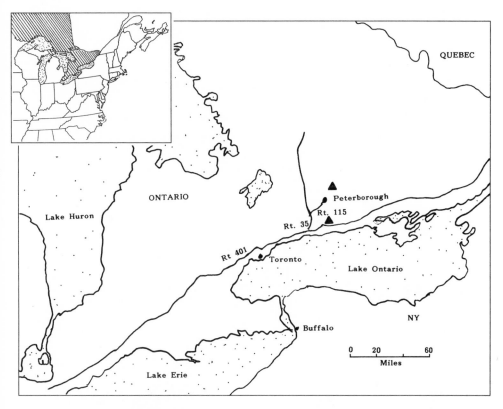

*Mysterious sites in southern Ontario*

### Contact Person(s) / Organization

Museum of the Sherbrooke Seminary
195 Marquette Street
Sherbrooke, Quebec
Canada
(819) 564–3200

### Total Magnetic Field / Inclination Angle
None taken at the museum site.

### Further Investigations in Area
Real inscribed stones (not modern fakes) never appear as isolated events. They seem to occur in multiples. With that in mind, a thorough search of the fields around Bromptonville, as well as the banks along the St. Francois, is in order. Of course, it wouldn't hurt to brush up on your Bulgarian *and* Libyan, either.

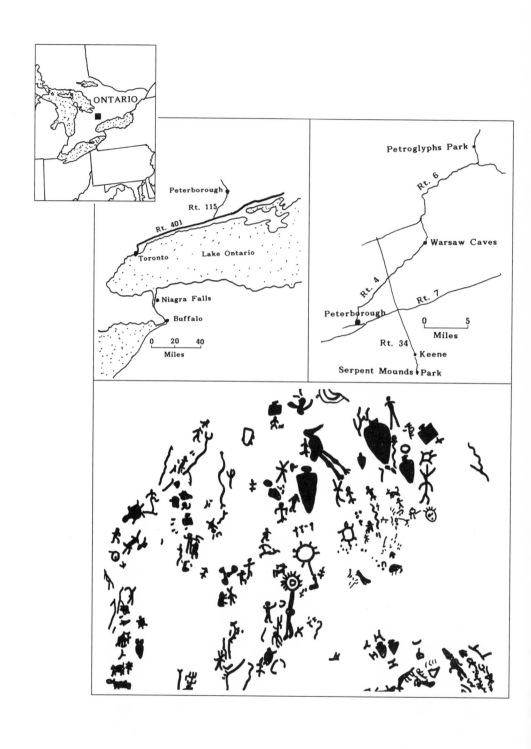

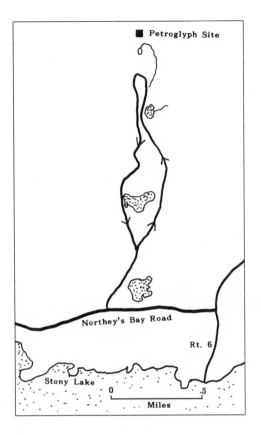

## PETROGLYPHS

Petroglyph Park, north of Peterborough, Ontario

### Site Synopsis

Strange markings on a sacred rock were found in the woods north of Peterborough, Ontario. Some of the glyphs are understandable. Most are not.

### Location

From Toronto, take Route 401 east for about 65 kilometers (40 miles). Turn off at Exit 436 going north on Route 115. Stay on Route 115 north for about 49 kilometers (30 miles). Once in Peterborough, take Route 4 north for about 40 kilometers (25 miles) until it intersects with Route 6. From the intersection, follow Route 6 north to Northey's Bay Road. Turn left here. Drive for about a kilometer (.6 miles) turning north (right) onto the Petroglyph Road. Stay on this road. In a little more than 2 kilometers (1.2 miles), you'll reach the parking lot. From this point, you'll need to walk about half a kilometer (⅛ of a mile) to the site.

## CONSIDERATIONS

The park is open from the second Friday of May to the end of October, from 10 A.M.–5 P.M. The gates are locked at 5:30 P.M. There's a daily vehicle permit fee charged.

Be careful of the poison ivy as you wander around the park. And remember to take only pictures. Nothing may be removed! All artifacts and natural objects of archeological or historical interest must be left in place.

### History / Background

Peterborough was settled in the nineteenth century. Then, in the 1820s, over 2,000 Irish immigrants moved into the region courtesy of a Peter Robinson who organized the migration. They showed their appreciation by naming their community after him.

Petroglyph Provincial Park is about 55 kilometers (34 miles) northeast of Peterborough. On a large, flat, sloping white marble rock over 63 feet long are 300 recognizable carvings and over 600 indecipherable glyphs. The petroglyph site was first discovered in 1924 by a member of the Peterborough Historical Society, although it didn't receive much attention at the time. Then, in 1954, a geological survey team rediscovered it, and since that time it's been the subject of much controversy. Extensive surveys were made in the vicinity, and two other small sites were uncovered near this large one.

During the initial search, archeologists uncovered about thirty hammerstones nearby. These are very hard yet shaped small stones that are believed to be some of the instruments used to peck out the rock carvings.

It is thought that the aboriginal Algonquian Indian peoples carved the shapes and figures here over a period from 500 to 1,000 years ago. Today, members of the Canadian Ojibwa Anishinabe Nation revere this as a sacred site. The shapes and figures have deep spiritual meaning to these people. They call it Kinomagewapkong, which means, "the rocks that teach" or, "teaching rock." They believe that the holes in the rocks are entrances to the spirit world, and that this site is a natural gateway.

From the historical record we know that Ojibwa youth went on vision quests for up to ten days. They walked into the forest to commune with spirits. It is possible that many of these young people came to this spot to carve the glyphs. There is disagreement, however, about this point. Scholars who have carefully studied the carvings here are convinced that they were done by very skilled artists—people who had done this *many* times before. After viewing the carvings up close, I'm inclined to agree with these experts. These are careful renditions of a variety of sacred images. They are too complex for the inexperienced carver, and appear to be the work of shamans.

It's been said that people who visit this site experience a range of emotions, from enlightenment to confusion. The Ojibwa have their own special interpretation of the symbols, but they don't say much. We are left with ghostly innuendo and heresay in our interpretation of the carvings.

The manitou is a spirit that dwells in sacred places. Many native people in North America were convinced that special rocks sites, hills, trees, and so on were the domains of different manitous. Some places were sought out by natives to get inspiration or strength from the residing manitou. The prolonged use of this rock ledge (over a 500-year period) attests to the highly spiritual nature of this place.

The following is a rather primitive interpretation of the carvings that's based on the late 1960s survey.

The thirteen turtle carvings on the rocks may have been a symbol of fertility and patience to the natives in the region. The five-foot-long bird symbol may have been a crane. Just why it was important to shamans is not known. The boatlike carvings do not look like the typical birch-bark canoes of Ontario's early residents. Some researchers think these boat images represent ancient European contact with Canadian natives. Other anthropologists, however, think the boats are some type of magical shaman vessel.

The triangular-shaped objects are quite prominent at the rock. Perhaps it represents a shaman in a large flowing skin cape. The snake motif is very common here. There's a very weird figure with a cone-shaped head holding some implement. Perhaps it's another shaman in headdress shaking a rattle. A rather large figure of a person with a sun head is thought to be a carving of Gitchi Manitou, or the Great Spirit, the all-powerful creator of the world.

The above comments are based on frequency of glyphs, oral legends, and contemporary native interpretation of the symbols. They may all be wrong. The best thing you can do is visit this site. Spend several hours roaming around the grounds. Stare at the petroglyphs and come to your own conclusion. It will be as valid as any stated in the most esteemed anthropological journal, since no one seems to have much of a clue to their true meaning.

### Contact Person(s) / Organization

*Summer Address:* May 12–October 9
Petroglyphs Provincial Park
General Delivery
Woodview, Ontario K0L 3EO
(705) 877–2552

*Winter Address:* October 10–May 11
Ministry of Natural Resources
PO Box 500
Bancroft, Ontario K0L 1C0
(613) 332–3940

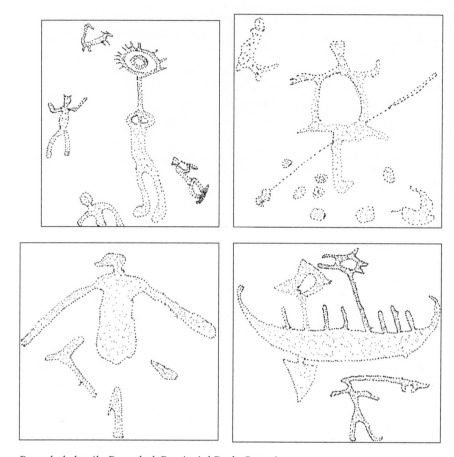

*Petroglyph details, Petroglyph Provincial Park, Ontario.*

Natural Resources Information Centre
Macdonald Block, Room M1–73
900 Bay Street, Toronto, Ontario M7A 2C1
(416) 314–1717

Peterborough Chamber of Commerce
(705) 748–9771

### Total Magnetic Field / Inclination Angle

The measurements I recorded here were intriguing: The area surrounding the park had a total magnetic field reading of around 550 milligauss, with an average inclination angle of 70 degrees. At the actual rock ledge, the total magnetic field reading was 320 milligauss, with a 50-degree inclination angle.

That's what happened the first time I measured here. I came back another day, and I couldn't get a stable reading! The magnetometer readout fluctuated wildly. It's possible that the underground stream near this ledge rock was in some way responsible. I suspect this rock was chosen due to its specific location.

### Further Investigation in Area

Although a major investigation launched soon after this site's rediscovery found no petroglyphs, some must still be hidden away. There are, however, many other sites scattered throughout Ontario that are accessible. Most are painted, not rock-carved sites: Mazinaw Lake, Bon Echo Provincial Park, Agawa Bay, Lake Superior Provincial Park, and Quetico Provincial Park.

The definitive publication on this site is: Joan and Ron Vastokas, *Sacred Art of the Algonkians* (Peterborough, Ontario: Mansard Press, 1973).

## SERPENT MOUND

Serpent Mounds Provincial Park, Keene, Ontario

### Site Synopsis

Near the shores of a glacial lake are nine burial mounds that date back over 2,000 years. One of them is in the zigzag form of a serpent. Does this sinuous outline have some mystical significance?

### Location

From Toronto, take Route 401 east for about 97 kilometers (60 miles). Take Exit 464, going north on Route 28 for about 19 kilometers (12 miles). Turn east onto Route 2 for 24 kilometers (15 miles) going into Keene. Once in Keene go south on Route 34 for a few kilometers. This leads directly to Serpent Mounds Provincial Park.

### Considerations

The Canadian government has leased this land from the Hiawatha Indians for over fifteen years. There is some concern among government archeologists that the lease will not be renewed. Call before driving out to this wonderful site.

### History / Background

Two thousand years ago native people annually congregated on a hill overlooking the shore of Rice Lake, gathering the wild rice that grew along the marshy banks and feasting on clams. They stayed long enough to construct several grave mounds before moving out to hunt and gather in different locales.

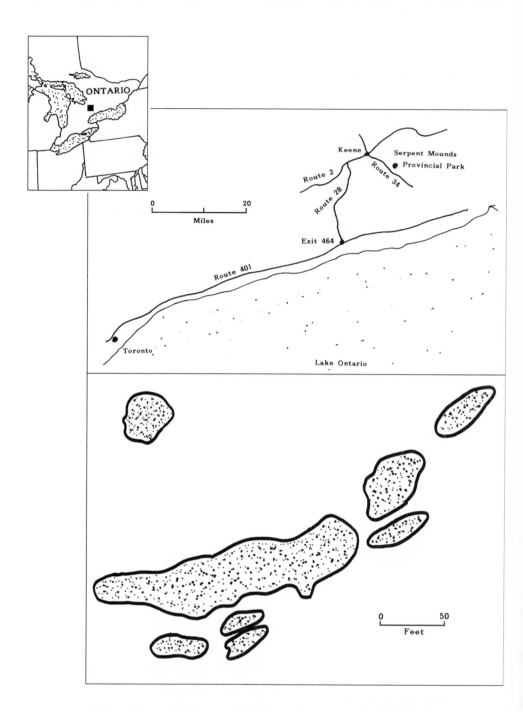

Eight of the mounds here are simple ovals. The ninth and largest mound is over 170 feet long, 24 feet wide, and 6 feet high. The angular zigzag along its length leads most to suspect that the mound was built in a serpent form. If so, then this would be only the second such mound ever found in North America. The other serpent mound is located in Ohio.

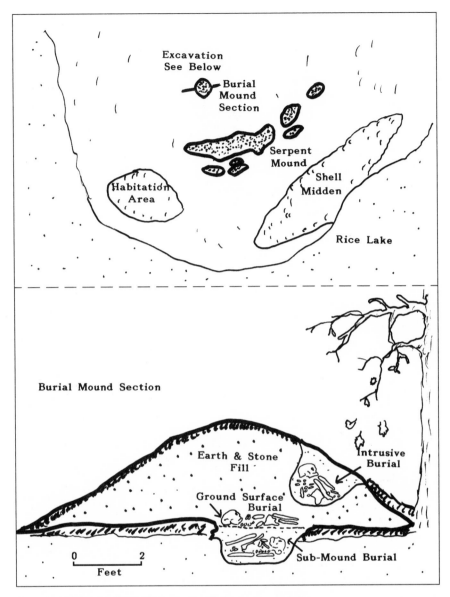

*Overview of Serpent Mound site and burial mount excavation*
*(Ontario Ministry of Natural Resources).*

Excavations since the late 1800s have revealed much about the people who built these strange mounds. Infant mortality was high. Most of the people died of natural causes, not from battle wounds. A good many people were afflicted with arthritis and tuberculosis.

Over 100 individuals were interred beneath the long Serpent Mound that was probably started around 128 A.D. The goods found at the burial site told some strange tales. Left with the bones were copper pins and conch shells. The pins came from the northern Lake Superior region, some 400 miles to the west, while the conch shells came from the Gulf of Mexico, some 630 miles to the south! These implements provide evidence of extensive trade routes in ancient America.

The Serpent Mounds site is intriguing for other reasons as well. Given the long use of the grave mounds, only a small number of people were buried there. Why? Who were these special people? While we can never fully answer that question, we can still appreciate the ancient fondness for this beautiful, sacred site.

### Contact Person(s) / Organization

Serpent Mounds Provincial Park
RR 3
Keene, Ontario K0L 2G0
(705) 295–6879
May 12–September 4

Park Superintendent
Ministry of Natural Resources
Lindsay District
(705) 324–6121
Fax: (705) 324–7619

Natural Resources Information Centre
Macdonald Block, Room M1–73
900 Bay Street
Toronto, Ontario M7A 2C1
(416) 314–2000

### Total Magnetic Field / Inclination Angle
None taken at this archeologically disturbed site.

### Further Investigations in Area
Two excellent references that will put these strange mounds into perspective are:

Richard B. Johnson, "The Archeology of the Serpent Mounds Site," *Ontario Art and Archeology Occasional Paper* 10 (1968). Ontario: Royal Ontario Museum.

David Boyle, "Mounds," *Annual Archeological Report.* Ontario: Royal Ontario Museum, pp. 14–57.

# FOUR

# Maine

**M**aine is a study in contrasts. Inland a heavy cover of pine trees graces rugged mountains as crystal blue lakes dot a countryside sometimes called "the last wilderness frontier in the East." Towns are few in the isolated northwest where giant mills pulverize trees into paper and toothpicks. Along the rockweed coastline, the Atlantic pounds against granite sea ledges. Raging storms called nor'easters sometimes keep vessels docked for days as they rip into high coastal headlands.

In the sixteenth century, soon after Europe realized that Columbus had not reached India, other explorers were employed to search for a northwest passage to the wealth of the Orient. While they all failed to find a waterway across the new frontier, they did manage to find, near the northeastern coast, one of the world's richest fishing grounds. Thriving seaports naturally grew as sailors forgot about spices and instead turned to fishing and its handsome profits.

A visit to the Maine coastline today can be disappointing for sunseekers. Creepy mists seem to roll in at odd hours of the day because of prevailing winds and the temperature of the ocean. To be closed in for several days in a "thick-o'fog," although great for blueberries, makes for a painful experience to those in need of stimulating sunshine.

Nevertheless, prepare yourself for a mystical experience along the rocky shores of Maine. The ancient petroglyphs and inscriptions seen in either brilliant sunshine or misty fog are guaranteed to raise you to another level.

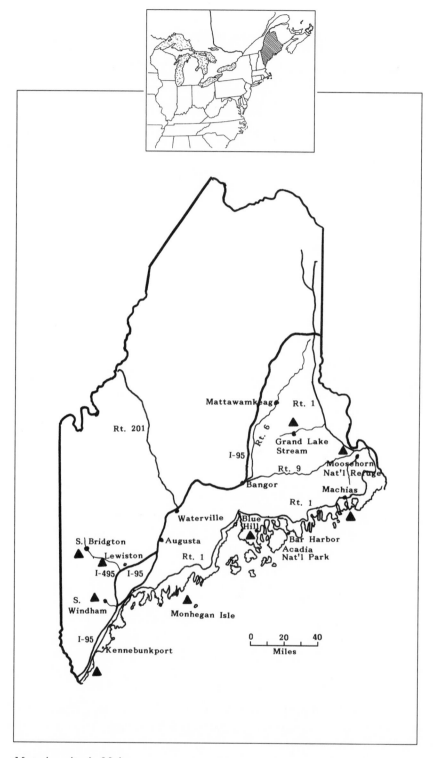

*Mysterious sites in Maine*

# NORTHEAST MAINE

Driving south from Canada into northeastern Maine is an interesting experience. Aside from road signs printed with miles instead of kilometers it is difficult, at first, to realize when you have entered the United States. The influence of Canada is pronounced. Fishing and lumbering is a year-round way of life. Canadian broadcasts on the day's catch and the day's cut are on local radio and television stations. As you venture north into the backwoods, the lakes and alderbush become dominant. The entire northeastern coastline must have once been like this section of Maine.

## PETROGLYPHS
Clark's Cove at Birch Point, Machiasport, Maine

### Site Synopsis
On several long, flat boulder slabs protruding from the water at low tide are dozens of strangely incised, or pecked images. Some seem to be rectangular-shaped people. Others are clearly animals, perhaps deer, while others have the shape of a person but the head of a bird. Who carved these?

### Location
From Bangor take Alternate Route 1 south for about 25 miles to Ellsworth. Continue on Route 1 going north for about 60 miles to Machias. Once in Machias, take a right turn onto Elm Street (Route 92) toward Machiasport. You'll be going in an southeasterly direction along the peninsula. From the Elm Street turnoff, you'll see the Gates House about 3 miles on your left. This early-nineteenth-century structure houses the Machiasport Historical Society.

From the Gates House, continue along the road very slowly, for it is exceedingly hazardous. After 2.7 miles, turn left at an intersection stop sign. Track your miles carefully, because this road's easy to miss. In fact, if you see a large white church on your left, you've just passed the road, one-tenth of a mile back. If you've overshot the road, stop at the church parking lot and look out toward the church "backyard." You'll see the little cove where the petroglyphs are.

From the stop sign proceed down the road for .7 miles. At that point the public road stops and the private driveway of the access-road owner begins. Park well off the road, away from any neighbor's driveway, and ask permission to walk to the site. One set of petroglyphs is at the bottom of the cove on a long rock that looks like a beached whale. The others are out on a long hump of rock a few yards from shore during low tide.

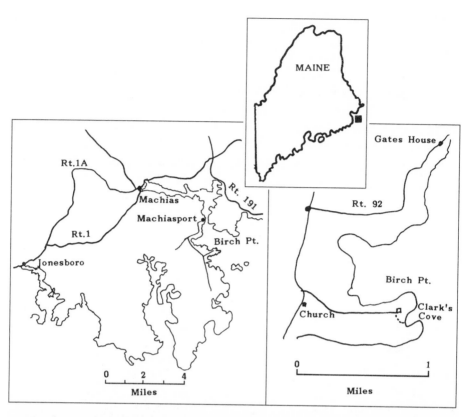

## Considerations

Plan on spending some time at the Machiasport Historical Society in the Gates House. On the second floor there's a wonderful display on the petro- glyphs and an article on the images by the archeologist, James Whittall. Study the images carefully. It will be helpful for later study at the rocks.

As access to this site is through private property, you absolutely, positively, *must* get the landowner's permission to walk down to the rocks. Failure to do so can result in some rather serious trespassing violations. Please contact the current owner of either access home.

The only other alternative is to access the rocks via boat during low tide.

It is important to keep track of the tides, since most of the glyphs will be exposed when the tide is low. Check with any marine shop along the coast for a tide chart.

The best time to actually see all of the petroglyphs is in late March/early April. The new harvest of rockweed has not yet taken hold of the rocks, so they will be barren in all their glory. While summer is more pleasant, it is sometimes difficult to see the markings and designs due to the seaweed cover- ing. Whatever season you go, however, plan on being at the site a little after dawn or a little before sunset. The angle of the sun will bring out the inscrip- tions in a way that the noonday sun will not.

These inscriptions are *very* difficult to see. They were made by pecking out the outer coating of the rock face. Their suspected extreme antiquity has slowly eroded both the pecked and nonpecked sections, making for difficult viewing. With careful study, however, you'll eventually see them all.

## History/Background

The area around Machiasport was settled in the 1760s. The region was a leader in the lumber and shipbuilding industries due to the swift-running Machias River and the primeval forest cover. Fishing, of course, was a growth industry at the time.

The rocks on which the petroglyphs appear is at Clark's Point on the northwestern side of Machias Bay. The main rock ledge is about 15 feet wide and 50 feet long from east to west. It's a blue-black, shist-slate composition. There are several more ledges that are exposed only at low tide.

Nineteenth century scholars believed the Abenaki people—a division of the eastern Algonquian Indians—carved the rocks. Professors at the time who in- terviewed the local Mechises Indians—a branch of the Abenaki—about the carvings reported that "all their old men knew of them, either by having seen them or by traditions handed down through many generations."[1]

In 1868 a Machias man made the first sketch of the petroglyphs and sent it off to the Smithsonian. Soon afterwards, curiosity seekers started pulling off slabs of the rock for mementos. In 1888, Garrick Mallery of the Smithsonian

*Looking toward Birch Point, Clarks Cove, Machiasport, Maine. Dozens of petroglyphs are pecked into the rocks scattered around this site.*

Institution got around to visiting the site and published the first detailed description of the petroglyphs. Almost a hundred years later James Whittall and a team from the Early Sites Research Society spent several days making exact reproductions of all of the petroglyphs. His work is on exhibit at the Machiasport Historical Society.

There are dozens of petroglyph markings along this cove. So many, in fact, that the usual questions arise: How old are they? What do they mean? Why are they all seemingly located along this cove? Mallery believed that the stone lay on a common line of communication between two major Indian tribes in the region. As he put it, they "were convenient as halting places."[2]

One of the images at this cove is the Thunderbird. Native Americans believed this creature was a powerful spirit whose flapping wings cause thunder across the land. It was also thought to be responsible for rain and, by association, the fertility of the earth.

Another image, of rectangular-shaped people, makes this cove quite special, since these figures are rarely found in this region. Perhaps this cove was a place of great spirituality. Perhaps it was a place to give thanks for past and future hunts. The bird-headed humanoid would seem to represent some type of

*A nineteenth-century sketch of Machiasport, Maine, petroglyphs*
(*Mallery,* 10th Annual Report).

deity or spirit. Again, why here? Measurement of magnetic flux may provide some of the answers.

### Contact Person(s)/Organization

Gates House, Home of the
Historical Society of Machiasport
(Built in 1807, this Federal-style house has a great
upstairs exhibit on the petroglyphs. On a clear day
you can see Birch Point.)
Open June–mid September; Tuesday–Saturday, 12:30–4:30 P.M.
Closed end of September–May.
(207) 255-8461

Early Sites Research Society
Rowley, Massachusetts 01969

### Total Magnetic Field/Inclination Angle

A sampling of the total magnetic field associated with this cove was pretty revealing. In general, the path leading down to the cove as well as the land surrounding the rocks had a higher TMF/IA reading than the petroglyphs themselves.

*Thunderbird petroglyph,*
*Machiasport, Maine.*

With respect to magnetic field, the area of the symbols seems quite different from the surrounding uplands. Was this change enough to influence the neurotransmitter secretion levels of the ancients? Did these particular rocks "feel" better than other rocks? I measured most of the large, flat exposed boulders in the vicinity of the cove and found, intriguingly, a TMF/IA that matched the upper vicinity. Only at the petroglyph rocks did I find a greatly reduced magnetic field!

### Further Investigations in Area

From Hog Island in Holmes Bay (a part of Machias Bay) comes a report of similarly styled petroglyphs. And there are further reports that many more petroglyphs exist on rocks a bit further out from Clark's Cove, but they are continuously underwater! If so, this brings up some intriguing speculation. The last time the sea level was low enough for people to carve symbols on rocks was more than 12,000 years ago.

A few years ago I joined an early spring survey team to search for a strange set of walls, stone shelters, and marks on cliff walls. The reputed site was about 25 to 30 miles northeast of Machias, up Route 191, near, but not in, the Moosehorn National Wildlife Refuge. We never found the chambers or walls, but we did find a lot of just-awakening bears. I'm convinced those lithic remains are out in the northeast corner of the state. Maine has some terrain that is very difficult to negotiate, and things simply get covered up.

Intriguingly, about 25 miles northwest of this suspected site a hunter found petroglyphs and a slab chamber that might have been used as a burial tomb.[3]

In the late 1980s, retired carpenter Walter Elliott of Grand Lake Stream, a village about 50 miles from the coast of northeastern Maine, uncovered hundreds of petroglyphs that no one in the area had seen before. On a rock ledge that slopes down into the water at the head of Big Falls, about a half mile from the village, Elliott noticed the marks. Some appear to be initials, perhaps of fishermen and loggers who worked in Grand Lake's hemlock tannery in the 1870s. It is said that some of the glyphs are the mystical symbols of Abenaki Indian shamans who lived here for thousands of years before white settlement. But some of the marks fit no category whatsoever. Others seem odd and out of place, resembling markings that appear in other parts of the East. Some even look similar to those found in a nearby chamber.

Just across from the petroglyph ledge, Elliott uncovered a series of slate slabs that were laid over an opening between another rock ledge and a row of

*Petroglyph and burial tomb site at Grand Lake Stream, Maine.*

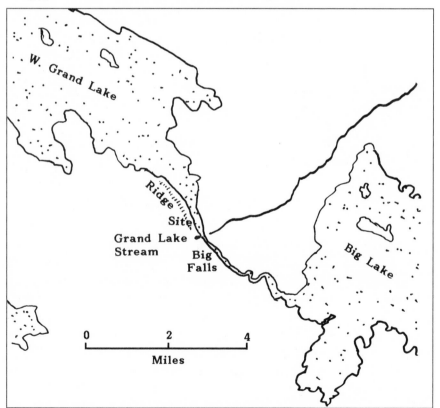

*Two-holed amulet with sun symbol and strange inscription that was found in burial tomb chamber at Grand Lake Stream, Maine.*

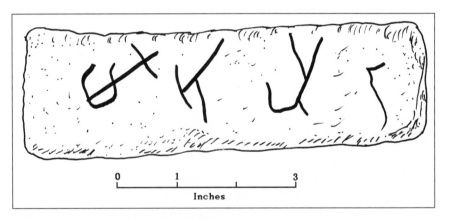

*Symbols found on stone taken from burial tomb chamber at Grand Lake Stream, Maine.*

stones. The inside of this "tunnel-like" chamber was coated in a yellowish orange slimy substance, now believed to be yellow ochre.

Ochre was a mixture of colored pigments that New England Maritime Indians placed on their dead before burial. This mysterious tribe, sometimes referred to as the Red-Paint people, were skilled sailors who lived along the northeastern coast for well over eight thousand years. They were superb craftsmen, shaping stone tools as easily as other cultures shaped clay. Just where these people came from and where they went to is a topic of great controversy. About the only other place in the world where this particular recipe of red ochre and stone tool design can be found is western Europe, circa eight thousand years ago.

From under the yellowish dirt, Elliott pulled out three stone artifacts that continue to defy rational explanation. Where they came from and what they mean is unknown. The symbols and "lettering" are unlike anything seen in traditional Maine Indian burials. If there was a burial inside this stone, boxlike chamber, the bones would have dissolved years ago, due to the highly acidic soil here. (See illustrations on preceding page.)

The story in this general vicinity gets even stranger when one considers another chance discovery.

In 1961 an amateur archeologist was poking around an ancient Indian rubbish heap—known as a midden—near Blue Hill, a coastal town just west of the Mount Desert Narrows near Acadia National Park. Inside the midden he uncovered a thin, badly worn, small disklike object that had a cross on one side and an animal head on the other. Initially, the Maine State Museum in Augusta identified the dime-sized object as a twelfth-century English coin. That alone would have been interesting enough. However, in 1978, a retired military historian who had always had doubts about this official identification discussed the find with a noted British numismatist (coin specialist). Incredibly, the numismatist said the coin was almost certainly a Norse penny, probably dating to the 1070s. The fact that the coin was found in a *coastal* Indian garbage pile suggests that someone who owned a Norse coin had sailed by and given or traded it to the Indians.[4]

*Slabs of rock covered this opening in the ledge rock at Grand Lake Stream, Maine.*

## SOUTHEAST MAINE

The southeastern sector of Maine was originally settled in the seventeenth
century by New England and British families who, attracted by the region's
economic potential—shipbuilding, timber, and fish—migrated into the Kennebec
River Valley and established the first towns. But as the settlers cut down and
cleared the woodland once believed to be impenetrable, the vestiges of an earlier age were brought to light. Farmers found the remains of chimneys and
moldered ruins which had been overgrown by the forest. These stone structures, at one time thought to be the shelters of settler fishermen, have since
been found in practically every part of northeastern America. Furthermore,
several other types of remains consistently found in the Maine region over the
past two centuries have led some scholars to suspect that the rock-clad coastline may have harbored boats and sheltered fishermen thousands of years before a certain Genoan claimed he had sailed to India.

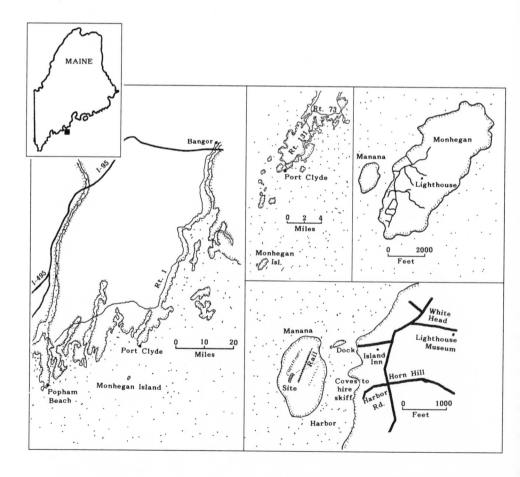

## INSCRIPTION
Manana Island, off Monhegan Island, Maine

### Site Synopsis
Weird markings, seemingly carved across the face of a rock, have caused excitement, controversy, and changing interpretation since their discovery more than one hundred years ago.

### Location
From Portland, Maine, take Route 95 to Exit 22 (Coastal Route 1). Follow Route 1 north for about 44 miles. At Thomaston turn right at Route 131 South. Follow this lovely winding highway for 15 miles to Port Clyde. Ferries leave on a regular basis from this port. (See Considerations below.)

Once you arrive on Monhegan, you'll need to find someone to take you to Manana Island. Walk down to the Sandy Beach Cove, or simply ask some of the fishermen if they know anyone who can get you across.

Once on Manana you'll need to climb up the hill, walking past the Coast Guard rail tracks. Just beyond the rail tracks the hill slopes downward. Walk south (toward the water) along this little valley depression for a few hundred feet, and on your right (west) you'll see a flat grayish rock face. You're at the inscription!

### Considerations
At Port Clyde, Captain James Barstow owns and operates the Monhegan Boat Line. Two 1950s-era converted island mail boats take passengers across the 12 miles to Monhegan. Following is a sample of their seasonal schedule, but be forewarned: Call and get the current version and book your reservation early (see phone number below). During the spring, summer, and fall the boats run seven days a week. The trip costs around $25–$30 for adults and $14–$18 per child (1–12 years).

Depending on the season, the boats run around four times per day, starting in the summer at 7:00 A.M. The last boat departing Monhegan in the summer is at 6:00 P.M. It's much earlier during the other seasons—either 12 noon or 4:30 P.M. Sailing time is around fifty to seventy minutes, depending on the boat and sea conditions.

There are several ferry runs from various places along the coast, such as Spruce Point south of Boothbay Harbor or from New Harbor on the Pemaquid Neck. I prefer Port Clyde because it's very low key and authentic—no toney art galleries there.

The only other opportunity to get to Monhegan is to hire a charter. Ask around at the dock or in the neighboring stores for a commercial charter. One warning: This can be very expensive for a 12-mile trip.

When you get to Monhegan, walk down past the Island Inn toward Harbor Road. Ask around for someone to row you across the small inlet to Manana Island. That's the only way to get there! Be patient. These people have their own schedules and things to do. The trip across the inlet takes about ten minutes and should cost around $5.00. Remember, there is *no* regularly scheduled boat that goes across. You are totally dependent upon the locals, so be very pleasant and undemanding!

If you have to wait for a while, I recommend that you head over to the lighthouse. It has a wonderful museum that will give you a great introduction to the area.

Prepare before embarking on this interesting journey. Coastal fog has a habit of suddenly appearing, so bring a warm sweater and a windbreaker. There are no banks on the island, and few of the eating places take credit cards. Carry a quantity of cash with you for hiring a skiff to Manana and for food and beverages while waiting. Public phones take no money and require a phone credit card. Bike riding is not allowed.

### History/Background

During the summer of 1971, Walter Elliott (see page 69), while strolling along the shore in Popham Beach State Park in southeastern Maine, found

*Overview of "inscription" on Manana Island, just west of Monhegan Island, Maine, as recorded by Henry Schoolcraft in 1857 (from Schoolcraft,* History of the Indian Tribes of the United States).

three runic stones in a gravel bank near the seaside. The stones contained characters that were used by tenth-century Norsemen. They were eventually turned over to the State Museum in Augusta, where they were analyzed and proclaimed authentic. How they got to Maine, however, is still a question that puzzles archeologists.

About 25 miles east of Popham Beach are two islands that may have been used as trading stops even before Vikings sailed west of Iceland. Monhegan Island is little more than one-and-a-half miles long and three-quarters of a mile wide. Across a tiny harbor on its southwestern end is Manana Island, which is even smaller, ranging less than half a mile in length and one-quarter of a mile in width. Both islands figure in the seventeenth-century history of the Maine coast, for they were used by fishermen as docking stations before their catches were transported to Europe.

Long before John Smith visited it in 1614, Native Americans knew the region as a great place to fish. There are shell middens scattered around the coastal region that testify to the type and amount of fish caught in ancient times. In fact, up until very recently it was common for Monhegan Island fishermen to catch so many 25-pound cod that they usually gave away what they couldn't sell. But now with changing ecosystems, overfishing, net dragging, and the increased seal population one is lucky to find even a four-pound cod in these waters.

In the mid 1850s, a Dr. Augustus C. Hamlin of Bangor, Maine, found

*Modern overview of "inscription" of Manana Island, Maine. Someone printed a large "X" near the site.*

what appeared to be an inscription carved along the face of a weathered rock outcropping near a high hilltop on Manana Island. Dr. Hamlin presented his finding at a scientific meeting in Albany, New York, where the general consensus among scholars was that the markings resembled "pointed runic characters." For many years afterwards, antiquarians proudly pointed to the Manana Island inscription as definite proof of early Viking contact. By the late nineteenth century, however, opinion had changed. A geologist traveled to the island and declared the so-called inscription to be a folly of nature. This idea was reaffirmed in 1971 by an authority from the Carnegie Museum in Pittsburgh who interpreted the carvings as a "mere erosion phenomenon."

In 1975 archeologists James Whittall and William Nisbet sent latex peels and photographs of the markings to Dr. Barry Fell for study. Fell's analysis was far different from those of previous scholars. He claimed that the seemingly random slashes and grooves from Manana Island were in reality examples of an unrecognized Celtic script known as Hinge-ogam. It differed from the seventy well-known varieties of Irish ogam recorded in an eight-hundred-year-old manuscript known as the *Book of Ballymote* in that it lacked symbols for vowels. Past epigraphers apparently had failed to understand these differences and therefore had seen runes or natural erosion instead. Barry Fell thought he had cracked the code of a previously unknown writing system! Amazing, if true.

Reading from right to left, he made the following translation: "Long-ships from Phoenicia: Cargo-lots (and) landing-quay." In other words, the symbols seemed to be a message to Phoenician merchant-sailors that Manana Island was a place to pick up merchandise, presumably fish. Similarly inscribed stones from northern Portugal and southern Spain, having been dated on the basis of associated archeological assemblages, imply that the Manana inscription was composed around 400 B.C.

Across the harbor on Monhegan, a tiny arrowhead, or possibly a small dagger, was recovered from an excavation of a rubbish heap by the island's archeologist. A carbon-14 test of the organic material associated with the de-

*Detail of "inscription" on Manana Island, Maine, as recorded by Henry Schoolcraft in 1857 (from Schoolcraft,* History of the Indian Tribes of the United States).

*Modern close-up of "inscription" on Manana Island, Maine. Betweem 1975 and 1980 someone hacked off a section of the markings.*

posited metal artifact gave an approximate date of 1800 B.C. The seemingly insignificant arrowhead was composed of copper and tin, which was *very* intriguing, for there are no tin deposits in either the eastern or middle states of America. The nearest mines are in Bolivia, but these deposits had not yet been worked in 1800 B.C. We must look elsewhere to explain how a copper and tin artifact found its way into an island trash pile that had remained undisturbed for perhaps over three-thousand seven hundred and fifty years.

Tin in the form of its alloy, bronze, was widely used in the Old World during ancient times. Tin mining was reported in central Europe as early as 2000 B.C., and later in Persia, Spain, France, and the British Isles. The Phoenicians are credited with spreading the bronze culture throughout the Mediterranean due to their tin trade. Phoenician ships, as early as 1300 B.C., regularly sailed from Cornish and Spanish tin mines to all parts of the known world.

If we accept the Manana Island translations of Barry Fell, then the copper-tin projectile point takes on a whole new meaning.

Then, again, it is also possible that the copper arrowhead was brought over to the island during the past two to three hundred years of exploration and settlement. Perhaps some pirate picked it up during trade with Spain and eventually threw it out in a rubbish heap.

Recently, some geologists (and locals) have argued again that the inscriptions are merely an eroded rock face. It's possible, because many of the other rocks in the vicinity have long vertical grooves. But the site in question is the only one that seems to have horizontal and vertical slashes in a form that *might* be script. Once again we are faced with a mysterious dilemma: Is it really an inscription? And, if so, who created it: Phoenicians, Celts, Iberians, Mother Nature? This one's very difficult to say for sure, though the magnetic field fluxes wildly.

In any event, this is a cool site to visit. Sit by the rock. Look out over the gorgeous ocean, visualize ancient (or "modern") sea vessels breaking by. You'll fall in love with the place.

### Contact Person(s)/Organization

Captain James Barstow
Monhegan Boat Line
PO Box 238
Port Clyde, Maine 04855
(207) 372-8848

Excellent background material on Maine's other sites, including an inscription on private property near the southeastern coastal town of York can be found in Robert Ellis Cahill's *New England's Ancient Mysteries*. This book will definitely whet your appetite for more. Unfortunately, no directions or location details are given for any of the sites listed.

### Total Magnetic Field/Inclination Angle

The total magnetic field and inclination angle decreased as I approached the inscription. It dropped from a general reading of 580 milligauss/73 degrees to 360 milligauss and 58 degrees.

### Further Investigations in Area

If this site is actually an inscription, then there must be more on other islands. Few people have visited *all* the islands in southern Maine. Perhaps as more people realize the potential of finding ancient markings on rocks, more will come to light.

There's also a report of a stone chamber, tunnels, and another carved stone stairway in Lewiston, Maine.

After a visit to America's Stonehenge—the Mystery Hill site at North Salem, New Hampshire—a visitor remarked that what he saw was "just like the stuff back in Lewiston." He claimed that for years teenagers have been flocking to this wooded site to drink beer and to make love.

According to the visitor, to get to the site from Augusta, you take Interstate 495 south. Take Exit 13 into Lewiston, getting on Route 196 west (Lisbon Street). After one-and-a-half miles, turn left (southwest) onto Sand Hill Road. The site is supposed to be somewhere up the hill.

If this place exists and is like the Mystery Hill site, then it will be a very important find. Perhaps the weirdness of the place has attracted young people over the years. Perhaps it's just out of the way. Let me know what you find.

# FIVE

# New Hampshire/Vermont

## NEW HAMPSHIRE

Geologically, New Hampshire can be broken up into a few distinct areas. The smallest of these regions, known as the Seaboard Lowland, is in the southeastern section of the state. This area includes a coastal area of the state exposed to the Atlantic Ocean and the fertile basin of the Merrimack River.

New Hampshire was settled a few decades after the Pilgrims sailed to the New World. The eastern Massachusetts area very quickly became filled with English immigrants soon after the Pilgrims landed at Plymouth Rock. Many of these land-hungry families pushed out into the then-wilderness searching for tillable land with a good water supply. The routes they took through a dense, overgrown forest had been cut over thousands of years by the indigenous Indian population. These major paths and trails conveniently led to the most desirable patches of land. Not surprisingly, the natives were not pleased with this encroachment upon their ancestral lands. There were a host of skirmishes and all-out Indian-settler wars throughout this period. Soon after most of the Native Americans were exterminated, due primarily to better colonial weaponry and by the influx of European diseases like smallpox, and trees were cut and fields tilled.

As they began to uncover mysterious stone ruins along the water route of the Merrimack, many of the new inhabitants of this old land realized that an earlier people had lived there a very long time ago.

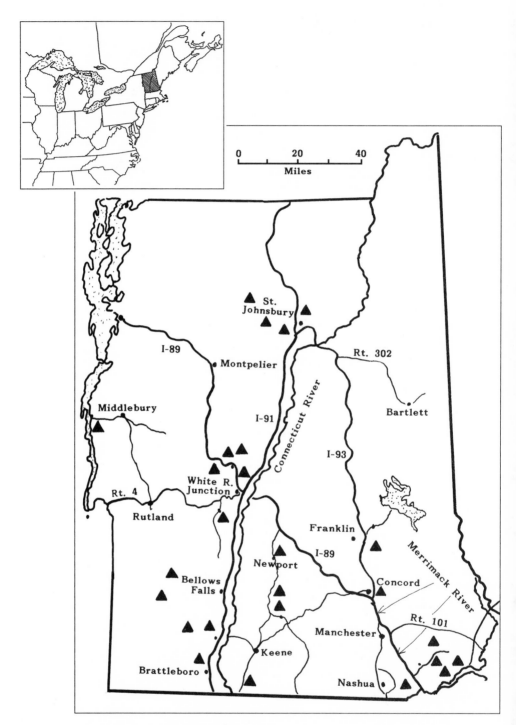

*Mysterious sites in New Hampshire and Vermont*

## SOUTH NEW HAMPSHIRE

Starting near the town of Franklin in south-central New Hampshire, at the confluence of the Pemigewasset and Winnepesaukee Rivers, the Merrimack River flows southward into Massachusetts, where it turns northeast, twisting along the corner of the state before emptying into the Atlantic Ocean at Newburyport. Its 110-mile course covers a drainage area of over 5,000 square miles. The lower Merrimack is a broad estuary that is navigable only by small boats for about the first fifteen miles. The main features of the middle and upper parts of the waterway during post-Colonial times were the many rapids and waterfalls. Scores of textile mills built along the churning waters brought great wealth to the area. Fortunes were made from gristmills as well.

The existence of the enormous quantity of stone ruins found along this water route, which was one of the major Indian trails in pre-Colonial New England, tends to be much better known to the general public because of the curious history of these ruins.

## MYSTERY HILL—AMERICA'S STONEHENGE
North Salem, New Hampshire

### Site Synopsis
On a hilltop in southern New Hampshire, a series of chambers, tunnels, standing stones, and other lithic remains have puzzled people for generations. No one knows who built them, what purpose they served, or when they were built.

### Location
From the Boston area, take Interstate 93 north for about 50 miles. Turn off at Exit 3 in New Hampshire. Stay on Route 111 going toward Canobie Lake. You'll cross the busy intersection of Route 28 in the process. From the Route 28 intersection, continue traveling for about 3½ miles on Route 111, turning right (southeast) on Haverhill Road. In a little less than a mile you'll see the right-hand turnoff into Mystery Hill. There are signs along the latter part of the route.

### Considerations
Mystery Hill is a privately run business. There is a small fee for entry to the grounds. The new and improved gateway building has a fabulous collection of books, articles, and audiovisual displays about the site as well as other New England mysteries. There's also a good set of exhibits showing the findings of several years of excavation.

Plan on spending several hours roaming around this intriguing place—and not just the main, fenced-off site. Wander the many trails that follow along the wallways. Ask if you can get a personal tour of the quarry site, which, for my money, puts the entire antiquity of this site into perspective. Look at the size of the monoliths they were blocking out. And with what tools? There are no chisel marks anywhere. The ancients must have used a fire/water technique: heating the rock and then splashing on cold water to crack it along the seams. Is there any record of English settlers doing that in the early 1700s when much simpler, more efficient techniques were available? I haven't found any.

Hours change by the season, but they generally are from 9:30 or 10:00 A.M. to around 5:00 or 7:00 P.M. Call or write first to get the correct times before going (see below).

Look past the tourist signs referring to a Sacrificial Table, America's Stonehenge, and the like. This place has nothing to do with Stonehenge. It's *far* more intriguing.

Wear good walking shoes, and if visiting in the summer, bring along a water bottle and some insect repellent—those hot, humid New Hampshire afternoons can bring out thousands of blood-sucking mosquitoes. Also, if venturing out to the quarry site, wear long pants and a long-sleeved shirt to protect against patches of poison oak and poison ivy. Topical skin barriers are marvelous products that allow you to actually touch toxic plant resins and not be affected. I use a product called Derma Plus which is manufactured by the Benchmark Company in Salt Lake City, Utah.

### History/Background

About 13 miles east of the Merrimack River, atop a wooded rise outside of North Salem, New Hampshire, an intriguing complex of granite walls, dry-stone chambers, underground passageways, standing monoliths, alignments, and inscriptions is spread over a 24-acre fenced hilltop. Known as Mystery Hill, the site has long fascinated the layperson and angered the professional archeologist, in part because of its previous history of exploration by inept researchers.

The first person known to be associated with the site was a Jonathan Pattee, who built a house amid the stone ruins in 1826. In the mid 1850s, a fire destroyed his brick farmhouse, forcing the family to settle elsewhere in the community. Left to the elements, the charred remains were eventually covered over with years of plant growth.

Residents referred to the stone structures adjoining the house foundation simply as Pattee's Caves. They erroneously assumed that the nineteenth-century farmer had a penchant for stone construction and was in some way responsible for all of the structures. Hunters used to hide within the chambers

*Inside view of a stone Chamber known as the "Oracle Chamber,"*
*America's Stonehenge, North Salem, New Hampshire.*

and wait for passing buck. And many young boys spent a summer afternoon exploring the overgrown man-made "caves."

That Jonathan Pattee utilized the stone structures strewn about his property cannot be denied. Many early nineteenth-century artifacts in the way of rusted nails, kitchen utensils, and broken china are scattered all over the surface of the site. That Jonathan Pattee erected all of the huge chambers is quite another matter, and is the subject of an ongoing debate.

The first person to challenge local folklore was William B. Goodwin, a wealthy insurance executive from Hartford, Connecticut, who purchased and "reconstructed" the former Pattee property in the 1930s, setting out to show the world that a Christian monastery had been built there in the tenth century by Irish Culdee monks fleeing from Viking raids. Goodwin also trekked throughout most of central Vermont and Massachusetts exploring similarly constructed "artificial caves." Understandably, a slew of outraged archeologists and historians on both sides of the Atlantic published scathing rebuttals to Goodwin's weak premises. When the dust finally settled, one sticky problem remained: namely, who built the stone chambers and underground passageways?

In 1945 Dr. Junius Bird of the New York Museum of Natural History was invited to conduct the first professional investigation of Pattee's Caves. The results of his five-day excavation—an incredibly short time to dig—were contradictory. He wrote: "There is the suggestion of age antedating Colonial times from the charcoal distribution in the soil in the hill slopes";[1] but at the same time the data from a slab-roofed chamber implied a historic date.

Dr. Bird did note something that archeologists today still fail to comprehend when they claim that no information can be obtained from a site that has been meddled with for so many years. He stated that "no structure could have been so thoroughly cleared or disturbed in recent times as to completely obliterate the evidence of several centuries' abandonment if they were constructed in pre-Colonial times. Even if the builders left no artifacts, there should be evidence of occupation, at least charcoal, which should be separated from subsequent material by sterile dirt."[2] He was enthusiastically in favor of future research.

In the 1950s, a Yale archeology graduate student undertook six weeks of digging at the North Salem site. He concluded, on very thin evidence, that the entire stone complex was initially constructed between the late seventeenth and early eighteenth centuries, and that Jonathan Pattee was probably the principal "reconstruction" architect in the nineteenth century.

After a few years, the property was purchased by Robert Stone, an electrical engineer who lived nearby. Stone eventually changed the name of the place from Pattee's Caves to Mystery Hill and subsequently established the first ongoing research project at the site. By the 1980s, the name was changed to America's Stonehenge. It is largely through the dedication of this farsighted man that Mystery Hill—America's Stonehenge—has been preserved from the bulldozer.

Throughout the sixties and seventies, Mystery Hill acquired something of a confusing reputation as each year a new investigator applying newly emerging concepts in European megalithic archeology presented a different interpretation of its stone structures. For example, a few years after the British astronomer Gerald Hawkins shocked archeologists throughout the world with his dramatic sunrise analysis of Stonehenge, Mystery Hill was thought to be a giant megalithic astronomical complex. When scientist Alexander Thom's high-powered statistical arguments for a standard megalithic unit of measurement finally filtered down into popular literature, the megalithic yard and all its variations were found in every nook and cranny at North Salem, (as well as elsewhere in the world). In 1975, when Barry Fell pointed out that stones at the site appeared to have markings that resembled Iberian Punic script, Mystery Hill suddenly was deemed to be a major outpost of Celtic-Iberian people.

Cast as an Irish Culdee Monk hideout, a Phoenician trading post, a Viking center, and, throughout the 1980s, as an ancient Celtic/Druidic enclave mixed in with astronomically aligned stones, this site in southeastern New Hampshire continues to astonish generations of people because it *is* a mystery of the highest order. It is impossible to discount the endless stream of ancient radiocarbon dates coming from the site after every season. The most recent is a 7,400 year-old-date for a standing fire pit. More conservative thinkers, however, claim that Yankee farmers in either the eighteenth or nineteenth century just happened to plop a rather cumbersome stone exactly into a fire pit that supposedly was started by lightening. Perhaps.

The explanation for Mystery Hill continues to change with cultural fashions. Depending on what's currently in vogue in academic and/or New Age circles, visitors keep seeing what they want to at this place. Ever since the site became accessible to tourists, the explanations miraculously have changed with the times, very much like the strange interpretations and reinterpretations of American inscriptions. Perhaps the overall mystery of the hill is actually its ability to confound, amuse, and make otherwise rational people behave somewhat erratically.

Look past the picnic tables and the chain-link fences, discount the Oracle Chamber description, and study the stones: There are percussion marks, not steel chisel marks. Think about the labor expended here and try to come up with a reason for the existence of this place. Either Jonathan Pattee or somebody pre-English was doing something very peculiar in the primordial woods of New England. The evidence is there somewhere.

A trench sunk by archeologist James Whittall over the so-called Oracle Chamber drain revealed tiny specks of charcoal from under one of the capstones. Radiocarbon dating yielded a date of around 520 A.D. From other excavations, Whittall obtained charcoal from *between* the slabs of a drystone walling. The samples gave a collected date of over 3,500 years! More recently an excavation at the northeastern section of the site revealed a 3,600-year-old date.

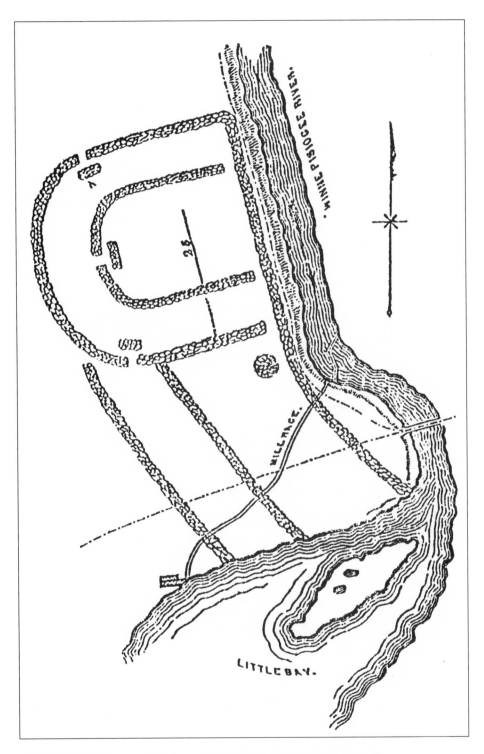

*An 1822 sketch of a stone ruin site—walls, mounds, earthworks—near Lochmere, New Hampshire.*

The people at Mystery Hill quickly released these remarkable dates and waited for the praise. Unfortunately, it never came. Archeologists criticized the radiocarbon dates, reasoning that when the walls were constructed in Colonial times, some charcoal and dirt from an earlier Indian occupation site on the hill must have mixed in with the stone slabs. In other words, they doubted the hill's antiquity merely because in their minds, it simply *couldn't* be older than white New England settlement.

Mystery Hill is intriguing. The fenced section comprises only a tiny portion of a site that rambles on for over 150 acres. Along the many infrequently traveled trails surrounding the hilltop is some impressive evidence of wedge and fire stone quarrying (methods of quarrying without the use of metal tools). On a high ridge a few hundred yards from the so-called Sacrificial Table, a series of long stone slabs lies amidst a patch of poison ivy plants. Some of these rectangular blocks are up to 15 feet long and 5 feet wide. Some are split and lying on their sides a few feet from a ledge. Other slabs are partially split from the bedrock, waiting to be removed by a combination of bashing, wedging, and heating.

There are a lot of large triangular-shaped blocks at Mystery Hill, some measuring up to 20 feet long by 10 feet wide. These stones are not naturally shaped glacial debris. Systematic maul markings and chipping along the edges are quite clear and impressive. A few of the stones stand upright in the midst of field walls.

Over the years, Mystery Hill has undergone an extensive examination with reference to possible astronomical alignments. The meticulous and oftentimes tedious work has paid off, for it seems that a number of major standing stones (more than one would expect by chance alone), when viewed from a particular spot, line up with key solar events such as the solstice and equinox sunrises and sunsets.

Since 1989, the crew at Mystery Hill has sunk over ninety test pits across the site to see what the soil levels reveal. Each hole, 50 centimeters in diameter, that has been dug down to bedrock has provided intriguing information about the hilltop. It seems that over 4,000 years ago the site was around 75 percent barren. It was clear and open to the heavens—the better to see various astronomically related events.

What do we make of all this? It is obvious that some serious chronological problems will remain at Mystery Hill until a continuously funded, long-term, major excavation is mounted. The work of scores of volunteers over the years, however, points to a time span ranging from 3,500 to 7,000 years of occupation.

Interestingly, Mystery Hill shares some superficial similarities to stone sites reported by scholars back in the 1850s. In 1851 surveyor E. G. Squier reported on some stone remains found thirty years earlier around the towns of

Concord, Franklin, and Lochmere, New Hampshire. Those towns are between thirty and fifty miles north of Mystery Hill, along the Merrimack River Valley. Squier states that a large stone fortification once stood on the bluffs east of the Merrimack River in Concord on what used to be called Sugar-Ball Plain. "The walls could readily be traced for some distance, though [they are now] crumbled nearly to the ground and overgrown with large trees."[3]

Squier quotes from an 1822 report of an ancient stone fortification on the west side of the Winnepesaukee River, near the head of Little Bay in the present-day Lochmere, New Hampshire:

The traces of the walls were at that time easily discerned, although most of the stones had been removed to the milldam near at hand, on the river. On approaching the site . . . the walls were two or three feet high, though in some places they had fallen down and the whole had evidently much diminished in height, since the first erection. They were about three feet in thickness, constructed of stones outwardly, and filled in with clay, shells, gravel, etc., from the bed of the river and shores of the bay. The stones . . . were placed together with much order and regularity and when of their primitive height the walls must have been very strong.

The site of the fortification is nearly level, descending a little from the walls to the bank of the river. West for the distance of nearly half a mile, the surface is quite even. In front, or east, on the opposite side of the river, are high banks, upon which at that time stood a thick growth of wood. When the first settlers discovered the fort, there were oak trees of large size standing within the walls. Within the enclosure and in the mound and vicinity, were found innumerable . . . ornaments, such as crystals cut into the rude shapes of diamonds, squares, pyramids. . . .

The small island in the bay appears to have been a burial-place from the great quantity of bone and other remains disclosed by the plough when settlements were commenced by the whites. Before the island was cultivated, there were several large excavations resembling cellars or walls discovered, for what purpose constructed or used, can only be conjectured.[4]

This is an astonishing report. It clearly points to weird things uncovered by the first settlers in New Hampshire. From this document we can also surmise that many of the in-place stone sites found by the first whites were convenient sources of building stone. Many were plundered, taken apart, and used for other Colonial constructions—like a milldam.

*Contact Person(s)/Organization*

Mystery Hill—America's Stonehenge
North Salem, New Hampshire 03073
(603) 893-8300

*Total Magnetic Field/Inclination Angle*

There are several areas at Mystery Hill that demand more detailed magne-tometer work. The patch of land ranging from the southeast of the north tri-angular stone to the stone and beyond it gave some interesting readings: As one approached the stone the TMF and IA increased. At the southwestern sector, near the so-called Sunset and Lunar Minor stone, the TMF from inside the walling to outside the walling were 342 to 559 milligauss. The IA reading was constant.

The other area of interest is the so-called Sacrificial Stone/Oracle Chamber sector. A radical decrease in TMF occurred from the mound over-looking the large, grooved stone and on through the stone base.

Five measurements were taken at the Oracle Chamber: at the south en-tranceway (342/73); three feet into the chamber (547/68); near the so-called speaking tube (550/69); at the extreme north end of the chamber (335/79); and midway at the Y-access tunnel (528/72).

The average total magnetic field/inclination angle *away* from any of the stonework at Mystery Hill was 500 milligauss units and 71 degrees. Bottom line? Specific stone structures at Mystery Hill appear to be located on top of areas of changing magnetic fields. A more detailed study is needed to com-pletely map out the contours of these fields.

*Further Investigation in Area*

It does not seem likely that Mystery Hill existed alone. Indeed, Jim Whittall of the Early Sites Research Society has documented some rather in-triguing stone chambers *outside* the Mystery Hill site. For example, within a ten-mile radius of Mystery Hill are the towns of Windham, Danville, and Plaistow, New Hampshire. Near each of these locales are some unusual stone chambers. Contact Whittall's group for more information.

If we are every to fully document the hillsides and valleys surrounding Mystery Hill, it had better be done quickly. The southern part of New Hampshire has experienced a building boom. New developments, strip malls, and convenience stores are popping up all over the area below this hill. The lack of a state income tax and relatively low property taxes have been luring neighboring Massachusetts residents for years. The stores, services industries, and other artifacts of late twentieth century have followed. Get out there and start looking before some site gets covered over by tons of asphalt.

# VERMONT

Vermont on a summer morning can be dreadfully hot or painfully humid. Or if you're *really* lucky, it can be a combination of both. Then a sweltering day can suddenly turn into a brutally cold night when an arctic Canadian air mass swoops down the state in savage defiance of summer, making one wonder why anyone settled here in the first place. The region was attractive to early 1700s settlers because the best land in lower New England was already taken, and Vermont was undeveloped. This infatuation with the state didn't last too long. The growing season was too short and the soil wasn't as fertile as that in southern New England, so when newer sites opened up in western New York and beyond, many farmers abandoned their homesteads in search of better opportunity. All of this happened before the American Revolution.

Many Native Americans found Vermont more hospitable because they were not bound to a plot of soil as white settlers were. When the annual harvest decreased due to overfarming, they simply picked up and left. They moved about the region searching for the best patches of land. There was an abundance of wild game, fish, berries, and wild plants for a culture that knew where to look for them.

Vermont today is but a shadow of what it once was. As you travel the main roads of this tiny state, you'll need to look beyond the hundreds of antique shops, cute stores with names like Scotland by the Yard, the plastic cows on lawns, and the weekly farmers' markets. Look past all of these twentieth-century trappings and imagine an ancient time when narrow trails through a dense forest led to stone ruins. As you walk around the descendants of that forest today, you'll see the remains of abandoned eighteenth-century farmsteads. You'll see stone walls snaking through the woods; walls that were originally built to pen farm animals. Continue walking beyond the homesteads and walls, and you will come face to face with some very unusual sites.

## EAST CENTRAL VERMONT

East central Vermont during the winter months is a fantasy world where valleys stretch away from snowcapped mountains and where granite and gneiss outcroppings make farming seem next to impossible. The warmer months, however, change the illusion strikingly. Many of the steep, precipitous hills, blanketed in shades of green and gold, have soil fertile enough to produce an assortment of vegetables, grains, apples, pears, plums, and cherries. But getting to the soil is not easy. New rocks seem to crop up after every season's plowing. Early farmers got rid of the surplus stones with typical Yankee ingenuity: They built miles of filed walls to retain their livestock and to maintain their property rights.

The region had a late start in getting settled. If we believe what one man had to say about it, then it is easy to understand why. An explorer of the Ottauquechee River Valley, where the town of Woodstock is presently situated, described the land as "savage-looking." And after carefully inspecting the countryside, he concluded that the valley was so far from any road and so much out of the world that no human being, except possibly an Indian, would ever live there. Nevertheless, by the mid 1700s the first historic settlements were rooted in the central Vermont district. After the Midwest opened up and news of lush, fertile soil reached the eastern states, many New Hampshire and Vermont settlers abandoned their hard rock farms and staked out a new life in the Ohio and Mississippi valleys. Today, it's not unusual to find the remnants of these first Colonial farms scattered throughout the region. In fact, seen from the air, it's astonishing how unpopulated central Vermont is. Vast stretches of green trees remain unbroken except for the occasional house. It's been that way for a long time.

Within a 600-square-mile area of the Connecticut River's western watershed, an area encompassing such towns as Woodstock, Royalton, and North Tunbridge and such waterways as the Black, Ottauquechee, and White rivers, there are vast numbers of corbeled and flat-roofed chambers, buried stone waterworks, alignments, massive walled complexes, and other lithic material. The following are but a few powerful examples of the strange array of stonework here.

## STONE CHAMBER
McIntosh Farm, South Royalton, Vermont

### Site Synopsis
Over sixty years ago a farmer accidentally uncovered a mysterious stone cave on land that had been in his family for over two hundred years. No one had ever seen this man-made ruin before.

### Location
From Brattleboro take Interstate 91 north to White River Junction. Exit onto Interstate 89 north. Exit at Sharon onto Route 14 north. In about 3 miles you'll come to Dairy Road, which leads to the Joseph Smith Birthplace Monument. Continue up this road for a little less than 2½ miles. Just before the turnoff to the monument, you'll see a farmhouse on the right. Park here and ask if it's all right to visit the stone chamber.

As one faces the house, the chamber is set in a tree line, across a field. Specifically, if you sight 180 degrees from the right front corner of the shed that sits next to the farmhouse toward the tree line, you'll be at the site.

### Consideration

Please get permission from the farmhouse to visit this chamber. And, as always, leave nothing and take only pictures.

### History/Background

The story about this chamber is that sometime in the 1920s or 1930s, one of the McIntosh landowners was tractor-plowing his field when a wheel sunk into a hole. After workers uprighted the vehicle, they dug down a bit and found a stone-lined "cave." This surprised the landowner. The land had been in his family since the 1700s, but he had never seen or heard about such a chamber on the property.

The McIntosh chamber is compact. There's a narrow entranceway leading into a circular "beehive interior" with corbeled (stone overlapping stone) walls. One massive capstone holds the entire structure together. It's an impressive bit of work.

This chamber was excavated in the 1980s by Massachusetts archeologist James Whittall and a team from the Early Sites Research Society. Three sections of the chamber were dug: on top, in front, and inside. The digging on top of the chamber exposed the upper capstone. The soil conditions suggested great age. The trench in front of the chamber revealed very little beyond twentieth-century glass jars and farm debris. But the interior was something else. Days of careful digging revealed a stone-lined floor. Flat stones were chinked into rectangular slabs and laid out wall to wall. In the cracks between the stones, Whittall found an assortment of American Indian tools: arrowheads, chopping stones, flakes, and the like. While it is difficult to date stone tools by design—many of these tool designs were repeated by early stone workers over thousands of years—the fact that he found Native American handiwork associated with the chamber was remarkable.

So what is the McIntosh chamber? Difficult to say, but it was one of the few excavated that had actual pre-settler artifacts associated with the design. My suspicion is that it was an ancient burial tomb. The stone-lined floor suggests that the chamber's builders were very concerned about what was placed inside. They didn't want whatever it was to touch the earth. This makes no sense for living things, be they root crops or people: During the winter the stone floor would easily conduct frost from the surrounding stones and make for rotten produce and miserable living quarters. This place has all the indications of a room for the dead.

*Interior view of chamber looking toward the entranceway, showing the circular inner space and superb stonework. Below the leaves is a flagstone floor. American Indian stone tools were found there during a 1980s excavation.*

### Contact Person(s)/Organization

Early Sites Research Society
Rowley, Massachusetts 01969

### Total Magnetic Field/Inclination Angle

The total magnetic field measured 558 milligauss with an inclination angle of 70 degrees for the area around this chamber. As I entered it the TMF decreased rapidly to 300 near the chambers rear while the IA increased to 86 degrees.

### Further Investigations in Area

There are reports of many more chambers on the McIntosh property. Once permission is secured a walk through the woods would be enlightening.

Behind the McIntosh chamber, in a field adjoining the farmhouse where the Mormon prophet Joseph Smith was born, are a series of small, saucer-shaped standing stones, averaging 1–2 feet high, 9–11 inches wide, and 4–5 inches thick. Strewn across a rolling meadow, more than ten of these curious stones have been placed into the ground at intervals of 50–100 yards from each other. Invariably, the long axes of these stones are parallel. Hundreds of similar groupings of small standing stones having triangular to parabolic shapes have been reported. Their purpose is unknown.

During the spring of 1982, a woman found a pair of Roman coins on her family farmstead in Bethel, Vermont, a town about three miles west of South Royalton. Using a metal detector, she found the coins about six inches below the ground surface near an old barn. The coins were minded in 72 A.D[5] What they were doing in central Vermont is a mystery. But this is no isolated incident. Throughout the history of American settlement, trappers, pioneers, and farmers, have all documented finding unusual caches of ancient coins.

## CHAMBER/INSCRIPTIONS
South Royalton, Vermont

### Site Synopsis

About 20 miles almost due north of South Woodstock, Vermont, within walking distance of the White River, there's a peculiar array of slab chambers, strange walls, and inscribed stones.

### Location

From Brattleboro take Interstate 91 north to White River Junction. Exit onto Interstate 89 north. Exit at Sharon onto Route 14 north. In about three miles you'll come to Dairy Road, which leads to the Joseph Smith Birthplace Monument. Take a left turn, instead of a right, which leads to the monument. Follow this curving road past McIntosh Pond. Just before the road ends at a farmhouse, you'll see a dirt road on your left. Drive down this road a short distance and pull over to the right, being careful not to block any driveways. Walk up the dirt road on your far left, *not* the one near the car. Just before reaching the house at the top of the hill, turn right onto the dirt logging road.

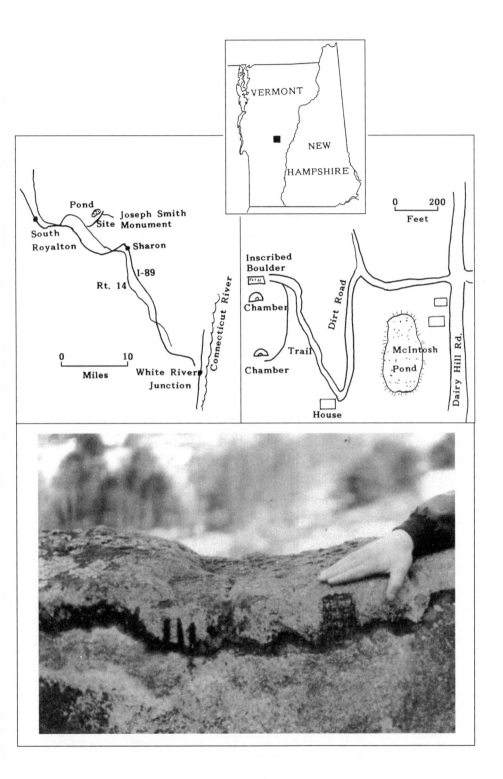

Continue on this road, taking care to avoid the deep ruts. Follow this trail until it breaks into a clearing. The chamber is on you left. As you are facing the chamber, the inscribed boulder is to your right. Follow the trail to his mysterious site. The walk from the car to the chamber/boulder site should take around thirty to forty-five minutes.

### Considerations

Getting to this site demands good walking shoes and stamina. If visiting during the summer months, bring along a water bottle, a skin barrier, and bug spray. I recommend long pants and a long-sleeved shirt.

The Vermont State archeologist came out with a report a number of years ago emphatically stating that Vermont stone chambers are of recent origin, that is from the eighteenth or nineteenth century. Readers/explorers should be aware of this interesting documentation, which is available from the State Archeological Office in Montpelier. It will set the stage for some mind-boggling alternatives, especially when you see the ancient radiocarbon dates amateur groups have gleaned from excavated sites. Some of these early dates make it difficult to believe the "official explanation."

*Excavation of the South Royalton, Vermont, stone chamber by James Mavor and Byron Dix. Mavor and Dix found that the chamber's side walls went into the ground some 13 feet before the bottom level was reached.*

Whatever the origins of these strange, artificial caves, no one has the definitive answer as to who built them or why.

### History/Background

Near the top of a 1,300-foot hill, within a vast, bowl-shaped depression that looks as though it had been scooped out by a giant shovel are stone platforms, a chamber, and a set of boulders with weird markings on them. From the bottom of this natural depression, one can see horizon monoliths that may have been placed so that an observer could watch the sun rise and set from the surrounding hillsides during the summer and winter solstices and the spring and fall equinoxes. This site could very well have acted as a huge calendar.

A number of intriguing inscribed stones were found at the site. Along a north-south wall, three elongated boulders had been placed adjacent to each other. On two of these boulders some prominent gridlike, or checkerboard, designs had been carved. Measuring approximately 2½ inches wide by 3½ inches long, the grids were made by carefully chiseling vertical and horizontal grooves into the surface of the stones. The checkerboard design has since been found throughout New England, and usually a solar alignment of stones is nearby.

Within the walled site is a long, narrow, partially collapsed, slab-roofed chamber. On the morning of the equinox, a person seated within the structure

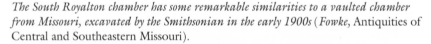

*The South Royalton chamber has some remarkable similarities to a vaulted chamber from Missouri, excavated by the Smithsonian in the early 1900s (Fowke,* Antiquities of Central and Southeastern Missouri).

would see the sun rise from a prominent horizon stone. On the ceiling of the chamber near the entranceway, a gridlike symbol has been carved. There have been numerous attempts to explain the significance of this symbol, all of which are still tentative.

Although many of the stone features at South Royalton are aligned with the major events of the solar year, there are, nevertheless, a few inherent problems with the astronomical calendar hypothesis. The most obvious, of course, is the general location of the site. The bottom of a natural amphitheater would seem to be the most unlikely place in which to set up a solar observatory when so many hilltops are in the immediate vicinity. Also, because of the sighting angle of the "observation point," during the solstices and equinoxes, the sun would be visible long after the initial moments of sunrise. Similarly, sunset during those days would be premature. One would think that a people aware of key astronomical events would have chosen a better locale. This said, it still cannot be denied that certain stones were indeed placed to take advantage of the general position of the sun.

### Contact Person(s)/Organization

Early Sites Research Society
Rowley, Massachusetts 01969

### Total Magnetic Field/Inclination Angle

I took extensive measurements in and around this chamber and found nothing unusual. The average total magnetic field/inclination angle both outside and inside this site was 550 milligauss and 70 degrees.

The grid stone inscription was another story. As I got closer to the stone, the total magnetic field significantly decreased.

### Further Investigations in Area

Research scientist James Mavor and the late Byron Dix studied the surrounding hilltop stone features in the 1980s. They found a variety of strange standing stones and platforms on the crests of those hills that can be seen from the stone chamber. Dix and Mavor spent years surveying the surrounding hilltops and found evidence of a highly sophisticated ritualistic placement of stone chambers and piles and rows of stone scattered throughout this region.

From a nearby hilltop, one that overlooks the vast bowl-shaped depression of the site, these two researchers found the remains of an Indian fort. The site consisted of a 200-square-meter enclosure of small wall stones. A group of stone mounds was found just west of the stone wall. This stone enclosure sits on a ridgetop northwest of the stone chamber.

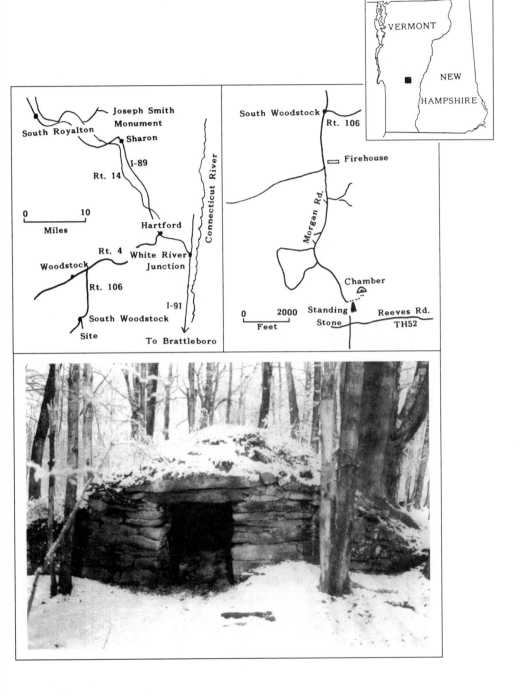

## WINTER SOLSTICE STONE CHAMBER/STANDING STONE
South Woodstock, Vermont

### Site Synopsis

In one of New England's largest stone chambers, on the shortest day of the year—the winter solstice—the sun's rays penetrate the structure's entranceway and greet an observer. Who designed this spectacular feat of solar-alignment engineering?

### Location

From Brattleboro take Interstate 91 north to White River Junction. Exit onto Interstate 89 north. In about three miles, exit at Hartford onto Route 4 going toward Woodstock. At Woodstock, turn onto Route 106 south. In a few miles you'll reach South Woodstock. Go through town. One-half mile past the South Woodstock Country Store, the road curves to the right. Follow the road straight ahead. There's a fire station on your left. From this intersection continue for 1.2 miles. Just over the top of the hill, you'll see to your left a large standing stone in front of a tree. The chamber is within these woods. Do not enter yet, however.

As this site is on private property you *must* ask the present owners permission to walk the land. Check the posted signs for a name and phone number. Call and ask for access rights. Failure to do so can result in trespassing charges. If granted, as at all sites, do not leave trash around or take any of the site's stones.

If visiting during the summer months wear a skin barrier (a cream that prevents you from getting poison ivy), long pants, long sleeves, and spray on liberal amounts of mosquito repellent.

### History/Background

This chamber is big. There are a host of peculiar standing stones, strange wall sites, stone platforms, and etched rocks in the surrounding fields.

The late aerospace engineer Byron Dix was the first researcher to realize the astronomical significance of the site. He proved through extensive documentations the existence of solar alignments.

On December 21, the sun's rays directly penetrate the length of the huge slab-roofed chamber. Anyone sitting within it on that morning would behold the awesome spectacle of the midwinter sun illuminating the dank crevices of the 19-by-10-foot-wide structure. I did so one winter solstice, and the memory of that glorious spectacle has remained vivid. Measurements taken from within also showed that the extreme rising and setting positions of the moon

*The enormous interior of the South Woodstock, Vermont, Stone Chamber. No one has any idea what this chamber was used for or why it is so big. Intriguingly, it is aligned toward the winter solstice sunrise: On the shortest day of the year, the sun's rays penetrate directly through the opening to light up the chamber's rear wall.*

during its 18.61 year cycle (known as the major and minor standstills) correlated with the length, width, and height of the chamber. No doubt, whoever the astronomer-builders were, they lived in central Vermont for a very long time, keeping track of heavenly bodies.

The standing stone near the entranceway to the site is over six feet tall. It's massive and inexplicable. What was its purpose? Who put it there? Was it part of a field wall? Was it merely decoration for some megalithic-minded Colonial farmer? There are a lot of mid-eighteenth-century walls and foundations in this area so it is possible.

I recently asked an elderly farmer from South Woodstock what he thought. "Ain't no damn Phoenician church, 'twas a dungeon! That's what it was!" he replied, eyes twinkling. That moment was symbolic of the problem with these things. No one really knows what they are, even old-timers who have worked the land for years.

*Contact Person(s)/Organization*

Woodstock Public Library
The Green
Woodstock, Vermont 05019
(802) 457-2295

New England Antiquities Research Association (NEARA)
Journal/Archival Information
2388 Whalley Road
Sharlot, Vermont 05445

or

305 Academy Road
Pembroke, New Hampshire 03275

*Total Magnetic Field/Inclination Angle*

This site had some peculiar geomagnetic flux aberrations. Near the road entranceway is a large standing stone. The total magnetic field and the inclination angle significantly decrease as one approaches the stone. A 20-foot radius around the stone gave a TMF reading of 570 milligauss and an IA of 80 degrees. Near the base of the stone, the TMF readings changed to 310. The IA read 50 degrees.

*Further Investigations in Area*

I received an interesting report about a large chamber/wall complex north of Norwich, Vermont. Norwich is about five miles north of White River Junction. From Norwich take the Turnpike Road leading out to Gile Mountain. Take this road for about six miles. About 300 yards past the Gile Mountain Trail on your left is the site. Park and walk into the western (your left) woods. The chamber/wall complex is about 20 yards off the road.

# SIX

# Massachusetts

I t is well known that Massachusetts was founded as an experiment in religious rights. After landing on Cape Cod, the Pilgrims located two great
harbors across the bay, and eventually set up a colony at Plymouth. To the north
near the present Boston Harbor, they visited an Algonquian village, named
Massachusetts, which means "place of big hills," and adopted the name for
their colony. They quickly set about to reshape the land to suit their needs.

The rapidity with which the early settlers spread themselves over the wide
area of Massachusetts and elsewhere in New England is surprising. Within ten
to twenty years of the founding of Plymouth Plantation in 1620, pioneers
were traveling along ancient Indian trails in search of open, fertile land. Many
of their early accounts speak of deserted Indian villages and cleared fields. To
these religious men and women, it seemed as though God was providing the
best land and the best rivers for his flock in this new world. The former inhabitants already had done the arduous task of tree cutting for garden farming. Actually, most of the eastern Massachusetts natives either had died or
were dying of a massive epidemic because they had no immunity to the diseases the white settlers carried. The result was the almost complete extermi-
nation of the eastern natives.

## NORTHEAST MASSACHUSETTS

This area of Massachusetts was one of the first regions to be settled. The
Merrimack River provided food and a means to transport goods inland and
out of the heart of New Hampshire. Coastal towns grew quickly as shipbuilding sailing ports, and major fishing and salting industries developed along the

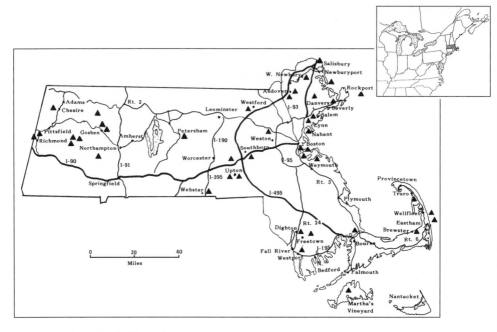

*Mysterious sites in Massachusetts*

estuaries. During the eighteenth and nineteenth centuries, the region north of Boston became a point of origin for whaling expeditions, and clipper ships traversed the seas with New England goods. A prosperous middle class developed. Life was orderly and well defined. Most people were comfortable in their surroundings, and they believed they knew the land. But every so often farmers would stumble upon mysterious things. Ditch diggers would find large stone chambers buried deep within the ground. Children would wander into tracts of forest and find strange symbols carved onto boulders. Legends were built up around these tangible remains of unknown origin.

## MOUND SITE
Morrill's Point, Salisbury, Massachusetts

### Site Synopsis
North of the town of Newburyport, within sight of the ocean along Massachusetts's northeastern shore, is a earthen burial mound that is 6 to 8 feet high and 200 feet in diameter. Excavations there show that over 7,500 years ago a mysterious, seagoing people buried their dead in this locale.

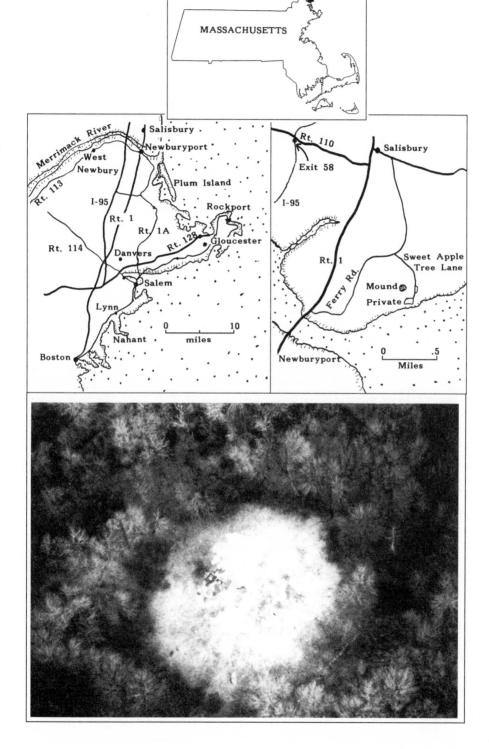

## Location

From Boston take I-95 north (via I-93 or Route 1) for about 45 miles. Turn off at Salisbury Beach exit (Exit 58). Take Route 110 east, turning south on Route 1. Just before the bridge going to Newburyport make a left turn (east). The road then splits. Take the left road (north)—Ferry Road. Travel on this winding road for 1.2 miles. Turn right on Sweet Apple Tree Lane. Go slowly. Take this road for .3 miles. Park at the dirt pulloff on the left side of the road. Note: Please do not continue on toward the road's end or park at the road's end, which is private property. Stop *well before* reaching the house at the end of the lane.

Once you've parked well off the road, take a compass bearing of 310 degrees North West and walk into the woods—there is no path these days because it's covered over by dense foliage. In about a quarter mile you'll see a clearing in the trees. This is the mound.

## Considerations

There are several things to consider before trekking off to see this mystical mound. If you go in the summer, do wear long pants and long-sleeves. Load up with insect repellent, containing at least 30 percent DEET, spraying it all over your body, your clothes, your hands, head, ears, and so on, because you'll be walking through muck and moist ferns—the perfect environment for mosquitoes, ticks, and greenhead flies and other blood-sucking insects. At the completion of the trip, have a friend check your body for ticks. There is a Lyme disease problem throughout New England, so check your body carefully. If you do have a tick, carefully pull it out without breaking off the imbedded part from the rest of the body. If that happens you risk further infection. If you develop ringlike skin discolorations at the site of the bite, or if you have flulike symptoms—pain in your neck, joints, vomiting, stomach cramps, get to your doctor. You may have the initial symptoms of Lyme disease, which is easily treatable in these early stages. Unfortunately, not everyone exhibits these symptoms so be careful.

The next thing you need to prepare for are the toxic plants—poison ivy is the most prevalent one along the mound's boundary. Use a good topical skin barrier.

The land that the mound is on is technically owned by the New England Power Company, although it is difficult if not impossible to ascertain this, as the land is not posted, nor is there a description of ownership posted. I had to track this fact down through tax records! I recommend, however, that you contact their corporate office to let them know you'll be wandering onto their property.

## History/Background

Long known as an "Indian" hill, this site was first actively investigated by the Early Sites Research Society in the late 1970s. Several seasons of excavation produced dramatic evidence of long-term use by generations of ancient Indians. The first few layers of the mound showed clear evidence of a feasting site: There were thousands of broken clam shells scattered throughout the black soil levels. This apparently was a spot where massive clambakes were held.

As the digging continued along the southern tier of the mound, the teams found several burials with skeletons that were almost perfectly preserved. Some were in a flexed, fetal position, having been arranged with great care, while others skeletons were found in ancient piles of shells. One young headless female skeleton was found about 12 inches below the ground surface. Based on the heavy incisions on the neck vertebrae, one can surmise that her decapitation was the cause of death. That find left an indelible impression on the archeologists there.

The age of these skeletons provided a perspective on both long term use and tradition. The earliest set of remains dated back over 6,000 years. People were using the mound as a burial site for countless generations.

Perhaps the most intriguing material found with these early burials was red ochre—sometimes called "red paint." (see Further Investigations in the Area under the Petroglyph site at Machiasport, Maine). Red ochre is found in many burials along the eastern coast of America. Why it was sometimes buried with the dead is unknown, although it probably had religious significance.

A few years ago I collected samples of red ochre from burials in New York State to Nova Scotia (including the mound site in Salisbury). The ages of these sites ranged from 2,000 to over 6,000 years old. I wanted to determine the exact composition of this reddish powdery material. The results of that study were intriguing. Working with Dr. Lawrence Nelson, then a senior scientist at International Nickel Laboratory at Sterling Forest, New York, I ran the materials through a mass spectrometer to determine the composition of the substance. While the sand/grain particles reflected local conditions we found that twenty specific elements made up red ochre.[1] Furthermore, we discovered that the proportions of these elements were the same. In other words, red ochre was manufactured based on a specific chemical formula! The fact that a recipe remained the same over a 4,000-year period in a 1,000-mile geographical area of the East suggests that the material was of prime importance to the early inhabitants' burial customs. This also indicates a complex level of oral tradition and contact. The remarkable similarity of the red paint composition surprised the technicians at International Nickel, for it indicated an advanced awareness of chemical compounds and mixtures far above anything previously reported in the archeological literature for the aboriginal tribes of eastern America.

The sophistication of the early tribes in eastern Massachusetts is further shown by a small copper bead found nearly 70 miles southwest in the center of the state at North Bookfield. This cremation burial mound was excavated by the Massachusetts Archeological Society more than 20 years ago. The site dated to over 2,500 years old, and there was no evidence of intrusion since that time. Found among the skeletal remains were tiny copper beads, which were thought to be similar in manufacture to hundreds of other copper artifacts found throughout the East. The belief among archeologists was that Indians took raw copper and banged it into little tubes and spheres. We, however, found something totally unexpected and strange.

The initial spectroscopic analysis suggested a very high copper content. Further analysis showed the bead had a purity level close to 99.98 percent—a very unusual situation even for the high-grade ore from the Upper Michigan peninsula. A thin section of the bead revealed why. The outer layer of the elliptical-shaped bead had a glassy, smooth form, indicating that it had been cooled rapidly. Just below the outer layer were markings of successive heat patterns, which could occur only if molten copper were dropped into cold water. Whoever made this bead had smelted ore to separate impurities from the copper. Melting copper ore requires temperatures of over 1,981 degrees Fahrenheit (1,083 Celsius), temperatures suggesting a blast furnace. All of this indicates a remarkable degree of technical sophistication among the people who built this mound in Massachusetts.

### Contact Person(s)/Organization

Early Sites Research Society
Rowley, Massachusetts 01969

New England Power Company
24 Fort Avenue
Salem, Massachusetts 01970
(508) 740-8200

Refuge Manager
Parker River National Wildlife Refuge Northern Boulevard, Plum Island
Newburyport, Massachusetts 01950
(508) 465-5753

### Total Magnetic Field/Inclination Angle

Magnetometer measurements around, across, and on the mound revealed no significant anomalies.

Perhaps this spot was chosen for its proximity to the tidal flats and the clams.

### Further Investigations In Area

There are hundreds of other potential mound sites up and down the Massachusetts coastline. A quick perusal of the *Massachusetts Archeological Bulletin* will reveal many of the coastal sites that have been excavated over the years.

Living by the ocean makes sense. The coastline is a great source of food. Early peoples used the mudflats like a supermarket. There were many things to consume here—from fish to birds. In the early 1980s, the Early Sites Research Society expanded their excavation to other parts of the coast. A few hundred yards from the mound, the teams found a male skeleton that was over 7,000 years old! (See illustration below.) This region has been home to people for an extraordinarily long time.

*Along the northeastern shore of Massachusetts, archeologists uncovered a 7,000-year-old burial in a sandy beach pit. The dark area above the burial is flecked with clam shells from centuries of feasting.*

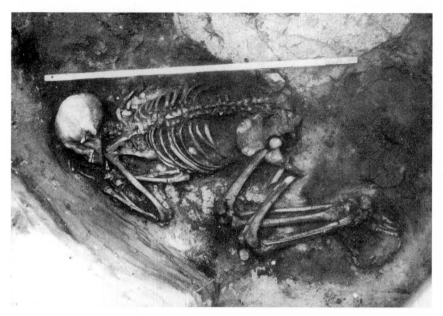

*The body was layed out in a flexed position, with the head pointing toward the East.*

A walk near a salt marsh will expose many intriguing things. Keep your eyes peeled for any slight moundlike protuberance. It may be a shell-heaped midden—a garbage pile from ancient times.

Many people in the Newburyport/Salisbury region never go to the mound site at night. They say it gives them the creeps—and this is from people who never knew about the burials there. One of the early excavators of the mound site refuses to spend time there in the evening. She claims it provokes too many bad feelings.

Another nearby site to examine is Plum Island, off Newburyport, Massachusetts. For years people have been finding ancient Roman coins along the southern tip of this large sand bar. I've even gotten reports of the occasional *gold* coin! To get there from the Boston area, take Route 1 north until the South Lynnfield region. The road will change to Interstate 95. Continue north on this road for another 30 miles. Take Exit 57, Route 113 toward Newburyport. In about 4 miles you'll be in downtown Newburyport. Drive toward the water, going in an easterly direction. This will be Water Street. Continue for another 4½ miles. You'll see the signs for Plum Island. Turn into the refuge. Once in, continue along the road until the end. The last 2.6 miles are unpaved, dusty gravel. Park at the very end.

There's a nominal fee for entry into this wildlife refuge. Do not drive above the posted 25 mph speed limit. The rangers will ticket you.

Bring along plenty of insect repellent because there are very irritating deer flies along this marshy coastline. Also take all valuables with you. Too often car thieves prey on tourists in isolated spots such as this.

So far it sounds pretty gruesome, but get to the beach and walk along the splash zone. The best time to find things that glitter and sparkle is after a severe storm—intense wave action tends to push material onto the shore from a mile or so out.

One more thing. All artifacts, precious or otherwise, found on refuge land are the property of the United States Government. Should the sea gods look upon you kindly and reward you with treasure, you'll have to relinquish it to a ranger upon leaving the park.

Finally, when leaving Plum Island, you'll note a small country airport on your left. Hire a plane to see the region from the air. It will put the entire coastline into perspective.

## WITCH ROCK
Danvers, Massachusetts

### Site Synopsis
A large granite boulder with several satanic drawings on it dates to the period of New England's witch-hunts. Evidence from here and elsewhere suggests that witchcraft *was* being practiced during the late 1600s.

### Location
From Boston take Interstate 93 north 10 miles before exiting north on Route 128 (Interstate 95). Take Exit 28, Forest Street. Follow the road to the left as it goes over Route 128. The Salem Country Club is on the right, and several housing developments are on the left. At Crestwood Lane turn left going to the end of the cul-de-sac. The unmarked path leading to Witch Rock is a public-access path that goes between two private homes. Several outcrops of granite are along the right. Witch Rock is the first large flat-faced outcrop on the right about 20 yards in.

### Considerations
As a courtesy, please inform the adjacent homeowners of your presence before proceeding along the public dirt path.

The faded black pigments on the rock are best seen after the fall season at sunset when the sun is at a low angle. Portable, optically triggered camera flashes (known as "slaves") tend to bring out the images. Try shooting the symbols with a video camera, again with side lighting. Be patient. The symbols are sometimes difficult to see.

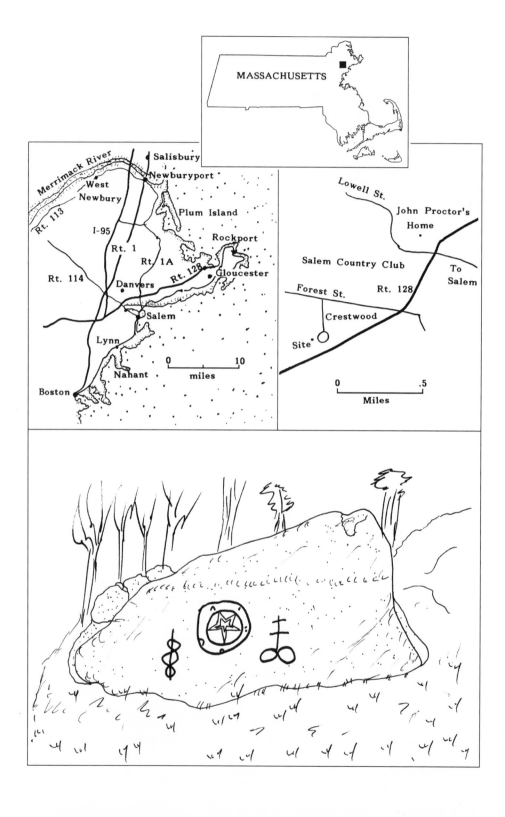

### History/Background

While strolling through Danvers, the old Salem Village location of the in-famous witch trials, it is easy to visit the refurbished homes of the people who were accused of practicing magic in 1692. Nearby Salem even has several "creep-shows" where unsuspecting tourists get a mini-lesson in revisionist history via soundtrack and mannequins in period dress. But one gets a truer feeling of the time by discovering the actual sites where the "witches" lived. If you are savvy enough to know where to look, you may encounter a ruined seventeenth-century foundation. You may even come across a large flat-sided boulder known as Witch Rock. If so, the reality of that three-century-old horror be-comes frighteningly clear.

*Map of Salem Village, 1692.*

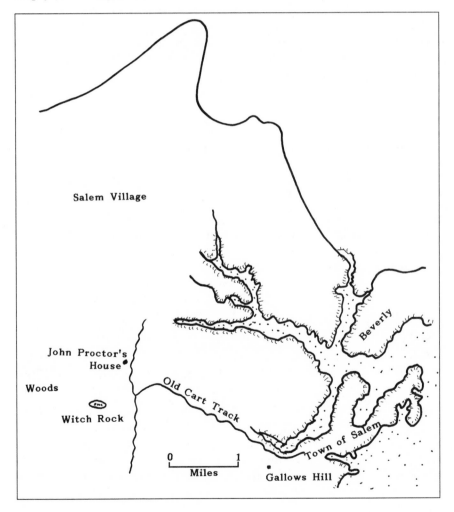

On August 19, 1692, John Proctor, a respectable farmer and landowner in Salem Village, was executed for witchcraft. Between June 10 and September 22 of that year, nineteen Massachusetts men and women and two dogs were hanged for witchcraft. One man was pressed to death for refusing to plead to the indictment. When the executions came to an end, fifty-five people had confessed that they were witches, and one-hundred fifty were in jail, either waiting to be tried or waiting, as several convicted women did, for reprieves, so that infants they had already conceived would not be executed with them.

What happened? How could an entire community become caught up in this so-called witch hysteria? For years scholars have been trying to understand why the accusations of witchcraft were rampant. Dozens of theories, ranging from the social to the psychological to the biological, have been generated to help make sense out of that senseless time. Early-twentieth-century scholars assumed it was an economic struggle: The accused lived on good farmland. Socialist-thinking professors reasoned that the city-based accusations were hysterically veiled attempts to grab land. Another researcher thought the entire village had been collectively deluded. Recently, scholars have argued that fungus-infested rye—the community's staple grain crop—was the culprit. It seems that all the springtime weather conditions were right for a strain of common yet virulent hallucinogenic fungus to grow on the Puritans' stored grain. Baking and boiling it only enhanced its potent effect, with young children being more susceptible than adults to the fungus's perception-altering powers.

There may be a simpler explanation, however. As the noted scholar Chadwick Hansen wrote in his 1969 bestseller *Witchcraft at Salem*: "The popular view holds that there was no witchcraft practiced at Salem; the danger was illusory from start to finish. It is comforting to think this, . . . but it is quite wrong. There was witchcraft at Salem and it worked."

It all started in February 1692, when Elizabeth Parris, the eleven-year-old daughter of the minister of Salem Village, and her cousin Abigail Williams began having violent fits. Soon afterward, other children began acting strangely. They told their elders that invisible "specters" or demons were pecking at their bodies. Within days, the witch hunt was on and townspeople were accused.

While the court transcripts of the trials are fascinatingly lurid, and while Professor Hansen's literary arguments on the reality of witchcraft make one shiver, they are too voluminous to be summarized here. What is of interest, however, are the real bits of data—the physical debris—that indicate something peculiar was happening in seventeenth-century northeastern Massachusetts.

In the early 1980s, when construction workers were clearing the lands off Route 128 near Danvers for an expansion and new exit, I spent a weekend crisscrossing the fields on my motorbike. Foundations and cellar walls that hadn't been seen in almost 300 years were now visible. A survey team reported finding dried out cornhusk dolls hidden between ruined fireplace stones. They had pins stuck in them. The area of most interest to me was a plot of land less than a mile from John Proctor's farmhouse where a large boulder with curious satanic markings dating to the witch hysteria was found during an archeological survey. When it was brought to light, many old residents recalled half-forgotten legends about the boulder. Folklore placed the stone at the center of black magic rituals.

The rock is a flat-sided granite boulder located in a regenerated forest area once strewn with wood trails that led to farmhouses. The pictographs, or rock symbols, are now visible only under direct sunlight or by photographing them at night with a flash.

Suspicion that the markings date to the 1600s is based on two pieces of evidence: the *composition* of the paint and the *location* of the stone. According to the archeological report, the paintings' black pigment composition, analyzed by the Fogg Museum at Harvard, was found to be a hematite resin "embedded in an organic binder," which was either casein (milk protein) or albumin (egg white). "The preservation of the paintings was no doubt due to the southern exposure" of the boulder and the inherent strength of the binder.

Based on period documents, the method of mixing hematite with milk or egg white was the classic Old Masters' technique for making a strong, blackish paint that would not crack or fade with age. This technique was widely used throughout the seventeenth century in England, interestingly, by rural people dabbling in Druidic rock symbology. By the early 1700s, as trade routes opened to different world markets, new products, particularly those from the eastern Mediterranean and the South Pacific made their way into paint technology. Hematite in an organic binder was rarely used thereafter.

The location of Witch Rock allows for some intriguing speculation when one looks at an early map of the village. Most of the accused lived in the vicinity of the boulder. The surrounding lands were reputedly where witches met. In fact, John Proctor's housemaid vehemently testified during the trials that Mr. Proctor frequently roamed the woods late at night. She and the village elders thought such behavior was strange. Proctor gave no explanation for his walks. Whether he had a good reason or not is unknown. But we do know that Witch Rock, located on Proctor's land, was a mere ten-minute walk from his home.

The central symbol of the boulder—a five-pointed star with the point projected downward—is over three feet in diameter. The star is surrounded by two concentric circles. Between the circles are several poorly preserved occult symbols. To the left and right of the star are a caduceus (a snake-entwined staff) and a composite figure made from the upside down astrological sign for Aries and the Archiepiscopal Cross (two ovals horizontally joined).

As with all cryptic symbols, their meanings are open to interpretation. The pentacle with its star pointing upward is used today by occult worshippers to increase personal power; when it is pointed downward it has evil connotations. It may represent the face of Satan. The caduceus, in its original form, was a staff of the divine messenger who used it to herald important communications. Throughout the Middle Ages it represented the mystery of healing—a craft for which many Middle Ages European witches were famous. The sign for Aries represents the ram, or Satan. But in its upside down form with a cross attached, it is a perversion of a Christian symbol. Reversing religious images or prayers was standard practice for devil worshippers. Examples include drawing an upside down cross or reciting verse backwards. The entire composition seems to be calling for Satan to appear in the woods. The combination of data at Witch Rock strongly suggests that it was indeed a seventeenth-century site used by people who practiced the arcane and forbidden symbology of devil worship.

On a recent visit to Witch Rock, I noticed startling things that I had never seen before. Near the top of the rock, above a sloping ledge on the main panel of the rock, I discovered a highly weathered carving of a face. Careful tracing of this image revealed a face with horns. It isn't painted, it is cut into the stone. The visage is very much eroded. Careful lighting with strobes or slaves exaggerated the features and shadows.

### Contact Person(s)/Organization

Peabody Essex Museum
132 Essex Street
Salem, Massachusetts 01970
(508) 745-1876

### Total Magnetic Field/Inclination Angle

Out of all the large, flat rocks in this area, why was this one chosen? Geomagnetic readings may provide some of the answers. As one approaches Witch Rock, the total magnetic field readings go from a high of 580 milligauss to a low of 300 at the base of the rock. Climbing to the alcove above the flat ground parcel reveals an even more dramatic decrease in milligauss units to 210. Clearly this rock sits above a geomagnetic hotspot. It probably induced all sorts of strange and wondrous feelings—of course a little homegrown herbal hallucinogen probably helped get the Black Sabbath going.

*Further Investigations in Area*

Witch Rock is quite special. It may be the only tangible artifact from that sordid time in our history. It may hold answers to many present-day, unanswered questions: What really did happen at Salem? What type of witchcraft was being practiced there? A full-scale archeological dig at the extended base of this rock will probably reveal the evidence of meetings and intriguing doings there. How can the Peabody and Massachusetts Historical societies let this slip by?

There is even more ominous news. Recent town meetings have brought up the possibility of extending a road *through* Crestwood Lane, just skirting Witch Rock! The town managers believe a new road will increase access to a new industrial park nearby. At whose expense? Destroy Witch Rock and a symbol, a reflection of all of us is destroyed. Go to any part of this country and everyone knows the Salem Witch Trial story. What would they think if they knew a road might be built at this spot?

A little more than fifteen miles northeast of Danvers is a prong of land known as Cape Ann. For years residents in communities all over this region have talked of weird lights coming up out of the ocean and zooming across the salt marshes. The Native Americans called them water spirits. Seventeenth-century fishermen said they were flying demons. Eighteenth- and nineteenth-century farmers knew them as swamp gas or ball lightening.

New England author Robert Cahill recounts an early-seventeenth-century sighting above Boston of a strange, unearthly sight. James Everell and his two friends ". . . saw a great light in the sky near Muddy River and said, 'when it stood still, it flamed up, and was about three yards square and when it ran it was contracted into the figure of a swine.'"[2]

One resident, a friend of mine, called me up in the middle of the night a few years back scared out of her mind and described "floating luminescent ghosts" hovering around her kitchen. She shrieked and told me her refrigerator was moving across the floor! I jumped in my car and drove the forty-five minutes to her beach house. Yes, there was the refrigerator in the middle of her kitchen, clearly out of place from its wall space. But I didn't see or experience anything out of the ordinary. I spent the next several hours talking with her, trying to understand what she had experienced.

She told me her grandmother had been born in the house and had lived there until recently. Her family had moved her to a nearby nursing home because of her increasing obsession with "nonexistent lights" appearing on her porch. The family assumed this was the progression of her Alzheimer's condition. My friend thought that perhaps she herself was experiencing some early indications of this dreadful degenerative disease. Perhaps. But it is intriguing to consider that for over three hundred years residents in this area have been chatting about inexplicable sights.

Geologists know that this part of New England was scraped, gouged, and depressed by a massive continental glacier over 20,000 years ago. As it melted, the bedrock uplifted. It continues to rise today. Movement of the "basement" rocks far below ground level may be causing unimaginable strain and pressure. It's possible that this rubbing of rocks may cause weird electrostatic excitement of surface air molecules. Maybe some type of gas is released and charged.

The region has long experienced earth movement. Beginning in 1727 and continuing for several years, the northeastern sector of Massachusetts experienced mild earthquake shocks that were accompanied by loud and terrifying sounds from the depths of the earth. The convulsions and earth groans eventually centered around Newbury, Massachusetts, where the alarmed residents prayed that the devil would stop his evil work. Whatever the cause of the strange lights and flying objects, this part of the Northeast historically has been prone to all sorts of visual and psychological anomalies.

A few years ago I received a report stating that near the towns of Beverly and Hamilton stands a stone structure known locally as the "Devil's Altar." A local resident described this strange ruin as a defined collection of stones more than 10 feet in diameter and height that was shaped like a huge wedding cake. Supposedly, the structure is terraced so that one can walk up to the top. The general feeling among those people who know of this structure is that it was used for witchcraft ceremonies.

Nearby this intriguing site are reports of stone "altars" and piles.

## GALLOWS HILL
Salem, Massachusetts

### Site Synopsis
On a hill that once overlooked Salem Harbor—it's now blocked by highrise apartments—is the actual site where twenty suspected witches were killed by their Puritan neighbors: nineteen were hanged and one man was pressed to death—progressively heavier rocks were placed on his chest until he died.

### Location
From Boston take Route 1 north. Exit at the Route 128 intersection going north. Take the Lowell Street exit going toward Salem. Stay on this road. The same road will change to Main Street then Boston Street. After entering the Salem Town Line, watch for Hanson Street. Turn right on Hanson, going to the top of the hill. There's a park at the top. Stop here and get ready to walk.

Walk down the paved path toward the baseball field—you'll see the huge Salem water tower in that general direction. As you are descending the paved

road toward the field, look over home plate for a hilltop. That's where young and old people were hanged.

From this direction there is no path to Gallows Hill. Make your way behind home plate and bushwhack through the ferns, poison sumac, and poison ivy to the hill. There's a dirt path at its base with residences surrounding it.

Don't be misled by signs in Salem that refer to "Gallows Hill Park." This is *not* the site of the hangings. When you park at Hanson Street you'll be walking *through* Gallows Hill Park to get to the actual site.

### Considerations

This is a powerful place. You can feel the anguish here. At the top of the hill, at the spot closest to the incongruous Salem water tower, is the very place where ropes were wound around a thick tree. The accused were led up a tall ladder that was anchored to the ground. Look closely and you may see some of the flagstones used to anchor the wooden posts. You'll note there is no plaque, no sign, no remembrance of the tragedy that happened here, although many town businesses have appropriated the witch motif into their logos and names. In fact, many residents don't even know where the actual hill is.

This is one of the few mysterious sites where I've felt overwhelmed. One sunny July afternoon, I was photographing the hill, looking at the stones and rocks and debris when I was inexplicably overcome by the most intense grief I've ever felt. It surprised me. I had been in an exceptionally happy mood. But as I got closer to the gallows section, I had to stop photographing and sit down. I cried! I know this sounds silly, but I could *feel* the sorrow and horror of a mob screaming for death. It was too overwhelming to continue. As soon as I stepped away from the hill, I felt fine again. Was my experience based on interpretive knowledge of the site, or did I actually pick up some 300-year-old lingering "memory" of the place? I've excavated hundreds of ancient burials, even some from 2,500-year-old Carthaginian tombs where they sacrificed young children, and felt nothing. Gallows Hill is different. There's something extraordinary here. Do be careful.

### History/Background

Cotton Mather was a Harvard-educated minister who firmly believed in the Devil's sly ways: "Witchcraft is a horrible plot against the country, which if not seasonably discovered, will probably blow up and pull down all the churches in the country."[3] By stoking the emotional fires of Salem's residents and officials, Mather was instrumental in providing the religious fervor necessary to accuse and execute witches. He even attended the hideous hanging of George Burroughs, a fellow minister and a Harvard College graduate.

Once convicted, the accused were placed in a cart and hauled through the streets of Salem to the top of Gallows Hill, where, before being marched up the ladder, they were given the chance to address the crowd. The minister Cotton Mather had called a devil made one of the most heartrending, rational

*Gallows Hill, Salem, Massachusetts, where twenty people were slaughtered in the name of God* (Picturesque America.)

speeches anyone had ever heard. He spoke calmly and eloquently about his innocence. But to no avail. Mather's words were more forceful.

Some in the huge crowd of spectators pleaded for the clergyman's life. Mather shouted out: "The Devil is most dangerous when appearing as an Angel of Light," as he watched his former colleague's body twist and shiver in a ghastly death.[4] The air immediately around the hanged body was foul. A body dangling from the neck relaxes the colon muscles, releasing intestinal gases and feces.

Martha Corey, one of the accused, turned to address her neighbors, repeatedly telling them of her innocence. Another woman, Mary Easty, spoke in such a "Serious, Religious, Distinct, and Affectionate," manner that the entire crowd burst into tears. They hanged her anyway. Once the hangings were over, the bodies were thrown into a crevice of rocks on the hill and covered with dirt. Some of the remains are probably still there. No doubt their souls still linger at this sad place.

### Contact Person(s)/Organization

Peabody Essex Museum
132 Essex Street
Salem, Massachusetts 01970
(508) 745-1876

This fine organization houses a major part of the original court documents pertaining to the Witch Trials. There's a small admission charge. Scholars must

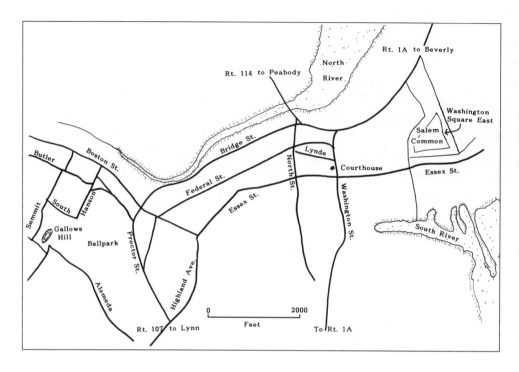

notify the institute in advance if they wish to conduct a detailed study of the documents.

### Total Magnetic Field/Inclination Angle

The southern end of Gallows Hill has a much lower total magnetic field than does the northern tip. The inclination angle changes as well. But I'm certain that the Puritan authorities did not choose this hill based on how they felt there. They chose it because it was outside of town and near open fields. Hanging witches in full view of the community was the civic thing to do, and this locale provided such an opportunity. Nonetheless, there *is* a noticeable deviation across the north-south axis. Perhaps this flux was what affected my neurotransmitter secretions and made me sad. Or maybe it was something not measurable.

### Further Investigations in Area

In all probability, the people killed at Gallows Hill were not witches, nor were they practicing witchcraft. But someone was. Someone or some group of people were doing strange things out in the forest away from the populated villages.

Every Halloween the town of Salem sponsors a Witch Ball. The event has turned into a grand affair of the absurd. You should attend one of these balls and experience the giddy side of this ominous place. Every stereotype of a witch is represented, from the old hag to the svelte sex goddess. During the times when I've attended this grand soiree, I've often wondered if are there any descendants of the *real* Salem witches there. Are there people who have maintained a 300-year silence about what really happened in 1692? I'm positive there are.

## EAST/SOUTHEAST MASSACHUSETTS

East of the Connecticut River in Massachusetts is a wooded central plateau that is actually a geological extension of the White Mountains of New Hampshire. East of the plateau, the hills slope away to a coastal lowland. The major waterway is the Charles River, which flows across 60 miles of eastern Massachusetts before emptying into Massachusetts Bay at Boston. This bay is but one example of the many protected harbors that have made the shoreline a favorite sailing spot for hundreds, perhaps even thousands, of years.

### BEEHIVE STONE CHAMBER
Upton, Massachusetts

#### Site Synopsis
Near the path of an ancient Indian trail leading from the coast is a massive stone chamber. A long passageway opens up into an enormous "beehive-shaped" room. This mysterious ruin has been a mystery since the first settlers cleared the forest.

#### Location
From Boston take the Massachusetts Turnpike (Interstate 90) west for about 27 miles to Interstate 495. Exit south on I-495. Continue for 3 miles to the Upton exit, 21B. Continue west on Route 135 for about 3½ miles, at which point the road will fork. Bear left just beyond the large pond. Continue on this road for ⁹⁄₁₀ of a mile until it intersects with River Street. Turn left on River Street, and take the next right turn. The site is off Elm Street.

#### Considerations
The site is on private property. You *must* get permission from the landowner before entering the chamber, or trespassing charges may be filed.

#### History/Background
We know from archeological excavations that Native Americans lived in the Massachusetts area for many centuries. But this fact wouldn't have sur-

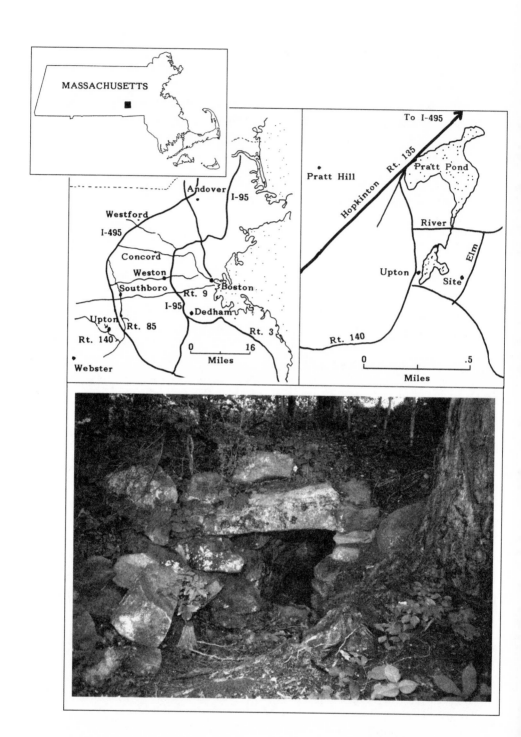

prised the early settlers for the first Englishmen came across countless trails crisscrossing the eastern seaboard. Some were a mere foot wide through the tangled underbrush, while others were close to three feet wide. A major trail, known as the Old Bay Path, extended from the Boston area (Massachusetts Bay) to Hopkinton, through Upton, and over to Hartford, Connecticut. Many of these Indian trails became Colonial roads.

*Inside Upton Chamber looking toward the entranceway. Note the massive, carefully arranged stone slabs.*

On one side trail of the Old Bay Path, the first Englishmen discovered an unusual stone cave, a large circular chamber with a domed roof.[5] The length of the entranceway measured over 15 feet, with the "beehive" chamber measuring about 11 feet in diameter and over 10 feet in height. It wasn't until the late 1800s that a local resident aroused public curiosity about the structure.

In 1893, the *Milford Journal* published a piece by Daniel Fiske under the pseudonym Pratt Pond, Jr. He wrote about a largely ignored buried chamber and pondered "its origin, its builders and purpose." He then put forward the proposition "that this relic was created as a place of refuge from the attacks of some warlike nation, previous to the Indian race."[6]

Daniel Fiske's article was the first written account of the chamber, and it caused several scholars to visit the site. Harvard Professor Hugh Hencken visited the site in the 1930s and was perplexed as to its function. A sketch of the chamber was done in the late 1940s by another scholar, Vincent Fagan. This prompted more visits and a litany of theories about its possible origin. In the early 1950s, an amateur archeological group got two graduate students to partially excavate the site, but the results of their dig were inconclusive.[7]

Nevertheless, some very interesting elements of the structure were uncovered. They completely excavated the entranceway of the chamber, and, to their surprise, found the remains of a rotting *wooden* floor. More intriguingly, they found a curious placement of large stones *above* the floor. The researchers speculated that the stones had been placed above the floor when the water table flooded the chamber entranceway.

My reading of this forty-year-old report suggests that someone other than the builders of this chamber tried to made use of it via a wooden flooring. This suspicion is based on the different layers of flooring in the main beehive. Also, the wooden floor seemed to rest on the *original* level of the chamber entranceway and beehive.

Whoever built and/or used this structure was careful to keep it very clean, so it is difficult to determine its age or occupants. The only artifact found near the wood floor was a silver-colored rim shard. And the context of the find suggested that it may have filtered down from a later time period. Nothing else was uncovered.

This chamber is intriguing. It is built entirely of dry-stone granite—no mortar was used to hold the stones together. They stay locked in due to the weight of one stone overlapping the other. A massive lintel stone peering out from the side of a hill is the only indication that something is there. Stepping down into the opening brings one into a 15-foot-long stone-lined passageway that's a little more than 4½ feet high. At its end is a round chamber that corbels upward a little more than 10 feet. This is an astonishing piece of construction.

During the late 1970s and 1980s, researchers across New England latched on to a form of investigation that seemed to work very well for sites in Great

Britain and Europe. Called archeoastronomy (archeological astronomy), the idea was to see if a given site had any association with the rising or setting of the sun or the moon, or the movements by other heavenly bodies.

Excited by another method to help uncover the reason why such mega-lithic sites were built, researchers around the world, including those in New England, dusted off their transits and resurveyed the chambers, standing stones, and the like with respect to which way they faced and what may have been observation points for at different times of the year. Amazingly, many of the structures, such as Stonehenge, seemed to be positioned to watch various solar/lunar/stellar phenomena. Suddenly, the people who had built these things were ancient astronomers! It was a pretty cool paradigm. Many of us fell for it; some more than others.

In the early 1980s, two researchers rushed to apply archeoastronomy to the Upton Chamber, recording a series of measurements, calculations, obser-vations and the like. They hypothesized that the chamber was constructed to watch the Pleiades star group pop up over some stone piles on a nearby hill-top. Based on their calculations, this had happened around 710 A.D., as that's the last time this stellar phenomenon could be observed from the Upton site (the earth wobbles a bit every few thousand years, changing the site lines for various astronomical events). Thus, the chamber may have been constructed sometime around 710 A.D. Pretty neat. Well, maybe. Constructing a chamber as large and as massive as this one for observing a bright star cluster is stretch-ing a point. Furthermore, what about the notoriously heavy cloud cover in New England, which makes it very difficult to observe astronomical events? Imagine ancient priests waiting for the special moment late at night, and sud-denly a layer of clouds drifts into the region from the ocean. This site is the worst possible place to observe anything astronomical.

If it *was* built to watch the stars, then my cap is off to the archeoas-tronomers. But I suspect something a tad stranger.

### Contact Person(s)/Organization

Upton Historical Society
Library Building/Corner of Main and Grove Street
Upton, Massachusetts 01568
(508) 529-6600

Open Wednesday mornings, or by appointment.

### Total Magnetic Field/Inclination Angle

I was unable to obtain a magnetic horizontal or vertical vector at this site, because the numbers kept moving all over the scale. Something weird was happening there. It was definitely a place of power.

On a recent visit to the site, I took a series of magnetic-field measurements around the vicinity of the chamber. As I continued into the chamber, the magnetic field changed significantly, as I have discovered at many stone chamber sites. But when I attempted four cardinal measurements *inside* the beehive structure, I was stymied. I could not get a stable horizontal or vertical vector. The digital readout kept displaying an assortment of numbers: 100 milligauss, 1400, 50, 358, 900, 20, 861, and so on. It would not stabilize. The same happened with the vertical vector.

I changed batteries, remeasured the outside points, got the same numbers, and then attempted, once again, to measure the inside of the beehive. The same phenomenon occurred. This curious anomaly also happened at the Petersham, Massachusetts, beehive structure.

My guess is that these two sites are geomagnetic hotspots: areas of the earth where intense aberrations exist. The causes could be many things, such as the soil/bedrock composition; the structure of the deep basement rocks; deep fault zones; and so on. It's difficult to believe that both the Petersham and the Upton sites were built on such impressive microregions by chance alone. Based on data collected throughout the eastern states, I think the placement of these sites was a conscious, well-thought-out decision. Perhaps these places were built to capitalize on the influence of geomagnetic flux on peoples' moods or feelings. If the work of Dr. Robert Becker and others is correct with respect to magnetism affecting the secretion of various neurotransmitters (see the Introduction), then the chambers, and the Upton and Petersham beehives in particular, take on new meaning.

### Further Investigations in Area

I have received reports of the existence of several large stone piles or cairns at the top of Pratt Hill, in clear view as one looks out and up from the chamber.

There are also vague reports about other stone chambers in the general vicinity of the beehive. This makes sense. Chambers are rarely found in isolation. It might prove worthwhile to thoroughly search the deep recesses of the state forest between Upton and Hopkinton.

Finally, in Daniel Fiske's 1893 *Milford Journal* article is the following enticing tidbit:

> It is but a few years since that one of our roadmasters and his men in excavating gravel from a hill on the Westboro Road, unearthed two wells in the bottom of which water remained. The wells remained intact, the top of which were several feet under the surface of the ground, there being no indication of ever having been disturbed. As it

was well known that Indians never dug wells, the minds of many citizens were full of conjecture in regard to their origin. There may have been a settlement in that section of a partially civilized race prior to the tomahawk and wigwam; but this is only conjecture and the mystery of their origin will ever remain.[8]

About 25 miles southwest of Upton, in the town of Webster, Massachusetts is a stone chamber. Constructed a few yards from a brook that empties into Lake Chaubunagungamaug, the chamber is located a short distance from the Great Indian Trail that ran through the dense forest of New England from Boston to the Hartford, Connecticut, area. The chamber is of interest because of its proximity to both the trail and the lake. To get there from downtown Worcester, Massachusetts, take Interstate 395 south for about 20 miles to Exit 2. Exit onto Route 16 traveling east for about 1½ miles. Bear right onto Gore Road when the road splits. Stay on Gore Road for about 300 feet, and turn right onto Community Road. There's a small embankment within a 100 feet. Park and walk south (to your left) toward Browns Brook, where you'll see the chamber.

## INSCRIBED STONE
Aptucxet Trading Post Museum, Bourne, Massachusetts

### Site Synopsis
A large stone etched with strange symbols, now housed in a Museum on Cape Cod, has evoked some bizarre explanations over the years.

### Location
Presently on display at the Aptucxet Trading Post Museum, Bourne, Massachusetts. From Boston take Route 3 south to the Sagamore Bridge. Turn west onto Route 6. Follow the road to the Bourne Bridge. After crossing over the Bourne Bridge, the road changes to Route 28 South. Turn off at the Trading Post Corner Exit. At the end of this road, turn left onto Trowbridge Road. Continue on until the intersection of County Road and Sandwich Roads. Continue going straight across the intersection for less than half a mile. Turn right onto Aptucxet Road, then make a quick left at the sign.

### Considerations
There's a small admission fee. It's well worth it. Spend time examining the wonderful array of artifacts on display. Walk out the back toward the canal and look to the south toward Buzzard's Bay.

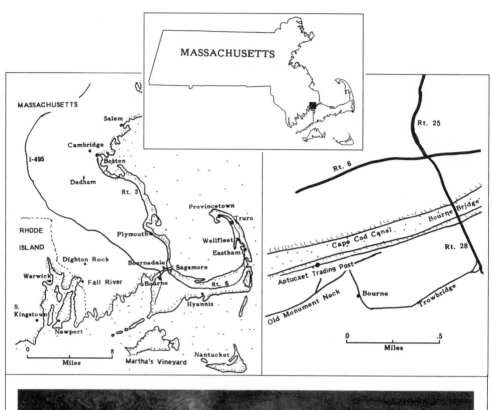

## History/Background

Cape Cod was formed around 10,000 years ago when a gigantic, continent-sized glacier made of ice, sand, and boulders stopped advancing. It had pushed an assortment of debris in front of it, like a massive bulldozer, so when the ice finally melted away, this front-end material of rock, sand, and boulders was left in place. While rising sea levels covered up a good portion of it, early Cape Cod, the Elizabeth Islands, Martha's Vineyard, and Nantucket were born.

It didn't take the Native Americans in the vicinity long to make the most of this new territory. Many made their way to the coastal regions, no doubt for the abundant fish. When the first Pilgrims landed on the northern tip of Cape Cod in 1620, before sailing across the bay to Plymouth Rock, they found many villages along this armlike spit of land.

After establishing a permanent settlement the following year at Plymouth, the Pilgrims began to explore their neighborhood. Difficulties during the first season's planting led them to go south in search of food. They found an Indian village called Manamet along the northwestern border of the cape, and eventually established a trading post farther south along the Manamet River at a place called Aptucxet, which means "little trap in the river." The museum there was constructed in the 1930s on the original site of this first trading post.

This northwestern tip of Cape Cod is intriguing. Before the Cape Cod Canal was dug in 1914, there were two rivers that allowed partial transit between Cape Cod Bay and Buzzard's Bay. The Scusset River emptied into Cape Cod Bay and was navigable for about a mile inland. The Manamet River's source was the Great Herring Pond, and it emptied into Buzzard's Bay. The hilly area where the Sagamore Bridge is today separated these two waterways. Instead of navigating 135 miles around the arm of Cape Cod—a very dangerous sail, given the ever-changing shoals and tempestuous Atlantic Ocean—natives and early settlers traveled up either river as far as they could, then they portaged, or carried their canoes, a few miles over to the other river. While this may seem terribly inconvenient—and it was—it did save time and lives. Many people passed this way for perhaps thousands of years. This region was also the intersection of many ancient Indian trails.

The Bourne Stone was actually found somewhere in the vicinity of Bournedale—about where the Manamet village used to be. It was regarded as sacred by the Manamets. This stone was incorporated into the entranceway steps of a church built for them in the late seventeenth century, and after the church was destroyed by fire in the late 1600s, the stone was incorporated into an Indian woman's dwelling, the ruins of which are tucked away in the woods to the west of the Great Herring Pond. In the early 1900s, the stone was retrieved from this dwelling by the Bourne Historical Society and is currently on display at the Aptucxet Trading Museum.

The stone is about four feet long and two feet thick. Along its broad-flat face are several deep incisions. The composition of the stone is like that of other stones found in the woods just to the north of Bournedale.

As is the case with most American inscriptions, the interpretation of this stone's markings has depended on when it has been examined. Early Puritans thought the markings had something to do with Indian devil worship. The local natives denied it, claiming to know nothing of the symbols' meaning. By the late nineteenth century, scholars were sure the markings were of Scandinavian or Viking origin. In fact, this stone was used as proof positive that the Vikings had sailed to New England and left their mark. By the 1970s, Vikings were out of style and in came the Phoenicians. Barry Fell saw two different Old World alphabets within the carvings, indicating to him prehistoric visitors to the Manamet Valley. Fell envisioned Iberian-Phoenician traders wandering about lower New England leaving carved stone messages for other literate sailors. His translation of the Bourne Stone? "A proclamation of annexation. Do not deface. By this Hanno takes possession."[9]

Recently, some scholars have been looking at the symbols and signs different Indian sachems (chiefs) used to "sign" a treaty and have found them to be strikingly similar to those found on the Bourne Stone and others like it (see the Yarmouth Stone, Nova Scotia). The suspicion is that the treaty symbols were merely the last vestiges of an ancient writing or pictorial system. Dr. Fell looked at those personal markings and concluded something entirely different. He claimed to see ancient Old World alphabetic symbols, which suggested to him that some early Native Americans learned or emulated that ancient European writing system. As you can see, there is great controversy over the origin and meaning of the symbols. But fear not, like the New England weather, wait a little bit and it will change.

### Contact Person(s)/Organization

Aptucxet Trading Post Museum
24 Aptucxet Road
PO Box 95
Bourne, Massachusetts 02532-0785
(508) 759-9487

### Total Magnetic Field/Inclination Angle
None taken at the Trading Post Museum.

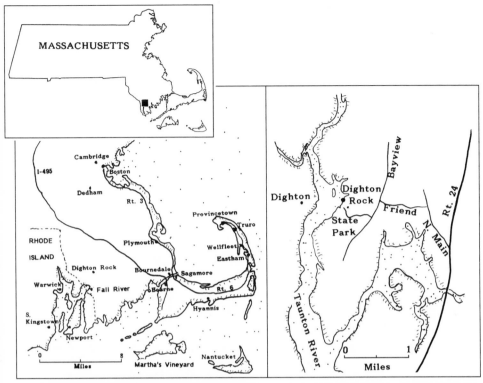

## Further Investigations in Area

There are several places that demand investigation in this fertile region. My work in the surrounding area was limited. But I did glean some good leads. Researchers should hike along the western side of Great Herring Pond. There are reports that other inscribed stones exist in old foundations.

## DIGHTON ROCK
Dighton State Forest, Massachusetts

### Site Synopsis

In the seventeenth century, settlers discovered a stone in the Taunton River that had an impressive array of inscriptions. Over the years, various researchers have attributed the inscriptions to the Phoenicians, the Vikings, American Indians, and early Portuguese explorers. A few years ago, the rock was removed from the river, and a small museum was constructed around it. The rock stands a few feet in from its former home in exactly the same orientation as when it was in the river. Nearby are small islands that have unusual earthen and stone formations.

### Location

From Fall River take Route 24 north, turning off at Exit 10. Follow the road north to the State Park.

### Considerations

Although the Dighton park is under the jurisdiction of the Department of Environmental Management, Division of Forests and Parks, the actual rock is now housed in a museum that's *not* open all the time. Call ahead to obtain opening schedules.

The gates to the park open at 10 A.M. and close at 6 P.M.

### History/Background

It's an easy sail up from Rhode Island Sound through the Sakonnet River and Mount Hope Bay up to the Taunton River. Continuing on from the mouth of the Taunton, the river eventually narrows and splits. Along the eastern banks of this waterway, at the head of Assonet Bay, a large, flat-faced boulder could be seen partially protruding from the water.

A number of years ago, a small museum was built on an artificial prong of land jutting into the riverbed. The stone was moved inside the structure for protection and now rests behind a wall of glass.

The stone is almost 12 feet long and about 5 feet high, although it slopes upward at about a 60-degree angle. The flat face of the rock is riddled with markings: images, glyph-like symbols, and so on. The meaning of those markings has been a mystery since Colonists first noticed this strangely inscribed stone.

As early as 1680, the Reverend John Danforth made a drawing of the marks that was widely distributed throughout Massachusetts. Danforth wrote that there was a "Tradition of old Indians yt yr came a wooden house, (& men of another country in it) swimming up the river Assonet, yt fought ye Indian & sley yr Saunchem, . . . Some recon the figures here to be Hieroglyphicall, the first figure representing a Ship, without masts, & a meer Wrack cast upon the Shoules, the second representing an head of land, possibly a cape with a peninsula, Hence a Gulf."[10] This piqued the interest of Boston clergyman Cotton Mather, who visited the site in 1712 and drew what he saw. Eighteen years later, a Dr. Greenwood apparently saw something different at Dighton Rock. His drawing looks nothing like the other two. Several other scholars made the trek to the stone to see what they could see. An examination of these on-the-spot sketches reveals more about the mind-set of the artists than the reality of the carvings. These renditions, however, influenced the interpretation of the symbols. Thus, Henry Rowe Schoolcraft, a historian and a United States Senator, concluded that the markings were a record of an Indian battle. Fur trapper William Pidgeon saw Phoenician symbols on the stone. A Danish historian saw Viking runes there. And on it went.

Currently, there are at least four theories concerning the origin of Dighton Rock's mysterious inscriptions. Each has its passionate and articulate defenders. The museum that houses the rock does a good job of illustrating most of these ideas with attractive and informative displays. The markings may be:

- American Indian symbols
- Ancient Phoenician script
- Viking or Norse runes, or
- Markings from a Portuguese vessel that strayed into the Taunton River sometime in the 1500s.

Which is the correct interpretation? Well, it all depends on what you want to believe. A funny thing about American inscribed stones is that there never is a consensus as to what they mean. Each person comes away with a different conclusion, probably based on what kind of cultural baggage he or she is carrying around. This is rather astonishing, for other cultures in different parts of the world have rigorously identified and deciphered ancient inscriptions on their soil. We have not. Perhaps it's something about our national character. Or maybe it's the water.

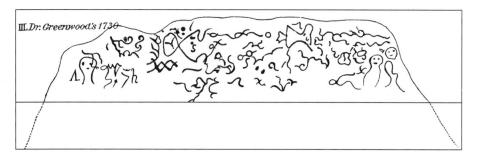

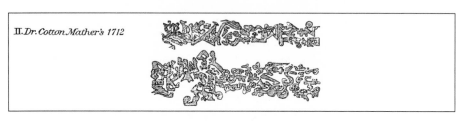

*Depiction of the Dighton Rock, inscriptions, 1680–1830* (10th Annual Report).

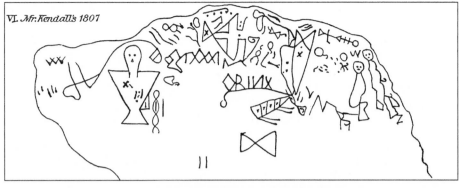

VII. *Mr. Kendall's 1807*

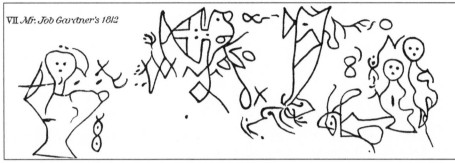

VII. *Mr. Job Gardner's 1812*

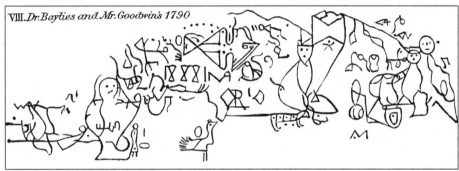

VIII. *Dr. Baylies and Mr. Goodwin's 1790*

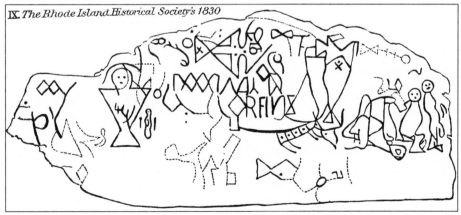

IX. *The Rhode Island Historical Society's 1830*

### Contact Person(s)/Organization

Freetown State Forest
Dighton Rock State Park
Bayview Road
Berkley, Massachusetts 02708
(508) 644-5522

Department of Environmental Management, Divisions of Forests and Parks
(617) 727-3180.

### Total Magnetic Field/Inclination Angle

None taken at this site because the stone was removed from its original riverbed location.

### Further Investigations in Area

There are a host of interesting sites nearby. Across the river, near North Dighton, there's an intriguing beehive-style stone chamber on Wheeler Street. Unfortunately, the chamber's top section is partially collapsed.

Southeast of Dighton Rock, deep in a wooded area off Chipaway Road in Freetown, are hundreds of sacred stone piles. Back in the early 1980s, a local resident contacted a member of the Tribal Council for southeastern Massachusetts. He claimed that he had found over 500 stone piles that might be ancient graves. When the tribal chief finally examined these stones, he became very emotional, for he was seeing a part of his heritage for the first time. There were many perfect circles of stones scattered throughout the forest, intermingled with stone piles.

Two researchers decided to excavate a similar stone mound site a few miles from the Freetown piles. The results of their excavation were remarkable. After finding a carefully laid out construction similar to many others they had examined throughout the East and an enormous amount of red ochre in the stone mound, the scientists concluded that ". . . some New England stone mounds are the remaining cultural components of an ancient and enduring religion . . ."[11] They believed that some of the strange stone remains found in New England and elsewhere in eastern America represented "primal architecture . . . in which the whole of space becomes ritualized.[12] The placement of stones on the land represented a symbolic connection with nature in a way that is fundamentally different from Western interpretation. Land was indeed sacred. And special places deserved special architecture.

Westport, Massachusetts, is almost due south of Dighton Rock. This old town is at the head of the east branch of the Westport River. About a quarter mile from the beach, in the backyard of a private home, is a large capstone supported by three smaller standing stones. This ruin looks like a stone table. It's origin is unknown.

And, finally, this area continues to surprise people. In recent years glass jars filled with pin-punctured dolls have washed ashore on the beach near Gooseberry Neck in Westport. Dozens of glass jars, sometimes sealed with black electrical tape, have been picked up by beach strollers. Some of the jars have pieces of clothing inside; others contain handmade effigy dolls with over one hundred pins stuck in them. Detectives in the area believe that someone could be practicing voodoo, or Santeria, an Afro-Hispanic religion practiced throughout the Caribbean. Based on tidal flow, many suspect the jars are being dropped late at night from a bridge on Route 88 near Horseneck Beach. Why here?

## WEST/CENTRAL MASSACHUSETTS

Cascading from a bog "in a trout hatchery near Canada," as New England poet Robert Frost once said, the headwaters of the Connecticut River flow 410 miles southward through forest and meadow, forming the state boundary between New Hampshire and Vermont, then weave across western Massachusetts and central Connecticut before emptying into Long Island Sound. Pioneer settlements along the Connecticut River Valley go back more than three hundred years. Dutch entrepreneurs set up trading posts along the marshes and salt flats of the lower reaches in order to buy beaver pelts from the Indians. But encroaching English immigrants, more interested in settling what would become one of the most productive farm valleys in the East, eventually expelled the Dutch traders.

The Puritans made their way from Massachusetts through a dense forest of giant white cathedral pines, described by one of the travelers as "a boundless contiguity of shade." Compared to the rocky soil of the eastern coast, the valley was indeed paradise, with its multitudes of river shad, salmon, and abundant wildlife along the broad, fertile floodplain. Shifting sandbars near the Connecticut's mouth at Old Saybrook have prevented large, deep-draft vessels from entering the waterway. As a result, heavy-shipping industry never developed in the valley, so many stretches of the riverbank have retained their wild, unspoiled beauty.

## BEEHIVE CHAMBER/TUNNELS
Petersham, Massachusetts

### Site Synopsis
Just off a lonely dirt road in central Massachusetts is a superbly engineered, underground beehive-style stone chamber. Snaking out from this stone room are several stone-lined tunnels. What their function was and where they go is unknown.

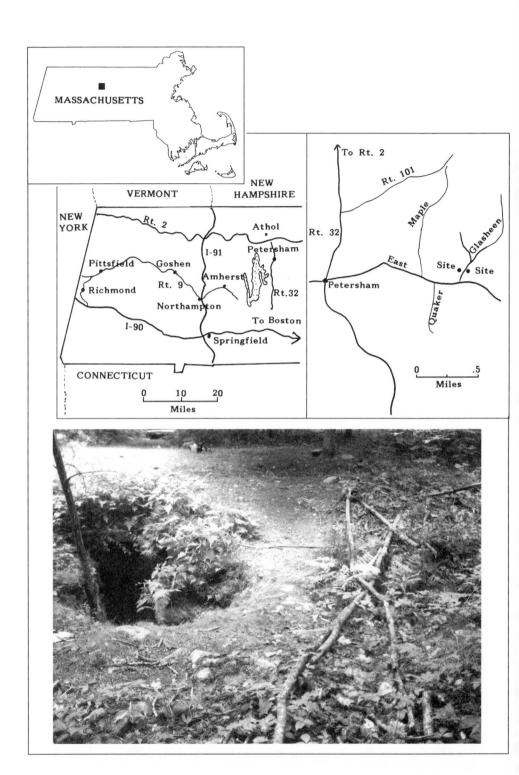

## Location

From Boston take Route 2 west for about 70 miles. Turn south onto Route 32. After 6 miles you'll be in the town center. Turn left (east) onto East Street. Continue for 2.3 miles. Turn left (north) onto Glasheen Road. This is an unpaved, dirt-graded road. Drive for .25 miles. Park in the opening path on your left. The beehive and tunnels are directly up this path.

## Considerations

If you visit this site during the summer months, take the usual precautions against poison ivy and mosquitoes: wear a skin barrier, use an insect repellent, and wear long pants and sleeves. The best time to see this site, however, is during the late fall, just before the snowfalls of winter.

The site is owned and protected by the Petersham Historical Society.

## History/Background

The 510 acres of the James W. Brooks Woodland Preserve once was the territory of the Nipmuck Indians. In the mid 1700s, it was deeded to a Daniel Spooner, one of Petersham's earliest settlers. Nearly a century later, the land was farmed by Charles Dudley and John Cornell. The foundations of their homesteads and the stone walls that marked their pastures are visible today as one drives around Petersham.

In 1907 industrialist James Willson Brooks accumulated large tracts of woodland to protect the Swift River Valley, including the old Dudley and Cornell properties. Brooks then gave Harvard University 2,000 acres to establish the Harvard Forest. Much of that original land became the Brooks Woodland Preserve, which is being managed to recreate the virgin forest of central New England.

A few miles from the Petersham town center is a series of tunnels that have baffled people for years. Hardly anything exists in print about them, and no one in town knows much about their origin. Sometime before 1940 in the small field to the left of Glasheen Road, the ground beneath a tractor hauling lumber across this spot collapsed, revealing the underground chamber and the tunnels.

Originally, one entered the chamber by dropping down 5 feet into a hole and crawling through the opening, but someone in the last few years has made it easier by removing some of the dirt surrounding the opening. The entranceway is made of large fieldstones capped by even larger granite slabs. A few feet ahead is a room about 10 feet in diameter and around 7 feet high. The bottom of the structure is filled with water. Off to the right is a tunnel that opens to the surface. Down below is another tunnel about 12 inches high and wide that leads to another site. At the surface there are depressions in the earth where the soil has slumped down to the tunnels. A few yards away, capstones can be seen.

*Interior of the beehive chamber, looking towards the entranceway,*
*Petersham, Massachusetts.*

The site has never been excavated, and we haven't a clue as to how many
tunnels there are or where they go! This complex of carefully laid stonework
makes absolutely no sense—that is, with respect to a twentieth-century outlook on things.

Some researchers have tried to make the case that this beehive and tunnel
system was an eighteenth-century hideout of some sort. While it is known that
a Colonial farmstead was definitely located there, a brief examination of the
stonework would put the hideout idea to rest: The tunnel system is great if

you're the size of a squirrel. The exposed stone passageways are simply too small for even a child to crawl through. All indications point to the presence of this mysterious stonework being in place *before* the first Colonial foundation was dug.

At present, this beehive stone chamber and assortment of tunnels remains a mystery. No one knows who built it, when it was built, or for what purpose. I suspect, however, the specific placement of the beehive was a carefully calculated endeavor.

### Contact Person(s)/Organization

Petersham Historical Society
c/o Petersham Library
Petersham, Massachusetts 01366
(508) 724-3405

As with many volunteer New England historical societies, this one is open only once or twice a week, and sometimes by appointment only. Contact the local library for details.

New England Antiquities Research Association (NEARA)
Journal/Archival Information
2388 Whalley Road
Sharlot, Vermont 05445

or

305 Academy Road
Pembroke, New Hampshire 03275

The Fisher Museum at Harvard Forests offers a wonderful introduction to life in central New England over the past three hundred years. It's open from 9 A.M.–5 P.M., M–F, year round, and 12–4 P.M. Saturdays and Sundays, May through October.

Harvard Forest
Petersham, Massachusetts 01366-0068
(508) 724-3302
Fax: (508) 724-3595

The Trustees of Reservations
527 Essex Street
Beverly, Massachusetts 01915
(508) 921-1944

The Trustees of Reservations is dedicated to preserving for public use properties of exceptional scenic, historic, and ecological value throughout Massachu-

*Interior of chamber, looking up at the magnificent beehive-style stonework leading to a single-rood slab. Rising from ground level, each successive layer of stone overlaps the layer beneath it.*

setts. Founded in 1891, it's a nonprofit organization and the oldest land trust in the world.

### Total Magnetic Field/Inclination Angle

As at the Upton, Massachusetts, chamber, I was unable to get an accurate reading *inside* the beehive structure. The outside readings, taken some 15 feet around the chamber, were consistent with others in the Petersham region: a total magnetic field of 530 milligauss with an inclination angle of 66 degrees. As I approached the entranceway and entered it, the TMF increased significantly, as did the IA. But once inside the beehive, the horizontal and vertical vectors fluctuated wildly: from 90 to 495 to 3 to 1,000. In a five-minute span, the magnetometer seemed to be randomly displaying numbers.

I left the chamber, checked the instrument, changed the power source, and repeated the outside measurements. They were consistent with my previous readings. I again attempted to measure the total magnetic field inside the beehive, but, again, was not able to get a stable reading. Conclusion: This site is on a geomagnetic hot zone. This chamber was built by a people who were taking advantage of a peculiarity in the earth's geomagnetic field.

Buried stone tunnels seem to be part of the ancient landscape in the eastern United States. People keep coming across them, and they continue to puzzle all who do.

### Further Investigations in Area

Across Glasheen Road from this site is another set of tunnels. Go to the entranceway of the pathway and Glasheen. Site 105 degrees across the road. Follow this orientation across the stone walls. You'll pass an early Colonial farm foundation. In the corner of the walling is a well-like structure. At the bottom of this laid-stone pit is a stone-lined tunnel that goes off into the distance. What was its purpose? Some researchers have suggested that the tunnels here link up with those across the road.

The New England Antiquities Research Association (NEARA) has files on many stone chambers in the area west and east of the Quabbin Reservoir. In an arc leading from Amherst, Massachusetts, up through East Leverett, to Shutesbury (via Shutesbury Road), NEARA has several site reports on bizarre stone chambers.

## STONE TUNNELS
Goshen, Massachusetts

### Site Synopsis

On a hillside just beyond the center of Goshen, a town of 700 people near the center of Massachusetts, a stone-lined shaft, 3½ feet in diameter plunges

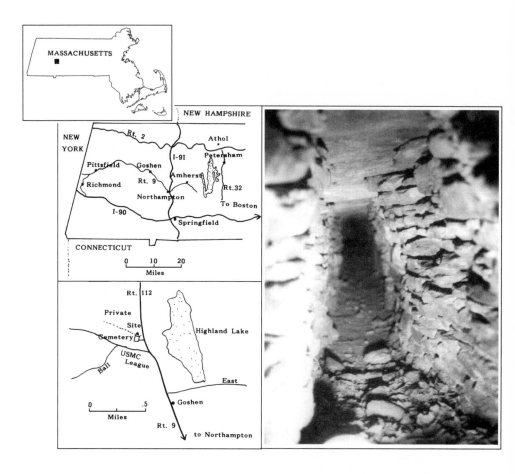

down through the ground. Seen from above, the cylinder-like "pit" gives every impression of being a simple, dry-stone well. Buried below 16 feet of dense "hardpan" clay soil, is an intriguing complex of stonework whose origins are shrouded in mystery. Near the bottom of the shaft, two stone-lined tunnels snake through the underground hillside for no apparent reason. One runs north for 16 feet, while the other runs south for 68 feet before narrowing into a collapsed sand pile. No one knows the exact length it continues beyond a neighboring cemetery wall. The tunnel's walls are built of stacked flagstones, rising to a height of around 3½ feet. Massive capstones weighing over 2,000 pounds span the underground walls, creating the two passageways.

### Location

From Boston take the Massachusetts Turnpike west for approximately 90 miles, just passing Springfield before exiting north on Interstate 91. Travel north on I-91 for another 15 miles exiting at Northhampton. Travel northwest on Route 9 for another 15 miles before stopping at Goshen. About a half mile before reaching the intersection of Route 9 and Route 112, there's a town cemetery on the right. Turn right into the cemetery. The road splits into two paths: The left one goes to the cemetery, while the right one leads up the hill to the property owner. Walk along the north cemetery wall (on your right). Follow this until you reach the newer section of the graveyard. Find the Sears tombstone against the stone wall and look into the woods. You'll see a large boulder covering the site. The entranceway shaft is about 70 feet from the wall.

### Considerations

The present owners of the tunnel have placed a large boulder on top of the main shaft, to guard against injuries and potential lawsuits. Needless to say, this is very disappointing for all interested parties. You can still view the site from the cemetery, however. With this book in hand, visualize the two tunnels deep under the ground. In fact, you may be standing on one.

### History/Background

There are lots of odd theories about the tunnels. Some locals once thought an enterprising pioneer built them to grow silkworms. Others thought it must have been part of the Underground Railroad. Still others believed it to be an escape tunnel used by Colonial settlers to flee from marauding Indians. James Whittall, director of the Early Sites Research Society, excavated the site in the 1980s and estimated that the tunnels had been there for over 5,000 years. No one really knows what the site was used for or who built it.

In the early 1980s, Jim Whittall and a crew began a two-phase program to map out and partially excavate the dense soil at the site. One team dug on the north side of the shaft above the smaller tunnel, while another team dug within. The results have some broad implications.

Above a capstone in the tunnel trench the archeological team uncovered a carefully made round stone disk about seven inches in diameter and one inch in thickness. Its position in the soil showed that it had been carefully placed at the time the tunnel capstones were covered with dirt. The edges of the disk had been intricately pressed and worked with a blunt instrument, causing the telltale indentations of what's known as pressure flaking. Arrowheads were made in the same manner. Someone went to much trouble to shape the disk. Although the function of this artifact is unknown, it allows one to crudely date the tunnel site by its association with the capstones. Round disk stones similar to the Goshen artifact have been recovered at several New England Indian sites that date to a period known as the late Archaic, around 5,000 years ago. Some other stone digging tools and hammerstones were found at Goshen that date to a much earlier period.

Digging down farther exposed the northern end of the tunnel that strangely came to a halt, almost as if the original builders just gave up con-

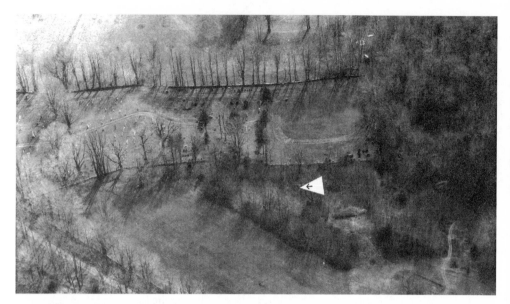

*Aerial view of the Goshen shaft/tunnel location. The arrow points toward the shaft opening within the cluster of trees (photo by Malcolm Pearson during a fly-by arranged by the author).*

*Plan and section views of the Goshen stone shaft and tunnels (after Whittall Excavation Report).*

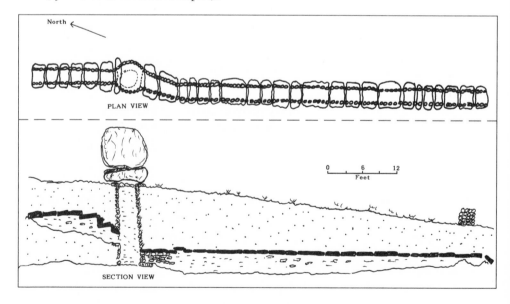

struction of the walls and capstones. Before they stopped, the builders quarried into ledgerock to keep the tunnel level.

The soil profile suggested the site is much older than the Archaic period. The excavation showed that the tunnel was constructed while soil was being deposited during the melting of the last glaciation, something that happened over 10,000 years ago!

It also appears likely that the Goshen tunnels are part of a larger complex of underground constructions yet to be found in the meadows surrounding the village. It is difficult to imagine such an isolated example of stonework unconnected to anything else in the immediate vicinity.

Aerial photographs revealed very long and straight soil discolorations near the tunnels. These ground disturbances may represent the obliterated outlines of a foundation structure six times as large as a modern house. The patterns, visible only from the air, were caused by the slow decomposition of wood foundations filling in with debris, humus, and moisture. During the last three hundred years nothing of that size ever existed in Goshen.

To date there are no known stoneworks of Colonial origin that even compare with the Goshen site. Clear, rational explanations concerning the tunnels' purpose continue to elude us. The site exudes an exotic, ceremonial feeling.

*The end of the northern tunnel. Excavators discovered that the tunnel's builders were carving into the bedrock, apparently to keep the floor level. Why they were doing this is unknown. The archeological team was unable to identify the builders of this complex.*

Perhaps it was used in an elaborate religious or fertility ritual, where adolescents descended far into of the earth, crawling deeper and deeper through the narrow passageways before returning to the surface.

Who were the people who built the Goshen tunnels? Where did they go? Why did they build them? While the stone disk found at the tunnels is similar to those uncovered at Archaic Indian sties in New England, no Indians from that period were known to have built anything like this. And the soil profile points to a tunnel age much older than the disk.

Could the stone-lined shaft and tunnels buried beneath 16 feet of clay on a hillside in Goshen be our first encounter with a newly discovered, strange and mysterious culture that vanished from America a long time ago?

### Contact Person(s)/Organization

Goshen Historical Commission
Route 9
Goshen, Massachusetts 01032
(413) 268-7026

The museum here is open on Sundays from Memorial Day through Labor Day, from 2–4 P.M.

Early Sites Research Society
Rowley, Massachusetts 01969

### Total Magnetic Field/Inclination Angle

I measured this site several years ago with a different magnetometer than the one used for this book. It would be helpful to remeasure it to compare the older data with the newer readings. Nonetheless, I list the readings here.

The area to the east and west of the shaft and tunnel gave total magnetic field readings that were typical of those around the Goshen region: 535 milligauss and 65 degrees. But inside the chamber I got completely different readings. Along the northern tunnel the TMF/IA was 320 milligauss and 40 degrees. Along the southern tunnel the TMF/IA readings dropped to 200 milligauss and 25 degrees throughout. Clearly this was another geomagnetic hot zone. Perhaps the complex was part of some intricate religious vision-quest ritual. After spending a few hours inside the tunnels—measuring, recording, excavating—one feels almost reborn upon entering daylight. Perhaps this is merely a function of going from cramped quarters bathed in artificial light to the openness of the outside world. But maybe that was the point.

### Further Investigations in Area

There are many other lithic remains in the Goshen area. A few years ago, Jim Whittall reported on a strange stone chamber on a ridge west of the tunnel site.

There's also a report of a 6-foot-high stone pile in Ashfield, Massachusetts, a town about 7 miles north of Goshen.

About 7 miles south of Goshen, near Westhampton, high atop Hanging Mountain near the Pine Island Lake Reservoir, is a stone house. The walls of this structure are made of massive slabs of granite.

Twenty miles west of Goshen near the town of Cheshire, Massachusetts, is a 6-foot-tall standing stone that was around when the current owner's early-eighteenth-century ancestors homesteaded the region. They never figured out what it was used for, although local Indian legend considered it a taboo stone—one that they never wanted to get close to.

# Rhode Island

R hode Island got started because of religious persecution. In 1635 the Massachusetts Bay Company banished Roger Williams, then a minister at Salem, out of their jurisdiction because his critical opinions on church government and notions about freedom of conscience and religious liberty were regarded as ungodly and dangerous. Williams went south of Boston and spent the winter on the Seekonk Plain with the local Indians. Later that spring, he and five other exiled men crossed the Seekonk River and landed on the eastern boundary of what would eventually be Providence, Rhode Island.

Within a few days, Williams and his friends started laying out a settlement that encouraged the initial population to have a variety of opinions and to express those thoughts without recrimination, in direct contrast to Massachusetts.

The southwestern tier—the Narragansett portion, across from Newport— is rural, quaint, and very old. Corn and squash fields abut gray-shingled, salt- box houses from the seventeenth century. As people cleared trees, plowed their fields, and built their boats, they began to notice peculiar remnants of an- other time. There were and still are a great number of mysterious structures and inscriptions scattered about this state.

## NEWPORT STONE TOWER
Newport, Rhode Island

### Site Synopsis
On a hilltop overlooking Newport Harbor stands a large stone tower. For more than three hundred years this round structure built on eight columns

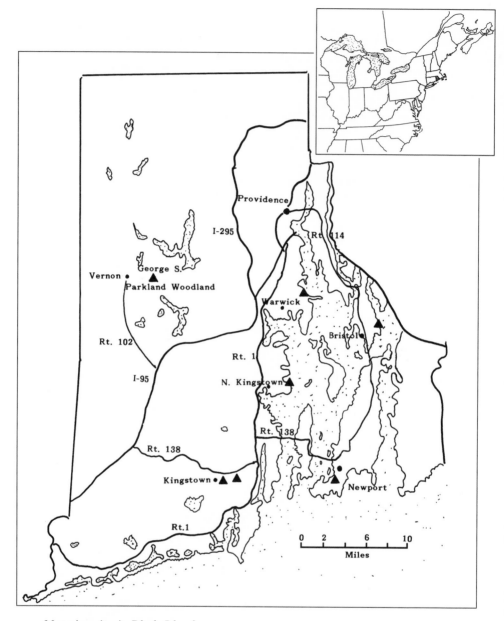

*Mysterious sites in Rhode Island.*

and arches has puzzled hundreds of people. No one knows when it was built or for what purpose. Over the years, researchers attributed this beautiful stonework to Vikings, Celt-Iberians, Phoenicians, or wandering Israelites. Recent work by an archeological ground survey team suggests the tower does not exist in isolation.

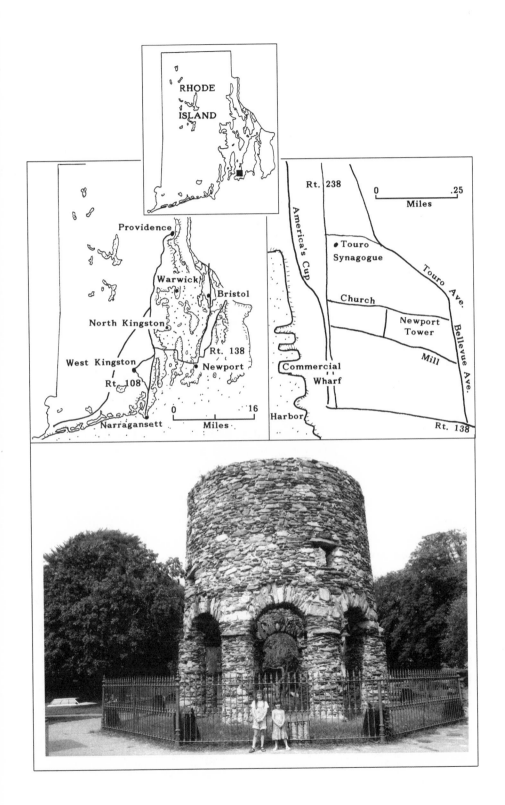

## Location

The tower is located in Touro Park off Mill Street just south of Bellevue Avenue in downtown Newport. From downtown Newport, near the shipyard, take Long Wharf Street east to America's Cup Avenue. Turn right (south) onto America's Cup Avenue, traveling for about a quarter of a mile before turning left (east) onto Mill Street. Stay on Mill Street for about half a mile. Touro Park is on your right (south).

## Considerations

Trying to park for free in Newport during the summer months will give you a headache. The streets are tiny, cramped, and filled with people. This is especially true around Touro Park. Vast numbers of tourists come to take in the gorgeous harbor, the yachts, the seaside restaurants, and the charm of this old port city. I recommend parking downtown near the harbor in one of the public lots and walking to the tower. It's not far, and it's much more pleasant than trying to negotiate very narrow seventeenth-century streets in a car. Besides, the trip up the hill will give you a fine perspective on the structure's location.

## History/Background

The Newport Stone Tower is one of those sites that refuses to give up its secrets. It's been the center of a long and continuous controversy.

The mystery began in the 1640s when Governor Coddington of Rhode Island wondered about the tower's origin. A later governor, Benedict Arnold, owned the tower in addition to a good deal of other prime real estate in Newport. When he died in 1678, he referred to the tower in his will as "my Stone Built Wind-miln."[1] But did Arnold *build* the structure, or was he merely making reference to a stone tower that he retrofitted as a windmill? Since that vague statement, controversy has raged over what Arnold meant. Some researchers think the Governor built the tower to remind him of one near his hometown in Chesterton, England. Others see the tower as a relic from Viking times—the reputed Norse exploration of New England in the eleventh or twelfth centuries.

In the early 1800s, Danish antiquarian Carl Christian Rafn believed the tower to be a Norse church. Over the years, minute details of the structure were endlessly dissected, discussed, and disputed: The windows meant one thing, the column's based supports meant something else; the arch clearly pointed to one culture, while an inscription found on one of the stones definitely dated the structure to the Vikings. And on it went. Many a scholar plunged into the controversy convinced he'd find the answer after a few weeks' study. All were humbled. One such scholar was Philip Ainsworth Means, who wrote the definitive historical book on the Newport Tower.[2]

Means's book prompted the Preservation Society of Newport County in

*The "Old Stone Mill," painted by Gilbert Stuart between 1770 and 1775
is the oldest image of the tower. Note its prominent place on a high hill (from Means,*
Newport Tower).

1948 to sponsor an archeological dig led by Harvard graduate student
William S. Godfrey. After two seasons of excavation, Godfrey couldn't say
who built the tower or when.

In 1993 Finnish Professor Hogne Jungner studied the tower by drilling
into its mortar and extracting samples. Jungner then analyzed the carbon
dioxide within the mortar and concluded that it dated between 1500 and
1630—clearly before Governor Arnold's time yet after the Vikings. End of the
story, right? Of course not!

Professor Jungner never released the details of his study in the form of a
peer-reviewed scientific paper. Those researchers familiar with Jungner's carbon dioxide–analyzing technique questioned its reliability. Furthermore,
when the results of a radar ground scan experiment were released in 1994,
they brought to light many weird subsurface structures.

A team from the Early Sites Research Society and the Weston Geophysical
Company used radar to "see" what was happening under the ground at Touro
Park. Scientists walked over the land surrounding the tower with a device that
looks like a metal detector. The scanner sent radar pulses into the ground and

recorded the resulting signals, which were then processed by an on-site computer. The findings? The Newport Tower does not exist in isolation. There are many underground features that suggests that the tower may be part of a larger complex of structures. Most of the anomalies are about three feet below ground. The area southeast of the tower had the greatest concentration of subsurface blips.

Unfortunately, ground-scanning radar can show only that something is below the ground. It cannot tell what that something is. Only a detailed archeological dig can do that. Hopefully the town of Newport will allow a competent team of researchers to penetrate the ground at Touro Park to finally solve this perplexing mystery.

### Contact Person(s)/Organization

Newport Chamber of Commerce
Newport, Rhode Island 02841
(800) 458-4843
(401) 847-1600

An excellent booklet on the ground-scanning experiment at Touro Park is: *Ground Penetrating Radar Survey: Newport Tower Site, Touro Park, Newport, Rhode Island*. Rowley, Massachusetts: Early Sites Research Society, 1994. It can be purchased from the: Early Sites Research Society Rowley, Massachusetts 01969

### Total Magnetic Field/Inclination Angle
None taken at this site.

### "RUNESTONE"
Narragansett Bay, North Kingstown, Rhode Island

### Site Synopsis
Twenty feet out in the water is a stone with symbols that look remarkably like Viking runes. Is this evidence of ancient Scandinavian contact with America?

### Location
From Providence take Route 1 south for about 15 miles. Exit left (east) at Essex Road. Continue on this road for about a mile and a half as it turns into Quidnessett Road. Turn left (north) into the long driveway at #860, which is the Scalabbrini Sisters Home—a Catholic nursing institution. Park at the main reception building and ask permission to go see the "Viking" rock.

Walk directly out to the beach from the reception building. Walk down to the splash zone. About 150 feet north on the beach, some 20 feet into the water is the rock.

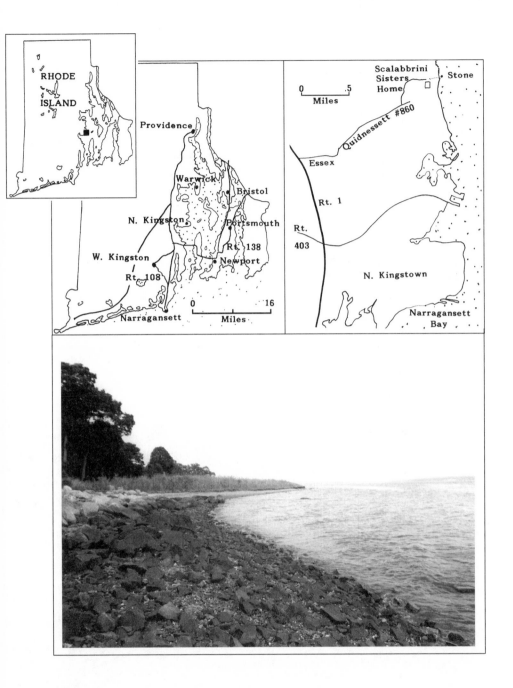

### Considerations

Walking on this beach is treacherous. Take your time getting out to the stone. Also plan on visiting the site when the tide is *very* low, as it is difficult to see anything with water splashing around it.

Bring along water sandals or sneakers you don't mind getting wet for wading out to the stone. If you plan on photographing the stone, obviously carry your camera well above your head as you walk out into a very muddy and mucky bottom.

### History/Background

This stone is conveniently located on the former beach property of a wealthy landowner who built the main mansion and matching barn in 1872—at the height of the Viking mania in America.

There are two takes on this stone: either it's a forgery by the landowner or some dubious "friend," or it was left by some Viking group.

If the stone is indeed an ancient Viking runestone, then New England writer Robert Cahill has added an interesting twist on its meaning. In 1993 he reported that the runic markings on this stone had finally been translated, and it supposedly reads: "Four victorious near the river."[3] While the Potowomut River is nearby, did Norsemen actually fight here? This site allows for some intriguing speculation.

*"Runestone," Narragansett Bay, North Kingstown, Rhode Island,
being covered up by water at the end of low tide.*

*Inscription on "Runestone" (after a photograph by Malcolm Pearson).*

### Contact Person(s)/Organization

Scalabbrini Village Sisters Home
#860 Quidnessett Road
North Kingstown, Rhode Island 02852
(401) 884-1242

### Total Magnetic Field/Inclination Angle

No significant geomagnetic aberrations were found at this site or along the beachfront.

### Further Investigations in Area

If this stone is real, then there must be more material scattered about the place. Recall the Yarmouth, Nova Scotia, inscribed stone and the many associated pieces of rock found in the same locale. It would be helpful to walk the entire beach, leaving no stone unturned. No doubt some odd bit of antiquity will show up.

I would also check along the mouth and banks of the Potowomut River. If there actually was a battle, then maybe someone dropped a battle ax or a buckle. Look carefully along the shoreline, particularly after heavy storm flooding. If you do find something, please leave it in place and contact the Rhode Island State Archeological Office. You may have stumbled upon the first documented Viking site in America, and you wouldn't want to disturb it.

# EIGHT

# Connecticut

The Indians who lived in the area of southern New England before colonial settlement referred to the region as Quinnetukut, which means "place of the long river." The state's name derives from this Algonquian term. This area, which touches Long Island Sound, was home to generations of indigenous tribes. Some more aggressive tribes, like the Pequots, who lived further to the east in Rhode Island, frequently ventured into the Connecticut area in search of Indian slaves.

The lower Connecticut River Valley is host to a variety of lithic structures. Among the most common are large stone piles. As early as 1705, at a spot three miles upriver from Old Saybrook, a map was drawn depicting "a heap of stones" as a boundary marker. The English assumed the pile separated the territory of two chiefs, but this was never confirmed by the Indians. In the 1950s, archeologist Frank Glynn excavated two large heaps along the Connecticut shoreline and found that they were constructed between three thousand and four thousand years ago by the mysterious Woodland Indians.

About five miles northeast of Old Saybrook, covering an area of over ten acres, is a group of meandering stone walls, several slab-roofed chambers, a few three-sided enclosures standing five feet high, some stone-lined cavities, and other dilapidated stone structures. The local interpretation is that they are the remains of a Colonial settlement, but there is no evidence for this. The lack of adequate ground soil coupled with the extreme rockiness of the site makes it difficult to imagine how an early settlement of English pioneers could have coaxed their cattle to graze or their plants to grow. The site has neither been properly surveyed nor excavated.

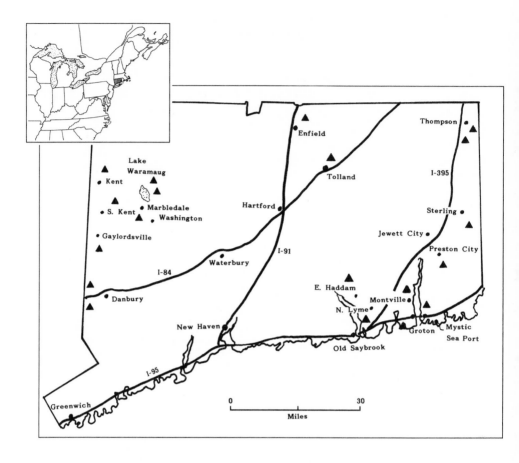

Another site of the same design lies but ten miles to the east, across the Thames River at Groton. At the entranceway to one of the longest river valleys in New England—one that could be used to travel 500 miles north to the Saint Lawrence River by following the headwater tributaries—a sophisticated array of stone chambers and enclosures was built at some time in the past. No Colonial records of this or any other similar site have been found.

## EAST/SOUTH CONNECTICUT

The Thames River in southeastern Connecticut is formed by a northeastern complex of tributaries. The Quinebaug, Shetucket, and Yantic Rivers unite into one waterway near the city of Norwich and flow south for about fifteen miles to Long Island Sound.

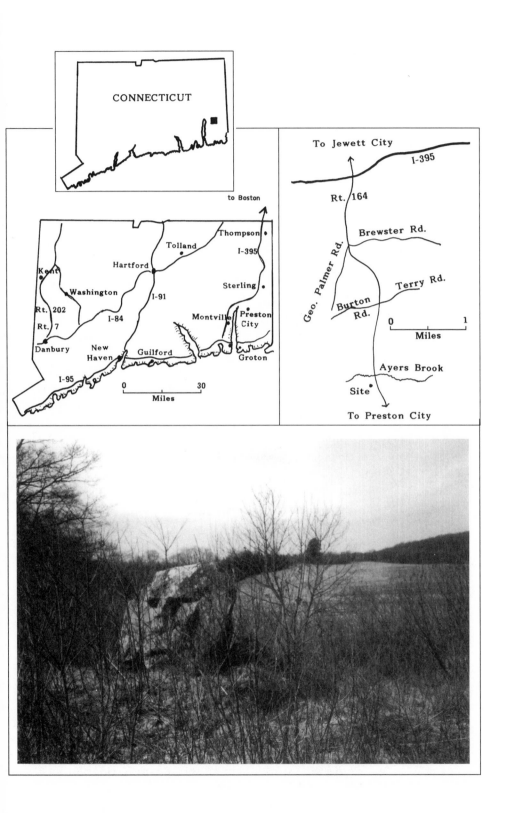

CONNECTICUT

to Boston

Thompson
I-395
Tolland
Hartford
Kent
Washington
Sterling
Rt. 202
I-91
Rt. 7
I-84
Montville
Preston City
Danbury
New Haven
Guilford
Groton
I-95
Miles
30

To Jewett City
I-395
Rt. 164
Brewster Rd.
Geo. Palmer Rd.
Burton Rd.
Terry Rd.
Miles
0          1
Ayers Brook
Site
To Preston City

## CARVED STONE HEAD
Preston City, Connecticut

### *Site Synopsis*

In a glacial outwash valley in southeastern Connecticut stands a 4-foot-high, 7-foot-wide granite boulder carved into the shape of a human head. It was first identified by a hiker in 1989. When it was carved and by whom is unknown.

### *Location*

From Boston take Interstate 90 west for about 45 miles to Interstate 395. Exit at I-395 traveling south for about 47 miles exiting on Rt. 164, south of Jewett City. Travel south on Rt. 164 for approximately 2¼ miles, passing Brewster Road and then Burton/Terry Road. A half mile south of Brewster Road, Ayers Brook undercuts Rt. 164. Park on the roadside. Follow the brook westward over the dirt pathway for approximately ¼ mile. The stone head is on the left.

### *Considerations*

Before entering the field do take the time to get permission from the landowner, who lives in the white farmhouse a short distance from Ayers Brook.

If visiting in the spring or summer when the field grass is high be aware of ticks. These insects are responsible for spreading Lyme disease (see page 110). Wear light-colored, tight-fitting pants and a long-sleeved shirt and a hat. Spray your clothing liberally with tick repellent. At day's end, have a friend thoroughly check your body for ticks, then jump in the shower.

### *History/Background*

In southern Connecticut, there is a 4-foot-high, 7-foot-wide stone head sitting out in a field. This fascinating carving was done from a massive block of fine-grained, very hard granite. The carvers apparently took pains to sculpt along a fractured bedding plane, intersecting the plane of the head.

The boulder is known as a glacial erratic—a stone that was picked up elsewhere by a glacier during the last Ice Age and redeposited when the ice melted.

In the fields surrounding the head are several examples of unexplained stone chambers and stone platforms.

The late date in reporting this carved head is odd. This part of Connecticut was settled in the late 1600s, and yet no written account of the site has been uncovered. To date no one has come forth with a suitable explanation, tall-tale, or otherwise to shed light on this bizarre carving. But one

*Close-up of carved stone head, Preston City, Connecticut.*

thing is certain. Late at night, under a full moon, the stone head site is an oppressive place.

### Contact Person(s)/Organization

No organizations presently are investigating this unusual site.

### Total Magnetic Field/Inclination Angle

This was another geomagnetic hotspot. There was a significant decrease in the total geomagnetic field as I got closer to the head compared to the surrounding region. A similar variation was observed with respect to inclination angles.

### Further Investigations in Area

There are reports of a stone-built chamber on a hillside farther south along a ridge near the stone head.

For reasons unknown the Thompson, Connecticut, region is home to the greatest cluster of inexplicable stonework yet found in New England.

On the eastern slope of a small hilltop outside of Thompson, near the Quinebaug River in northeastern Connecticut, about 35 miles north of the stone head an impressive cluster of conical stone piles rest on large base boulders. Covering an area of over 10,000 square yards, more than fifty of the structures are still visible. Closer inspection reveals the toppled remains of at least twenty more. About 60 yards from the cairns, at the foot of the hill, a tiny brook ebbs its way into a thick swamp.

The piles are typical of others found throughout New England in that all of them have been carefully constructed near a source of water on flat base rocks. The Thompson structures have also been placed on the eastern side of a rise in what seems to be a linear pattern. That is, the cairns are situated at intervals of about 25 yards from each other in more or less straight lines from the water source. Two stone-lined pits averaging about 4 feet in depth were found beneath the base supports of a couple of the toppled cairns. There is some evidence, in the way of chiseled caves, to suggest that small-scale copper and iron ore mining took place in the Thompson area; but at this time the information is too meager to define the time period of the shallow, mountainside troughs.

Colonial records make no mention of the Thompson stone piles. It is known, however, that around 30 miles downriver, just north of the present village of Greenville in Norwich, Connecticut, there used to be a stone heap on the western bank of the Shetucket River. The site supposedly marked the spot where an Indian sachem was captured and slain by an enemy tribe. Although it is no longer standing, eighteenth-century documents make it clear that the Greenville cairn in no way resembled the carefully built conical stone piles of Thompson. The sachem's memorial was described as a large heap of stones thrown together by wandering Indians.

About 4 miles southeast of the Thompson site, a grouping of five slab-roofed, beehive chambers has been reported. More undoubtedly existed in the region until building activity destroyed many of them. The beehives open to the southeast, in full view of the winter solstice sunrise. They are relatively small structures, measuring approximately 10 feet in diameter and 4 feet in height. The stones have been laid with great skill.

Small, rectangular enclosures adjoin all of the chambers, ranging from 30 to 100 feet in length and width. Upon seeing these interesting structures, one is reminded of the prehistoric earth houses of Scotland. In parts of Aberdeenshire, for example, similar dirt and stone enclosures, believed to have been constructed to pen sheep or cattle, are often found next to the corbeled structures. A surface collection in the Thompson chambers exposed several chicken bones.

One of the stone chambers in Thompson is on the north side of Cortiss Road, just past the Anderson Road intersection. In East Thompson there is another chamber that sits on the east side of East Thompson Road about three-quarters of a mile east of the New Road intersection.

James Whittall reports that one of the largest beehive-shaped chambers yet found in New England is in the Thompson, Connecticut, region. Built on a hillside, the structure faces almost due south.

A 7-foot, stone-lined entranceway leads into a circular chamber that's over 17 feet in diameter and over 11 feet high. The chamber is constructed of slightly overlapping stone slabs leading to a domed "beehive" shape. Whittall notes that due to vibrations of a nearby nineteenth-century rail track, the chamber is in danger of collapsing.[1]

Near the southeastern Connecticut town of Sterling, deep within the Pachaug State Forest off Interstate 395, is an alignment of three boulders with mysterious carvings. Two of the several-ton boulders are on a north-south axis, while the third is about 200 feet to the west. They are covered with strange circles and other animal-type figures. The markings appear to be painted on the boulders with a form of iron oxide pigment. The lineup of the boulders is intriguing. Local researchers suspect that a person standing at the most westerly boulders could watch the sun rise up over one of the boulders on April 25. This date is significant, for it is the safest time of the year to start planting corn in New England. One hundred and twenty days later, while standing at the same rock, one could view the sun rise up over the southern boulder on September 6, the date when corn should be harvested.

Who was responsible for this site? Any one of four different Indian tribes that occupied the area—the Mohegans, the Narragansets, the Nipmucs, or the Pequots—could have been the architects. Whoever it was they certainly knew a lot about astronomy. Based on what we know about other Native American tribes in ancient America, this is not surprising. But what do the painted circles mean?

About 30 miles west of the stone head is Mount Tom, located on the banks of the Connecticut River in East Haddam, Connecticut. This mountain was sacred to the Wangunk Indians of the region, who called it Machemoodus, or "place of noises." Called the Moodus Noises by Colonists who arrived in 1670, the site was the gathering place for powwows. The Wangunk believed an angry god created the "terrible roarings of the atmosphere" by blowing air out of a cave on the nearby mountain. This area is one of the most seismically active places in New England. Since 1979, when Boston College's Weston Observatory set up a network of seismometers near the neighboring town of Moodus, scientists have recorded hundreds of tiny earthquakes, some lasting up to several months long. All of these originated from a tiny spot in the earth's crust near the north end of Moodus.

It is difficult to explain why all these earthquakes occur there. Most other seismically active places in America don't have the regularity of the Moodus quakes. Perhaps it's difficult to quantify the actions of an angry god.

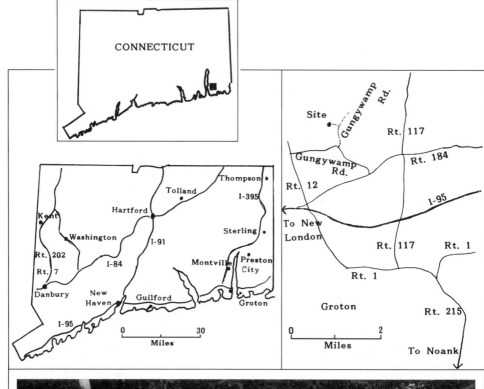

CONNECTICUT

## GUNGYWAMP STONE RUINS
North Groton, Connecticut

### Site Synopsis

North of Groton, Connecticut, are a series of large stone chambers, rows of standing stones, concentric circles of stone, earthen mounds, a ridge of cliffs, stone piles, and meandering walls. They represent one of the more unusual spots found anywhere in the East. After twenty years of excavation, the builder's identity and the function of these stones remain unknown.

### Location

This is a private site, but guided tours can be arranged by calling David P. Barron, founder and president of the Gungywamp Society at (203) 536-2887 in the early evening. This is a must see on your journey to eastern mysterious sites. From the Mystic Seaport area take Route 1 west for approximately 5 miles to Route 117. Turn north on Route 117 traveling for about 2½ miles. Exit west onto the Gold Star Memorial Highway (Route 184), traveling for about a mile before turning northwest (right) onto Gungywamp Road. In about another mile, just before the road curves to the left, bear right onto Gungywamp Road. Drive *slowly* on this dirt road. Park well off to the side. The site is on your left through the bushes.

### Considerations

The Gungywamp Society offers a variety of publications about the site and sponsors seasonal excavations of this archeologically fertile spot.

In addition to the Gungywamp Society, several private families and the local YMCA, among others, share the ownership of the Gungywamp archeological site. Tours and field work have been carried out only through their collective benevolence. Please do not enter the grounds unless you are accompanied by a member of the society or have explicit permission from the landowners. Failure to comply will result in trespassing charges.

There are no toilet facilities on this two- to three-hour hike through the ruins. Bring along plenty of water. In the summer wear protective clothing and insect repellent. Flashlights are helpful for peering into dark stone chambers. As usual, take nothing but pictures and haul out what you take in—leave no garbage or debris behind.

The Gungywamp Society's superb guidebook to the complex is mandatory field reading while visiting the site. Copies can be obtained from the Society at the address listed below. The society also has available a complete photocopied record of its superb publication *Stonewatch*. This unique database of strange Connecticut sites has been published monthly since 1979. Contact the society for details.

*History/Background*

The town of Groton is tucked away in the southeastern corner of Connecticut. Long a fishing community, Groton is situated on the eastern bank of the Thames River across from the town of New London, about 2½ miles north of Long Island Sound. During the last century, an active whaling industry brought much wealth to this portion of the Connecticut coast. The port of Mystic, famous in days gone by for shipbuilding, lies about 8 miles to the east.

New London was founded in 1646 by John Winthrop, Jr. Noted throughout the colonies for his extensive knowledge of the geography of southeastern New England, Winthrop was sent the following letter by a gentleman residing in Springfield, Massachusetts, on November 30, 1654:

> Sir, I heare a report of a stonewall and strong fort in it, made of stone, which is newly discovered atop near Pequot. [Pequot is a hill near Groton named after the Pequot Indians, who occupied the territory between the Thames and Mystic Rivers.] I should be glad to know the truth of it from your self, here being many strange reports about it.[2]

Winthrop never responded to the inquiry.

Extensive field surveys conducted by archeologist James Whittall of the Early Sites Research Society have shown that the letter was probably referring to a peculiar arrangement of stone walls, slab-roofed chambers, enclosures, standing stones, and other lithic material strewn across a 24-acre hilltop about 2 miles east of the Thames River. Known as the Gungywamp site (which may mean "a place of ledges" or a "swampy place"—there are many roads scattered throughout this area with the name "Gungy"), the walled complex lies on top of a sheer 30-foot cliff, 6 miles north of Long Island Sound. A 3-foot-high stone wall follows the western cliff face for about 1,000 feet before meeting with several crude enclosures and other irregular stone walls. East of the cliff, the land slopes downward toward a large swamp. A number of slab-roofed chambers and inexplicable rows of standing stones are scattered throughout the intervening acres.

In the 1960s, John E. Dodge, a resident of the nearby town of Stonington, spent several years surveying the site. He reported four chambers, two concentric stone circles, and a crude, dry-stone foundation within the Gungywamp. Dodge believed that the chambers were root cellars. He also felt that a set of concentric stone circles represented an early tanbark mill and that the foundation was simply the remains of a Colonial barn. Dodge also found two distinct clusters of strange stonework: a southern and a northern complex.

James Whittall visited the Gungywamp site in the early 1970s to take up

*Row of standing stones. These stones were built along a very peculiar geomagnetic field.*

where Dodge had left off. His detailed measurements of the chambers show that they are of the same design and construction as others found throughout New England. Known as the Large Chamber (Sector A—Site #1 in the guide-book), this unusual structure has a stone-lined passageway that precisely lets the equinox sunset light up the chamber's interior. Geomagnetic measure-ments made outside and inside this chamber show some intriguing flux. As one enters the chamber, the total magnetic field quickly changes from a high milligauss reading to a low reading at the midpoint of the structure, to a high reading near the rear wall: an up and down measurement, like a sine wave. The same pattern occurred with the incident angle.

A few yards away, another structure, oriented toward the east, measured 1½ feet high by 3 feet wide at the entranceway, with about 3½ to 4 feet of headroom in the interior. The small shape of the chamber suggested to Whittall that it might have been used as a "sealed and covered" tomb. Known as the Tomb Chamber (Sector A—Site Marker #2), this small, dry-walled chamber built into the side of a hill was first opened in the 1950s after a coastal storm washed away some of the surrounding dirt. Previously, it had gone undetected.

Magnetometer readings at this site were also strange. The base-line reading outside of the chamber was around 556 milligauss and 74 degrees. Yet 10 yards outside the entranceway, the reading was 380 milligauss/68 degrees! Directly under the capstone the reading changed to 700 milligauss/59 degrees. Inside the structure, about 5 feet in, the reading changed to 330 milligauss/80 degrees. Within a very short distance the readings radically changed. Recently, I wandered through the complex taking random readings over straight-line areas at 10- to 20-foot intervals. In every case where there was chamber or standing stone present, I got consistent readings. It was only at these constructed stone caves and erected stones (and one other category of site that will be referred to shortly) that I got unusual magnetometer readings. All indications are that the structures were purposely built on top of these weird geomagnetic hotspots.

High on a ridgetop overlooking the Tomb Chamber is a double circle of stones (Sector A—Site #5). The outer ring of slabs has a diameter of close to 11 feet, while the inner arrangement of stone measures almost 9 feet in diameter. The stones were worked to create a continuous inner curve. An excavation in the late 1980s revealed a stone floor between the two circles. The dig also revealed small quartz arrowheads and flakes—the cast off debris of arrowhead manufacture. Using radiocarbon dating, charcoal discovered at the site was found to be from the time period ranging from 280 A.D. to 630 A.D. In other words, the circle may have been laid out sometime during that time span.

As Dodge had suggested, the double circle of stones could have been used as a primitive mill to crush hemlock bark, which was used in the tanning process. But why in such a strange hilltop location, well away from a water source. I doubt this structure had anything to do with a mill processing operation. If anything, the double stone circles strongly suggest a ritualistic, sacred place. Measurements taken here support this. Moving west to east across the double circle of stones showed a consistent decrease in TMF. Going south to north showed a series of low, high, low, high readings: 540, 665, 540, 600. All of this change occurred within a radius of 30 feet.

On the eastern side of the site, an unusual row of standing stones has been placed in the ground at regular intervals (Sector C—Site #8, south complex). They stand slightly more than 2½ feet apart from each other. Since the tallest stone is only about 1½ feet high, it is unlikely that they were used as a wall to enclose animals. The purpose of this true-north alignment is not yet known.

Magnetometer readings along the outside boundaries of the row were the same throughout: 545 milligauss/65 degrees. But measurements taken along the long axis of the stones fluctuated. The magnetic field varied along the row, first dropping, then increasing, then dropping again, almost in a wavelike pattern. All of this occurred within a space of around 30 feet.

Perhaps one of the strangest aspects of this complex is located in the northern section. Known as the Cliff of Tears, located just west of Slag Iron Creek, there is an assortment of stone piles and boat-shaped cairns. But it is the trail near the stone ledge that is the most intriguing spot at Gungywamp. At some time long ago this rock ledge was quarried. The suspicion is that this activity was done in ancient times. There are no drill-hole marks that would clearly place it in Colonial times. The site was named a number of years back because of its peculiar physiological effects on people walking past it. For many years, the Gungywamp Society guides had been noticing that people at this part of the hike would invariably start crying or feel depressed. Some even reported bleeding gums and noses. With the assistance of local nurses, the society even went so far as to record changes in the menstrual flow of seventeen women walking past the cliff—none of the women had any knowledge of anything peculiar here—it was their first trip. Incredibly, all were reported to have experienced an unusual amount of blood flow while walking past "that large cliff rock."

Armed with this information, I took over fifteen magnetometer readings at regular intervals in and around the pathway leading around the cliff rock. I also took readings at the base of the cliff. In general, along the path the total magnetic field again fluctuated in a wavelike pattern, starting low then high, then low, high, and so on. The angle of incidence followed the same wave pattern. Twenty-five yards to the base of the cliff, the geomagnetic readings were completely different. But they, in turn, fluctuated in a wavelike pattern: very high, low, high, low, and so on. This is an extremely unusual pattern, and anyone stepping into this geomagnetic hot zone would be faced with radical natural changes in the earth's total magnetic field. Perhaps people are feeling the effects of a pineal gland rapidly secreting neurotransmitters into the blood. This hormonal change would clearly influence people's moods, and in some cases it would upset a variety of body mechanisms. If you do go to this site, prepare yourself.

So what is this Gungywamp complex? Seen in perspective with other sites throughout the East, it has all the earmarks of an ancient American Indian sacred place: tomb chambers, alignments of stone, cairns, standing slabs, unusual cliffs, bogs, swamps, and a tendency to locate all of this oddness at areas of extreme geomagnetic flux. In fact, the deeper excavations at this site by the Gungywamp Society have revealed ancient Indian pottery and sharp points (arrow and spear heads) dating to over 3,500 years. Yet, the scarcity of any quantity of debris emphasizes the site's unusual quality. The entire complex gives the impression of a ritualistic or ceremonial center.

The oral tradition of the Mohegans and Pequots indicates that this general area was a sacred burial site. The wide array of strange stones at this very weird place coupled with the bizarre geomagnetic anomalies found at key locations here makes this an intriguing yet unsettling place to visit.

### Contact Person(s)/Organization

David P. Barron
The Gungywamp Society
Noank, Connecticut 06340
(203) 536-2887

Ask about purchasing a copy of *The Greater Gungywamp: A Guidebook*. Also inquire about the complete collection of *Stonewatch*.

### Total Magnetic Field/Inclination Angle

The many magnetic measurements taken at this site allowed me to incorporate the findings directly into the text above. In general, the readings here were very unusual. The site is measurably strange.

### Further Investigations in Area

In the early 1980s, David Barron was asked to interpret a strange stone tunnel found in New London.

Eight feet below the ground, midway between the property of the New London Fire Department and 14 Tilly Street, contractors uncovered a small (3 × 3 foot square), mortarless, stone-lined tunnel. Barron partially excavated one end of the mysterious structure before it was covered over. All indications from his work suggested the tunnel was in place well before the region was settled in the early 1600s. Local officials either didn't understand the implications of Barron's excavation report, or else they didn't care. The tunnel was sealed up with a concrete partition.

Barron and his team haven't a clue as to who built this tunnel or for what purpose. But this mysterious tunnel is similar to others found throughout the Northeast.

Northwest of the Gungywamp site, about 3 miles from the town of North Lyme, Connecticut, is a series of unusual stone piles, chambers, and mysterious stonework. From North Lyme center take Beaver Brook Road east for about 2½ miles. At Gungy Road turn left (north). In about a mile, Gungy Road splits. Take the dirt road to your left. Within a few hundred feet, you'll see an opening in the stone wall. The area beyond the wall is bounded by two ridges. There's an enormous amount of stonework—piles, enclosures, and so on in the area bordered by the ridges. Most of the enclosure-like structures are set against the south face of the northern ridge. No one is sure what these stones mean.

## HILLSIDE STONE TUNNEL/CHAMBER
Montville, Connecticut

### Site Synopsis
In 1938, a hiker in a desolate area north of Montville, Connecticut, noticed that a large oak tree had fallen. While examining the roots, he saw a long, stone-lined tunnel about 3 feet wide and 6 feet high. The 30-foot tunnel, completely hidden inside the surrounding hill, opened up into a bell-shaped, stone-laid room. Archeologists have absolutely no idea who built this structure, why it was built, or when.

### Location
While this is a difficult site to find during the summer months, it's much easier to spot during early spring or late fall, when there are no leaves on the surrounding trees. One afternoon I spent several hours with the site's original investigator searching for the tunnel, and missing it by a few feet. It's well hidden, which makes it one of the most intriguing and mysterious in southeastern Connecticut. Nonetheless, here's the best set of directions, barring neon signs and billboards:

From Mystic, Connecticut, take Interstate 95 south. Take Exit 83 to Vauxhall Street. Turn left (northwest) on Vauxhall Street and stay on it until reaching Hunt's Brook Street. Bear right on Hunt's Brook Road. You'll pass the Waterford School on your left with a set of high-transmission wires overhead. From the Vauxhall/Hunt's Brook Road turnoff you'll need to travel ⁹⁄₁₀ of a mile. Just past the high-transmission wires there's a jumble of large boulders on your left. An intermittent stream flows over these and under a road conduit. Park and position yourself at this drain area. Sight into the woods 240 degrees southwest. Follow this line two thirds up the hillside. This should put you into the general vicinity of the tunnel/chamber. Be on the lookout for a "turtle-shaped" boulder. The entrance to this bizarre tunnel/chamber is about 5 feet to the right of it.

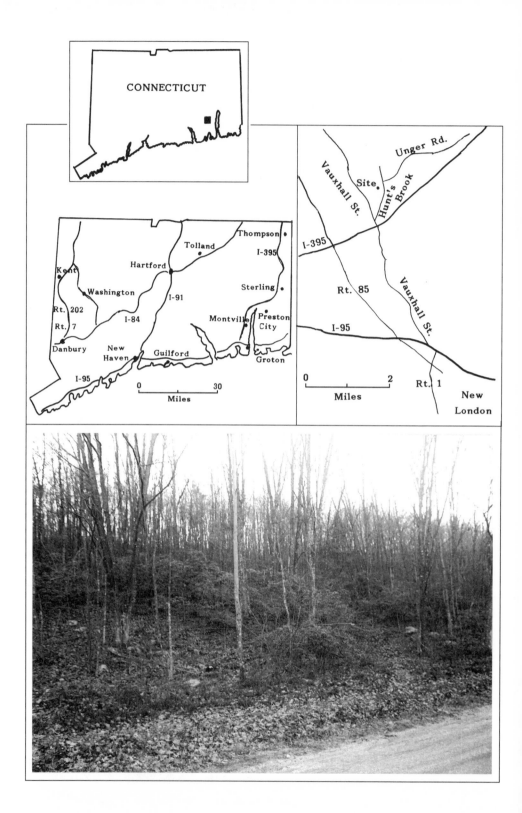

## Considerations

You'll need a good compass and a lot of patience to find this site. Press on, preferably with a few good friends. It's well worth it!

Once you find the site, plan on spending the rest of the afternoon exploring this strange hillside. There are dozens of ancient lithic remains scattered at the hilltop.

## History/Background

In 1938, a few months after a ferocious storm lashed New England, a hiker noticed a large oak tree had been blow over. Peering into the root system, he spotted a tunnel. The amazed hiker contacted local authorities who proceeded to climb into the structure. The entranceway below the toppled tree allowed access to a 3-foot-high, 30-foot-long stone tunnel system that ended in a bell-like chamber built well into the hillside. The chamber opened up to a height of over 5 feet. No one in the neighboring community of Montville had ever heard of such a structure. In fact, as far as anyone could remember, no one had ever homesteaded on this property.

The chamber became the focus of great interest among young children. Parents used it as a crude disciplining tool: "If you don't behave I'll send you to the chamber."

Within a few years, however, the chamber was forgotten and "lost." In the early 1980s, a local hiker rediscovered it and contacted David Barron of the

*Hillside Stone tunnel/chamber (after Whittall exploratory report).*

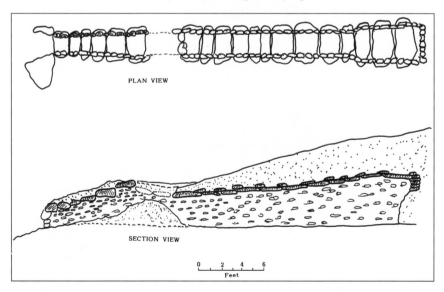

Gungywamp Society in Noank, Connecticut, to investigate. Barron drew the first plan illustrations of this site. It has great similarity to other underground tunnel systems scattered throughout the Northeast—from Nova Scotia to Massachusetts. The origins of this structure are unknown. Strangely, there are no records of farms in the vicinity or of anyone ever having a deed to this property.

David Barron has found that the land was originally owned in the 1600s by a John Brown, who was a crew mate of John Winthrop, the early governor of Massachusetts. When Brown died he had no heirs, and he did not leave the land to any of his friends. For unknown reasons, no one during the last 360 years squatted on or claimed the land. It has mysteriously avoided ownership, almost as if it were cursed soil.

During the early 1600s, the land west of the Thames River where the tunnel/chamber is located was controlled by the Mohegan Indians under their sachem, or chief, Uncas. Land east of the river was controlled by the belligerent Pequot Indians. By the time white settlers arrived, the Mohegans and Pequots were already in a centuries-old battle. These two tribes hated each other, although most of the horrific battles and forays were instigated by the Pequots, and perhaps for good reason. The Mohegans occupied land that was the ancestral burial ground of the Pequots. This last bit of historical information is very interesting. Could the Montville tunnel and the other chambers and stones found there (see Further Investigations below) be remnants of

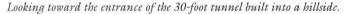

*Looking toward the entrance of the 30-foot tunnel built into a hillside.*

some ancient, ceremonial burial site? Its isolated location, far into the side of a hill, makes this a very plausible explanation.

### Contact Person(s)/Organization

David P. Barron
The Gungywamp Society
Noank, Connecticut 06340
(203) 536-2887

### Total Magnetic Field/Inclination Angle
None taken at this site.

### Further Investigations in Area
At the top of the hill there are dozens of small stone piles (cairns). There are also balanced rocks, large cut-stone blocks partially buried in the soil. Some are scattered throughout the slope as if thrown about by some giant hand. Take your time here. There are many pieces of this mysterious puzzle that haven't been put together yet.

Reports of hidden stone tunnels and buried walls are not new. They've been reported since the first white settlement of America (see New York State section).

Not far from the hillside stone tunnel/chamber are two very peculiar stone chambers. One has an atrium entranceway, while the other is built along a 12-foot glacial erratic boulder. Both are almost a mile from any habitation and are located on a hillside slope.

## WEST CONNECTICUT

To the settlers living in western Connecticut, the coastal prong of land stretching west from the Housatonic to the Hudson rivers was a 3,000-square-mile tract of uncharted wilderness. Known as the western forest, the land was the terror of the settlers, for it was the territory of the dreaded Mohawk Indians. In the early 1600s, few dared venture into this terrifying region.

As Native Americans in New England were hunted down and killed, the Colonists set out to systematically clear the land for pasture and farming. In sweeping away age-old trees and rotting brush, they uncovered the half-obliterated remains of an ancient agricultural operation. Amid the clearings were dim traces left by unknown farmers whose skill had surpassed anything currently practiced. Along the fertile valleys, the settlers thankfully built their homes and outbuildings on the foundations of another age.

As the seasons wore on, the once fertile soil lost its nutrients. Low crop yields forced families to move westward into the Ohio and Mississippi valleys, and by the early 1800s, a good many eastern farms were abandoned. Generations passed by; old surveys and land rights were misplaced or destroyed as successive waves of migrating Europeans took over these lands. But this time, the stone mysteries that had greeted the original pioneers were overlooked. Some of the structures were so intertwined within the Colonial settlements that their uniqueness remained hidden to all but the most keen-eyed antiquarians. Other telltale signs of ancient doings lay buried beneath years of forest growth.

Occasionally, however, the past crept into the present.

## HEBREW INSCRIPTIONS
New Preston, Connecticut

### Site Synopsis
On a mountain top overlooking a glacial lake, someone carved a series of Hebrew inscriptions into the bedrock. All evidence indicates that it was done a very long time ago.

### Location
From Greenwich, Connecticut, take the access road to Route 15 east (Merritt Parkway). Continue until Exit 40, and then take Route 7 north. Stay on Route 7 to Danbury, Connecticut, where you'll take Interstate 84 east until Exit 7. At Exit 7, take Route 202 north for about 12 miles. At New Milford, Connecticut, bear right to continue on Route 202 north. Take this until New Preston, Connecticut. Near the town's center, take Route 45 (East Shore or Lake Road) north for about three-quarters of a mile. At that point, make a right turn onto June Road. In a few hundred feet you'll see a dirt parking area and a trail head. Park and walk up the trail. Get to the highest point on the mountain and look for a semicircular arrangement of boulders. The inscriptions are a short distance from the open end of this arc. Look carefully; they are especially difficult to see during midday, when the sun is directly overhead. Splashing water on the flat surface rocks will help.

### Considerations
Caution is the operative word here. With the popularity of mountain biking, one will find many weekend warriors testing their mettle against the mountains. That means a sometimes dangerous hike—it's tough to avoid flying mountain bikes—and walking through rutted mud. There's a turf war going on between bikers and hikers.

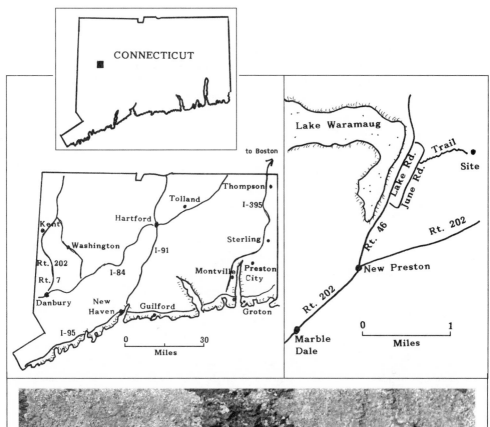

## History/Background

Almost two hundred years ago, Dr. Ezra Stiles, president of Yale College from 1778 to 1795, traveled to New Preston, Connecticut, and recorded in his *Itineraries and Memoirs* a "Hebrew Inscription" engraved on the summit of a nearby mountain peak—Pinnacle Rock—above Lake Waramaug. On October 8, 1789, the energetic scholar scurried up a weatherworn hilltop to measure and sketch the mysterious carvings. On the northwestern side of the mountain peak, Stiles found four separate inscriptions, each enclosed within a semicircle. Two of the enclosed engravings formed a northerly set, while the other two formed a southerly set. The carved semicircles opened at approximately 325 degrees NW.

The report, among others of Dr. Stiles's, eventually found its way into the manuscript collection of the Yale University library. It remained there until the early 1970s, when an archeologist happened upon Dr. Stiles's original documentation.

In the mid 1970s, a hiker from Washington, Connecticut, guided the archeologist to the inscriptions. Although severely damaged by modern graffiti, the inscriptions described by Stiles more than one hundred eighty-seven years ago were still plainly visible.

The letters of the inscriptions are not ancient. They are in a style of Hebrew that is readily understandable to modern students of the language. Severe weather erosion, however, has worn away the nuances of the carvings, thereby making an exact translation next to impossible. Based on casts made at the site, the northern set of carvings has been interpreted as "Abram" and "Isaac," while the southerly pair translates as "Moses" and "Adam."

Stiles reputedly attributed the inscriptions to Jewish miners who inhabited the Cornwall, Kent, and New Milford vicinity in the mid-eighteenth century and were thought to be searching for precious metals. The semicircles around each word give us a clue as to the inscriptions' purpose—they were probably memorial carvings to four Jews who died in the region sometime before 1789. The exclusion of a woman's name from the interpretation increases the likelihood that an exploratory band of men was indeed searching for something in the rugged wilderness of western Connecticut. It is nonetheless still puzzling that such an inaccessible spot on a particular mountaintop should merit the names of four individuals. An extraordinary degree of care went into the placement and execution of the carvings. Furthermore, a nearby grouping of man-made lithic features has ritualistic overtones.

A few yards southwest of the inscriptions are six glacial erratics that have been positioned in a 20-foot-wide semicircle. The boulders range in size from 2 to 3 feet high, 5 to 8 feet wide, and 3 to 4 feet deep. In front of the boulders are two shallow troughs that have been cracked by burning fires. This part of the mountainside commands a magnificent view of the distant southern horizon.

### Contact Person(s)/Organization

New Milford Historical Society
North of the Green
New Milford, Connecticut 06776
(203) 354-3069
(Open Memorial Day weekend through October 28, Thursday–Saturday,
1–4 P.M., or by appointment)

### Total Magnetic Field/Inclination Angle

No significant geomagnetic deviations were recorded at this site.

### Further Investigations in Area

I recently found a fifty-year-old report of a stone chamber in Marble Dale, a town a few miles south of Pinnacle Mountain. The chamber is supposedly located behind a house just down from St. Andrew's Rectory on Wheaton Road. Directly behind the house and built into the hillside is a stone-lined chamber. The structure consists of three rooms, two of which are below and behind the first. If this report is accurate, then it suggests the existence of one of the more interesting stone chambers. Go look for it!

# NINE

# New York

Italian explorer Giovanni da Verrazano visited the site of New York in 1524, but nothing came of it. Eighty-five years later, Henry Hudson sailed into the deep harbor and wrote glowing reports about the magnificent port and surrounding green hills to his employers, the Dutch West India Company. Within a few years, the enterprising company set up a trading post farther up the Hudson River, near Albany. A short while after that, another trading fort was built at the tip of Manhattan. Peter Minuit, director general of the province then called New Netherland, bought Manhattan Island from the local chieftains for the equivalent of twenty-four dollars.

This must qualify as one of the best real estate swindles in history. It prompted over thirty years of bloody clashes with Manhattan Indians, who tried to reconcile their mistake. They couldn't. Dutch and later English firepower proved too strong. The native peoples that inhabited New York just prior to the white invasion were divided into two main groups: the Algonquian of the Hudson Valley/Long Island region and the Iroquois of the western area. The Iroquois were a powerful federation of five upper New York State tribes who formed a highly organized political and military group that, given enough time, no doubt would have evolved into a city state comparable to that found in Central America. The arrival of Dutch and English settlers put a stop to all that.

New York has a wide range of geological regions set in a relatively small area. The southeastern sector includes the spectacular Hudson Highlands that swoop southwest across the Hudson River. Just west of these hills is a long valley that extends to the plateau region of eastern Pennsylvania. The famed

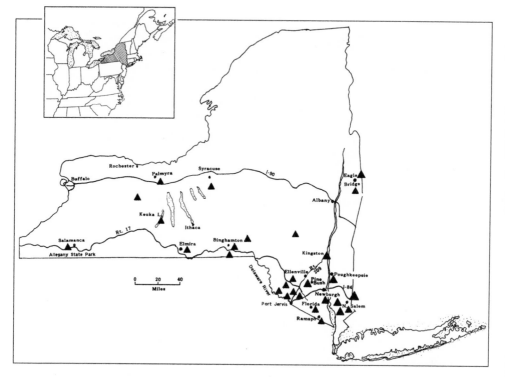

*Mysterious sites in New York.*

Catskill Mountain region is part of the Appalachian plateau that extends south into many eastern states. The central/western part of the state is comprised of drumlins, low, egg-shaped hills left by the last melting glaciers that heavily scarred the region. The deep Finger Lakes of this region were carved out by scooping tongues of ice.

The first pioneers who pushed into the wilderness north of Manhattan and those who later rode into the fertile valleys of central New York State recorded in their diaries and Bibles peculiar earth embankments, stone piles, and perched rocks. More often than not, the indigenous peoples of the region claimed to know nothing about the ruins, but recounted legends that told of strange ruins being there when their ancestors wandered into region.

## SOUTH/SOUTHEAST NEW YORK

From a Coney Island co-op it is possible to see the New York Narrows, the water divide between the boroughs of Brooklyn and Staten Island, where the Atlantic Ocean meets the upper bay of New York Harbor. Here, in 1524, the Italian explorer Giovanni da Verrazano sailed past the Canarsie Indians to discover New York. Eighty-five years later, Henry Hudson entered the "great river" and sailed as far north as Albany. During the journey, he frequently commented to his ship's diarist about the beautiful scenery, bountiful lands, and pleasant water in and around the river that would eventually be given his name. Subsequent travelers also marveled at the numerous springs, wells, and other attributes of the lower Hudson Valley. Much later, New York Harbor came to be known throughout the shipping industry as one of the world's best natural water inlets.

The Hudson begins as a trout stream in the Adirondack Mountains of New York State and flows southward, widening and deepening its channel. For much of its course, the Hudson is actually a great estuary in which fresh mountain waters mix with the salt tides of the Atlantic.

While most of the islands and land masses in New York Harbor have long been covered over with asphalt and concrete, there are tantalizing tidbits of the ancient mystery of the place. As a New York contractor once told me, "When you bulldoze in lower Manhattan, you *never* know what you'll find." Indeed. There is not much to be seen these days, but if you search through the archives of the main branch of the New York Public Library you will find some fascinating hints of unexplained constructions and objects.

## BALANCED ROCK
North Salem, New York

### Site Synopsis
On the side of a road near a great-looking nineteenth-century barn, a 90-ton boulder sits atop several cone-shaped stones. Some claim it is an example of a dolmen—an ancient European burial tomb—while others argue that it is an eleven- to twelve-thousand-year-old remnant of a melting glacier.

### Location
The upper part of Westchester County is strewn with lanes, byways, and roads having very similar, and even the same, names. It can be *very* confusing to find house addresses, let alone weird stone ruins. Take a deep breath, load up on some patience, and follow the maps *and* the text very carefully.

From New York City take the Saw Mill River Parkway north to Katonah. At Katonah pick up Route 684 north to North Salem—Exit 8. Take Hardscrabble Road east to the end and then bear right onto June Road. Take the next *left* onto Baxter Road (there are *two* Baxter Roads here. One goes south, the other, southeast—take the southeast road—a *left* turn off June Road). Follow Baxter Road to Crane Corner. Turn right onto Titicus Road (Route 116). Stay to the right on Titicus Road when the road forks. Just past Keeler Lane is the Balanced Rock.

### Considerations

When visiting this unusual site be careful to park well off the road because a high volume of traffic zooms past. Take only pictures and don't leave any trash.

### History/Background

The terrain east of the upper Croton Reservoir is not as rocky or steep as the jagged Highlands to the immediate west. Consequently, the first farms were sprawling enterprises spreading across many acres of flat-topped rises. Settled sometime prior to 1685, North Salem, like many villages in America, was built near a former Indian path, this one leading south to Manhattan. English immigrants later widened the trail to accommodate oxen teams and coaches.

Today, not more than a few hundred yards from the post office, and 30 feet from the main road, a 16-by-14-by-10-foot pink granite boulder rests in perfect equilibrium on several stone supports. Known as the Balanced Rock, it is located on Route 116 near Keeler Lane. As early as 1790, visiting European geologists were riding through North Salem and commenting on the peculiar stone. Most of them believed the rock to be the result of natural decomposition or, as they put it, "of primeval diluvian torrents." A century later, when geology was better understood, the few American scholars who visited the site argued that glaciers grinding their way to the sea had carried the rock chunk

*Aeriel shot of Balanced Rock, North Salem, New York.*

from New Hampshire's White Mountains, the nearest known pink granite deposit. As the ice melted, the encased boulder supposedly settled on top of a mass of rock debris. Over thousands of years, erosion weathered off the lighter debris beneath the boulder, leaving the more resistant base rocks in place.

One of the first specialists to question the natural origin of the Balanced Rock was John Finch, a professor of mineralogy. In an 1824 issue of the *American Journal of Science*, Professor Finch put forward the idea that the stone was actually a Celtic monument. He didn't believe the formation could be attributed to nature, since "primitive limestone never appears above the surface of the ground in the shape of small, conical pillars, but in large massy blocks."[1] He was right. The supporting stones are crystalline limestone.

In Finch's day, there were people who thought the Balanced Rock was a contemporary fake, but he dismissed this notion on the grounds that "the immense weight of the upper stone renders this improbable."[2] Based on the cubic density of pink granite, the upper boulder weighs approximately 90 tons, which was beyond the lifting capabilities of engineering techniques being used in 1824. The professor was expressing the utter amazement people have when gazing upon megalithic monuments. That is, how did the ancients lift so much tonnage?

Visually, the Balance Rock is remarkably similar to a class of tombs known

*Close-up of the Balanced Rock.*

*An 1824 illustration of the Balanced Rock. Antiquarian John Finch was the first scholar to question the glacial origins of this intriguing site (Finch,* American Journal of Science).

as dolmens, or stone tables. (See illustration on following page.) Found throughout the British Isles, Europe, the Middle East, and Asia, dolmens were tomb constructions in vogue for an incredibly long period of time, from around 5000 B.C. to 1200 B.C.—7000 to 3200 years ago. Dolmens consist of a huge capstone supported by upright stone slabs or, in some cases, by smaller stacks of untrimmed stones. The idea was to create a chamber in the space between the base stones. Depending on the size of the tomb, one or more bodies were placed below the capstone.

Archeologists think that most dolmens were covered with a mound of dirt. Throughout the centuries, however, both nature and people have removed the earth and exposed the inner stone coffins.

Because many of the world's dolmens occur along coastal lands, some authorities believe that megalithic fever—the insatiable urge to build with inexplicably huge stone—was spread by a seafaring merchant society. The associated cultural debris scattered along the western coast of Europe from Spain to Ireland, for example, makes it difficult to dispute this theory, as some have tried to do. The archeological and linguistic links between these regions are impressive. When we add to this the research data of physical anthropology, we find that similarities in the frequencies of certain genetic markers, like blood type, indicate that at some distant time populations of Mediterranean origin did live in Ireland and Scotland, leaving their genetic legacy to people still there today.

Unlike the other perched rocks in the East, the North Salem stone *does* have a layer of ground soil present. Today, we see the necks of deeply sunk base stones. Over the years, surplus soil from a nearby barn foundation and a widened road has banked more earth against the limestone supports. This clearly can be seen from early-nineteenth-century illustrations of the stone.

*Large dolmen from Portugal. These six- to seven-thousand-year-old tombs were often incorporated into more modern dwellings. (DeNadaillac,* Manners and Monuments of Prehistoric Peoples).

Aerial views of the site clearly show a stream/marsh nearby that formed at the end of the last Ice Age, lending support to a chance deposition. But, nearby, massive circular ground discolorations suggest something deliberate (see next section: Circular Ground Discolorations). So is the North Salem Balanced Rock a glacial aberration or a megalithic dolmen? Was it left by melting ice, or did some unknown people construct it as a burial tomb? Difficult to say without a proper excavation in and around the site. Until a full-scale archeological dig is mounted, the most anyone can do is take a side and argue ferociously.

### Contact Person(s)/Organization

North Salem Public Library
276 Titicus Road
North Salem, New York 10560
(914) 669-5161

### Total Magnetic Field/Inclination Angle

No geomagnetic readings were taken here.

### Further Investigations in Area

There are several reports of stone chambers in and around the North Salem, New York vicinity. To find them, see the associated section under Stone Chambers later in this chapter.

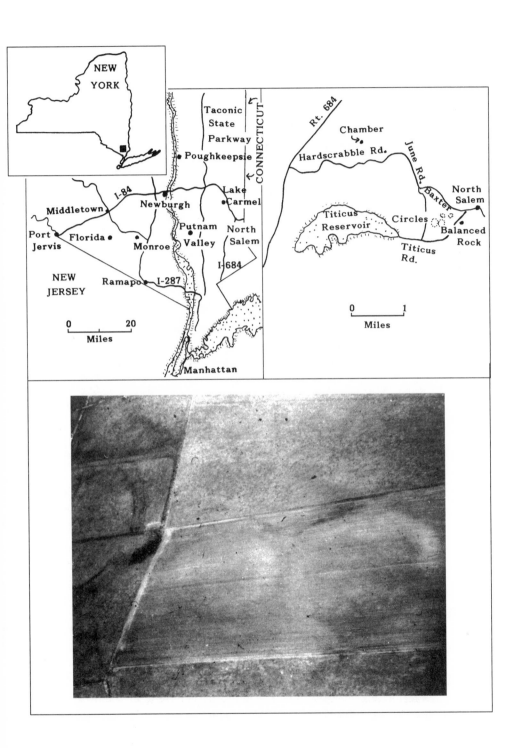

# CIRCULAR GROUND DISCOLORATION
North Salem, New York

### Site Synopsis

A short distance from the Balanced Rock at North Salem are massive ground discolorations. They may represent the filled-in ditches of a gigantic earthen complex.

### Location

This is one of the few sites listed in this book that must be seen from the air. The discolorations are impossible to see from the ground. You need perspective.

### Considerations

The only time of year when you will be able to see these strange ground markings is after the autumn harvest, when the crops have been picked and the soil replowed. To actually see these rings, you need to hire a plane with a pilot who's used to banking and flying around a ground feature. Check the local phone book for available planes and pilots.

### History/Background

Just west of North Salem, in a harvested field, are two circular ground-disturbance rings. They are adjacent to one another and average between 290 and 330 feet in diameter, the band of each ring averaging about 50 feet in width. The circular impressions run contrary to the field's plowed paths, suggesting that whatever left the soil stains was there long before seventeenth-century English immigrants cleared the Westchester forests and planted the seeds of modern agriculture.

The impressions may be the remains of circular earthworks, with ditches completely filled in and obliterated except when viewed from the air, where the roots of plants and groundwater can be seen following the ditch outlines, revealing subtle shading differences in soil colorations.

In other parts of America there are sites whose features parallel those surrounding the North Salem stone. In the Kanawha Valley of West Virginia is a double circular embankment. Excavated in the late 1800s by the Smithsonian Institution, the embankment consisted of two concentric walls, the outer being 295 feet in diameter, the inner reaching 213 feet. Between them was a narrow ditch filled in with dirt. Locally, they were known as "sacred enclosures," and nothing was ever found within them to explain their puzzling structure. Nearby, however, many stone graves were discovered as farmers dug into their fields.

American scholars in the 1800s were surprised to find Indians buried within these box-shaped slab tombs. The stone graves, often covered over by a mound of earth, were widespread, being found along the Mississippi, Ohio, Tennessee, Susquehanna, and Delaware river valleys. The cists titillated the imagination of American scholars, who saw within them a definite link to Old World burials. Dr. Joseph Jones, a respected nineteenth-century antiquarian at the Smithsonian, wrote:

> In looking at the rude, stone coffins of Tennessee, I have again and again been impressed with the idea that in former ages this ancient race [the builders of America's mysterious earthworks] must have come in contact with Europeans and derived this mode of burial from them.[3]

The circular ground structure might have been built by ancient Europeans, ancient Indians, or a group we haven't even imagined yet, but the point is they exist and they are mysterious. Hire a plane and zoom over North Salem during late autumn. Bring your camera!

### Contact Person(s)/Organization:

As very few people are aware of this strange ground feature, you may want to focus attention on any surrounding stone debris. Any land surveyor who works in the North Salem vicinity should have a wealth of stories to share with you.

### Total Magnetic Field/Inclination Angle

None taken at this site.

### Further Investigations in Area

As with all weird sites, these rings can't be the only examples. There must be more evidence of circular embankments and the like. A careful examination of early tax-map information, deeds, and survey records should yield impressive information for the curious investigator. Give it a go.

## STONE CHAMBERS

Oscawana Lake, Lake Carmel, Mohegan Lake, Peach Lake, New York

### Site Synopsis

An enormous number of stone chambers are scattered throughout this part of the Northeast. They variously have been deemed to be eighteenth- to nineteenth-century root cellars, Viking houses, Celtic temples, or Indian tombs.

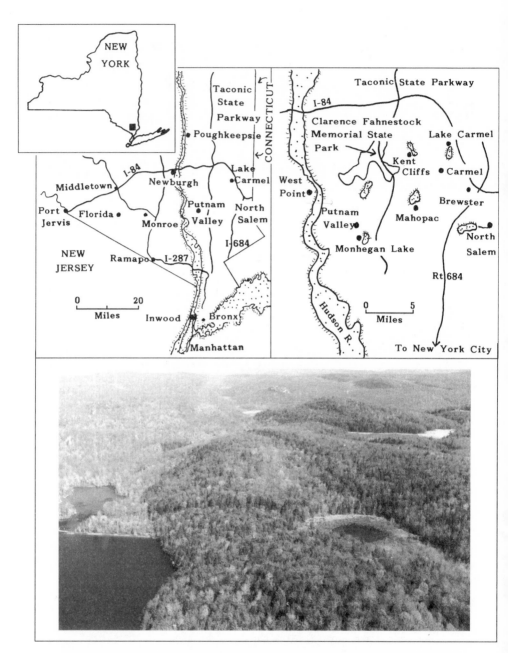

*Aerial view of the terrain surrounding the Boyds Corners Reservoir. This is one of the many water storage lakes near the Croton Reservoir System. Many slab-roofed chambers are hidden beneath the trees of these hills. The Clarence Fahnestock Memorial State Park is in the extreme upper left section of the photograph. Several impressive slab-roofed chambers were discovered there.*

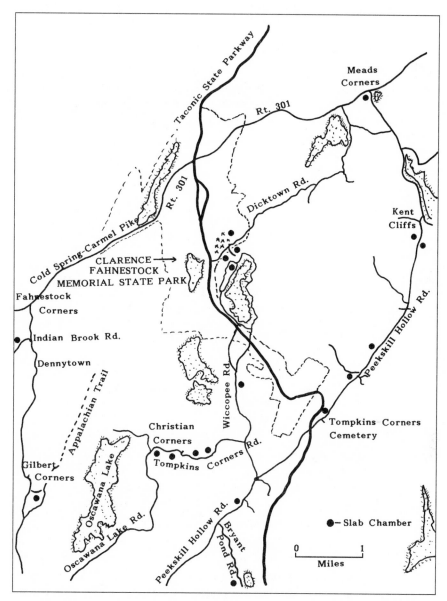

*Oscawana Lake, New York, slab-chamber map*

## Location

Finding these chambers is tricky, especially during the summer months when the heavy foliage covers up everything. Go during late autumn or early spring to lessen the frustration factor. To facilitate locating these fascinating structures, I've divided the southeastern sector of New York into several sections based on easily available topographic maps. The selection of chambers given here does not represent the full array of structures in the region. These are but a sampling of what's out in these strangely beautiful hills.

The best way to get to these sites is to follow both the text and illustrations. It also helps to purchase specific topographic maps, which are available in any good sporting/hunting store. They can also be purchased directly from:

U.S. Geological Survey
1200 South Eads Street
Arlington, Virginia 22202

Prices vary depending on the type of map required. Indexes showing plans for each state are available free on request from the same address. If you've never used these maps, then also get a copy of the free booklet entitled *Topographic Maps*. It explains everything you need to know about them.

The illustrated maps that follow are based on the 7½ minute series, with scale of 1:24,000. This means that one inch on these standard maps represents 2,000 feet.

## Oscawana Lake, New York

There is quite a variety of slab chambers in this quadrant. As with many throughout Putnam Valley and other towns nearby, I'm not convinced that all are ancient. The mystery here is the differing explanations for these peculiar structures.

The most accessible chambers are located along Peekskill Hollow Road. About 2,500 feet past Bryant Pond Road, along the western side of Peekskill Hollow is a stone chamber. (Turning south onto Bryant Pond Road and driving a little more than a mile will bring you to a slab chamber just off the west side of the road, a few hundred yards west of Bryant Pond.) Continuing north along the road for a little more than 2 miles, 1,000 feet past the Tompkins Corners Cemetery is another chamber on the western side of the road. Three-quarters of a mile north of here is a chamber on the western side of the road. It sits opposite two intersecting roads leading to homes. A half mile north of here, again on the western side of the road, just past a road leading to a home is a slab chamber. Three-quarters of a mile beyond this site, on the eastern side of the road, sits another chamber. Continuing past Boyds Corners Reservoir, two miles from the junction of Peekskill Hollow Road and Route 301, about 50 yards south of Meads Corners is a good-sized stone chamber. There are several noticeable chisel tool marks. These rock cuts may date this structure and others like it to the late eighteenth/early nineteenth centuries. But what were they used for? No one has any definitive answers.

*Stone Chamber off Meads Corners, Oscawana Lake, New York.*

The next set of chambers are within and south of the Clarence Fahnestock Memorial State Park. The best way to reach them is to travel west from Meads Corner along the Cold Spring-Carmel Pike (Route 301) for 3 miles to the Taconic State Parkway. Travel south on the parkway for 1½ miles and make the eastern turnoff at Dicktown Road. Drive for about 1,000 feet along Dicktown Road and park. There are four chambers and a large, elliptical stone wall complex within this area. The first chamber is up a small hill just south of the road from where you parked. Five-hundred feet northeast of there is the stone wall complex. Continuing brings you to the second slab chamber. Several immense slab-roofed chambers, all facing the same direction, are a short distance away. Reaching a height of 20 feet, the four walls enclose empty space; no foundations or remains can be seen within. Three stone-lined cavities 3 feet in diameter, and just as many feet apart, grace one side of the enclosure. A swamp is close by. The incredible height of the enclosure presupposes a deep footing, probably reaching well below the frost level. It also represents a major undertaking in the way of clearing land, quarrying, transporting, and building with large stone blocks.

One thousand feet north of here, along the eastern edge of a swamp is another stone chamber. The last site in this area is about 1,000 feet south of the stone wall complex, just south of the Lakeside Road loop, a few hundred feet from Roaring Brook Lake.

Continuing south for 1½ miles on the Taconic Parkway from the Dicktown Road intersection, turn right (south) onto Wiccopee Road. Three-quarters of a mile south, about 1,000 feet beyond the junction of Pudding Street, along the east side of the road are several stone piles.

Almost a mile south of here turn right (west) onto Tompkins Corners Road. There are four slab chambers along this road. The first is about three-quarters of a mile west in from Wiccopee Road. The second slab chamber is about 1,000 feet farther along the road. Two thousand feet west of here is the third chamber, and another 1,000 feet will bring you to the fourth chamber.

The last region of the Oscawana Lake Topographic Map to explore is the southwestern quadrant. You'll need to head back north on the Taconic State Parkway to Route 301. Travel south along Route 301 for a little over three miles to Fahnestock Corners. At this intersection take Dennytown Road directly south. In about half a mile turn west onto Indian Brook Road. There's a slab chamber 1,000 feet in from the northern end of the road. Watch for posted signs and get the landowner's permission before walking onto the property.

Drive back out to Dennytown Road and continue south for about 2½ miles, past Gilbert Corners, where you will make an almost 180-degree left turn onto the joining road. Travel north on this trail for about 2,000 feet. This site consists of a slab chamber and a stone wall complex with three circular depressions within it. Nearby, there are undisturbed slag heaps of nineteenth-century farm implements and shards of 300-year-old Dutch pottery, appearing as if they had been left just yesterday.

Evidently, some of the quarried stone walls were built during the post-Colonial era to harness the swiftly flowing Canopus Creek. The iron mines probably represent extensive eighteenth-century attempts to tap the region's rich mineral sources. But other mining shafts, the cavitied walls, and a few equinox-facing slab-roofed chambers found farther up the hillside seem to tell a different story. Although later incorporated within a Colonial enterprise, they probably date back to a different time period. Indeed, a mid-nineteenth-century document tells of an obscure silver mine being worked in ancient times and containing "old tools with the handles rotted out."

This is very reminiscent of the mysterious walled complexes found farther south in West Virginia. This road eventually turns into the Appalachian Trail.

## Lake Carmel, New York

This region is located east of Oscawana Lake.

One mile south of Meads Corners on Route 301 the road splits. Follow the left fork (east)—East Boyds Road—around Boyd Corners Reservoir. Continue for another mile turning left (east) onto Colesheare Road. There are

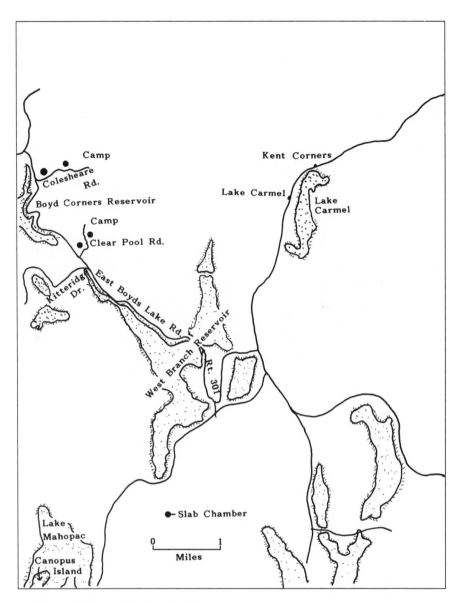

*Lake Carmel, New York, slab-chamber map*

two intriguing slab chambers along this road that leads to a summer camp. Please get permission to walk the land, and be aware of the posted signs.

Get back to East Boyds Road and continue traveling south. In a mile and a half turn left (north) onto Clear Pool Road. Two slab chambers are just off this road. This road also leads to a summer camp. Obtain permission to walk the land.

E. M. Ruttenber, an early historian of New York State, claimed that strange, pagan ceremonies were held on Canopus Island in Lake Mahopac,

*Stone chamber along Colesheare Road, Lake Carmel, New York.*

along the southwestern sector of the Lake Carmel map. It would be intriguing to spend time there.

There are reports of many other slab chambers in this area. Please check with the Putnam Valley library for details.

## Mohegan Lake, New York

This region is located south of Oscawana Lake.

Traveling south on Oscawana Lake Road from Oscawana Corners brings you past Kramers Pond Road. Along the northwestern sector of the land bordering Oscawana Lake Road and Kramers Pond Road, about 100 yards north of a school parking lot, is a large, double slab-chamber. Nearby are several massive stone walls and boulders placed atop others. This site was once a tannery mill. But what was it before that? Did the leather tanners actually quarry and transport gigantic slabs of granite, or did they merely use what was already in place? This is a nagging problem associated with these southern New York State chambers. Which came first: the cut slabs or the chambers?

The northern section of the enclosure is covered by a graded earthway. Parallel to this side, across a rectangular enclave littered with the plastic trash of twentieth-century man, are two more dry-stone walls. The southern sec-

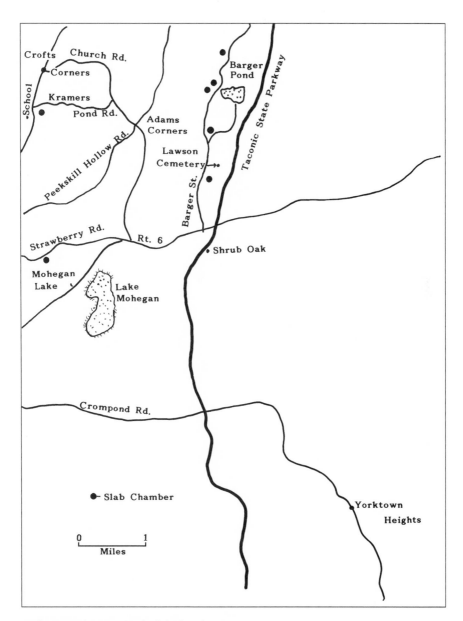

*Mohegan Lake, New York, slab-chamber map*

tion stands alone, uncovered by earth and grass. Measuring more than 8 feet in width along the top and 14 feet at the base, the walls, standing 6 feet tall, gradually increase in height as they stretch along—one for 50 feet, the other for 67 feet—eventually converging to form the extreme southern corner of the enclosure. Here, as the walls join in a squared corner, crudely hewn stones, some estimated to weigh more than 2,000 pounds, have been piled 12 feet high.

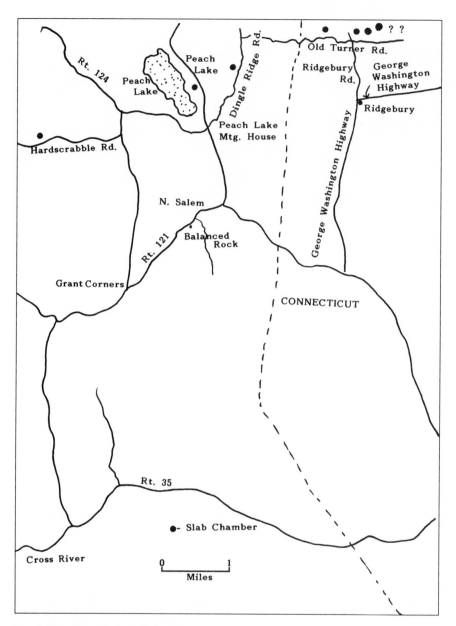

*Peach Lake, New York, slab-chamber map.*

Many of the following sites are probably nineteenth-century constructions. While they *seem* related to others found in the Northeast, careful inspection of these sites will reveal distinct differences: modern chisel marks, association with farmhouses, and the use of iron and mortar (cement) in their construction. So why list them? There is little agreement over their reputed nineteenth-century function.

Take Kramers Pond Road east to Church Road. Continue through Adams Corners south onto Mill Street. Turn east (left) onto Route 6. You'll pass through some heavily populated areas. Look for Barger Road. Turn left (north) onto Barger Road. There are several slab chambers along this rural road.

Three-quarters of a mile after the turn is a slab-roofed chamber on the east side of the road. It's about 1,000 feet south of the Lawson Cemetery entrance. Continuing north on Barger Road, in a half a mile the road forks. The eastern (right) fork leads to a private residence. On the property next to the house is a "root cellar."

A little more than half a mile north along Barger Road, opposite Barger Pond on the west side of the road are two slab chambers. One of them has an "1832" date chiseled into the ceiling lintel slab. Inside the name Barrett is carved along one of the stones. Great. We now know the date of this structure. But what was it used for: icehouse, root cellar, witches' hovel, storage bin, temporary housing . . . ?

Two thousand feet north is another slab chamber on the west side of the road.

## Peach Lake, New York

This region is east of Mohegan Lake.

Several interesting chambers exist here but beware—some roads share the same name and many are not marked. It almost seems as if the residents prefer it that way. (The North Salem Balanced Rock can also be found on this map.)

About two miles north of North Salem, in Peach Lake near the town cemetery, is a slab chamber. At the Peach Lake Meetinghouse, take Dingle Ridge Road north to find an intriguing slab chamber. Continuing north along Dingle Ridge Road, take the first right turn onto Turner Road. Two slab-roofed chambers were once located on this rural road, but they may have been destroyed by recent industrial development in the region. It is hard to ascertain if they still exist because the many large corporations that own the land prohibit entry into this once highly accessible region.

Almost due south of the North Salem Balanced Rock are two slab-roofed chambers. From the Balanced Rock drive south to Grant Corner. Bear left onto Hawley Road. Continue for a mile and a half, at which point there will be a trail road on your left (north). Go about a 1,000 feet and park. A slab chamber is off the northern end of the road in the woods. Two thousand feet east of this spot is another intriguing slab chamber. Both are near small ponds.

### *Considerations*

Give yourself plenty of time to visit these structures. Some are road-accessible; others are way off the beaten path. For the best view, I recommend a late autumn or early spring visit when the foliage is off.

As usual, get permission from landowners before visiting stone chambers on private property. For those sites on public property, take only pictures and nothing else.

As with all sites in the Northeast, watch for poison ivy and rattlesnakes. Yes, rattlesnakes *do* exist in many parts of the Northeast, particularly around flat ledge-rock.

### History/Background

To many of the residents living in southeastern New York State, the vaulted chambers strewn along the upper crests of the Highland Mountains are nothing more than the dirt cellars that for years held their ancestors' winter supply of the autumn harvest. Roofed with immense, overlapping stones and covered by thick mounds of turf, the cellars present no mystery to their contemporary owners. "We used to store potatoes in 'em," said one old-timer. "Been here as long as I can remember," replied another.

While there is no reason to doubt that the chambers were at one time or another refashioned as root cellars, there is an accumulating body of data that suggests that they were not all built solely for that purpose. The number of chambers frequently found together, as well as their general shape and layout, appears inconsistent with the idea that they were built as mere granaries or animal shelters.

Individually, the chambers say very little. But when grouped together, they tell an intriguing story. The best way to understand their meaning, then, is to diverge from the usual format of individually listing each stone structure and instead to discuss them as an aggregate.

Five clusters, each consisting of nine to twelve chambers, were found distributed approximately 3 miles from each other in the dense woods outside the towns of Putnam Valley, Kent Cliffs, Patterson, Mahopac, North Salem, and Danbury. Within each cluster, the chambers tended to be approximately 2,500 to 3,000 feet apart. This may be a local peculiarity, for although some of our site reports from New England suggest a parallel situation, archeologist James Whittall tells us that in areas of Massachusetts and New Hampshire the interchamber distance exceeds 1½ miles.

Practically all of the chambers surveyed are fashioned from massive chunks of stone. Here's where it gets curious: Some have chisel marks, suggesting construction in the last 200 years, while others do not and were clearly built before this time.

In the latter category, the slabs were pried out of bedrock with devices that left no traces. One such quarrying technique that's been around for at least six thousand years involved putting dry wooden wedges into the natural cracks of a stone. When the wedges were in place, water was poured over them. As the wood swelled, the fracture widened, making it easier to whack off a chunk with a big stick. Another method of quarrying without metal was to build a very hot fire on a stone surface and then douse it with water or vinegar to produce cleavage.

Because many of the chambers had dirt floors, it was impossible to accurately measure interior height. But even with this restriction, the average interior height was around six feet.

The chambers had some interesting orientation patterns. Some were built facing the southeastern sky, and others facing the southwestern sky but both tended to be situated near the crests of mountain peaks in full view of the local horizon. They were always constructed of enormous dry-stone slabs of granite, some reaching 15 feet in length and 5 feet in width. Still other structures faced the northwest and northeast and tended to look out at mountain ridges and other natural features. They were usually constructed of small field stones. Building mortar was usually present. I suspect we're dealing with two different cultural designs or two different functions.

American farmers routinely built their wooden homes and dirt outbuildings with entranceways facing the east and south to avoid cold northwesterly winds. This orientation also allowed the structures to absorb most of the limited, but potent, heat radiation from a low winter sun. (Colonial New England homes always had the kitchen on the cold north side, while the living room and bedrooms basked in the more comfortable southern exposure.) The slab-roofed chambers seem designed to take full advantage of the winter sun's diffused light at the expense of its heating potential.

If it weren't for the chambers' peculiar placement, it could be argued that they were icehouses—early refrigerators. Perhaps the ones close to the valley roads *were* used to store winter ice: Their orientation would prevent the summer sun from entering them, making them perfect for this use. Some, however, were found well up the sides of hills. Why haul large chunks of ice uphill?

What does all this mean? Could they have been burial crypts? Absolutely. And there is some interesting evidence from other parts of the country to support this theory.

In the 1890s the Smithsonian reported finding great numbers of corbeled chambers filled with human skeletal debris in Minnesota, Iowa, and western Pennsylvania. The were classified as Indian graves. Earlier, settlers trekking into West Virginia came across other stone-chamber burial vaults. Similar stone vaults were also found in Missouri. What's the difference between all of those known crypts and the slab chambers in southeastern New York? No bones. If anyone ever found skeletons in these ruins, they never wrote about it.

After many years of research, historians still disagree about the origin and function of New York's slab-roofed chambers. Some are convinced that they represent the ruins of an ancient culture. Others are equally convinced that they are the outbuildings of the first white settlers.

*Exit view of a stone vault from southern Missouri. Burned skeletal remains were found when this structure was opened in the early 1900s (Fowke,* Antiquities of Central and Southeastern Missouri).

### Contact Person(s)/Organization

The library in Putnam Valley, New York, has organized many forums for scholars to speculate over the nature of stone chambers. They have a good resource file on who's doing what in the region:

Putnam Valley Library
Oscawana Lake Road
Putnam Valley, New York 10579
(914) 528-3242

Mailing Address:

Putnam Valley Library
PO Box 425
Putnam Valley, New York 10579

### Total Magnetic Field/Inclination Angle

The gravity-flux measurements in this area were skewed by the presence of massive quantities of iron ore in the region. So much of this element in the hills and valleys makes the data unusable.

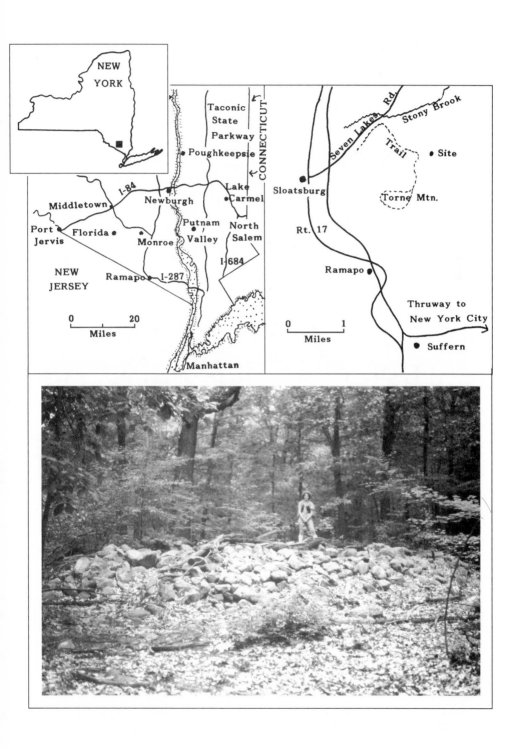

## Further Investigations in Area

Soon after I first wrote about these structures several years ago, many people started finding little-known structures deep in the wooded hillsides of the region. A large number of chambers exist in this area that I have not yet visited. Spend time in this special part of New York and locate a few of your own.

## PREHISTORIC WALLS, MOUNDS
Ramapo, New York

### Site Synopsis

Northwest of Manhattan in a small set of mountain ridges are a cluster of stone walls, double-cavity mounds, and other assorted stone constructions. It isn't clear who built these ruins, but the going bet is that they represent some type of ancient ritualistic site.

### Location

This is a difficult site to find in the summer. From New York City take the New York State Thruway (Route 87) north to Suffern, New York. At Suffern take Route 17 north to Sloatsburg. At Sloatsburg go east on Seven Lakes Road, crossing over the Ramapo River. In a little less than a mile the road will cross Stony Brook Stream. Park here and due south is a wood trail that you will follow for about a mile and a half, bearing right each time the trail forks. This trail leads to the highest point on the mountain—Torne. Look to your left into the woods. Once you see the first massive set of piles, you'll quickly find the rest.

If you get lost or confused, look for a telephone line to the south of the entry trail head. Follow that in a southeasterly direction for about 1½ miles, then turn north (left). That should also get you to the site.

### Considerations

Wear good hiking shoes, and in the summer watch for rattlesnakes. *In the fall wear very bright, preferably neon orange, clothes.* Hunters frequent this spot both in and off season, so beware. A colleague and I once were shot at along this route. Take note!

### History/Background

Northeast of Manhattan Island is a range of mountains that begins in Pennsylvania and continues through northern New Jersey and southern New York State. In the Hudson River region they're known as the Highlands.

If it weren't for several prominent passageways that breach the mountains, the Highlands would cut off the seaboard from the rich valleys to the west known as the Great Valley. In the northern part of the range, known locally as the Ramapo Mountains, a winding path cut eons ago by the Ramapo River provides a natural river highway for people traveling into the Great Valley and beyond. Along a hilltop overlooking the Ramapo Pass, a massive complex of stone walls meanders over some 200 acres of ground. The strange stonework, consisting of gigantic elliptical mounds and circular stone piles, as well as an assortment of haphazardly placed walls, has defied explanation since 1845, when an anonymous surveyor drew a fascinating map of the site entitled "Supposed Prehistoric Walls in the Wrightman Fields, Ramapo, New York."

On the heavily wooded and swampy hilltop there are, aside from the rambling walls, several stone piles. Field teams have recorded eight mounds varying in diameter from 43 to 45 feet and in height from 3 to 4 feet. Eight other mounds were found to be generally smaller, varying in diameter from 20 to 43 feet and in height from 3 to 4 feet. One intriguing mound measured a spectacular 60 feet in diameter, while another measured a remarkable 8 feet in height. Several of the larger piles were found to contain rectangular and circular cavities or carefully laid-out depressions. These gaping vertical openings were usually no deeper than 2 to 3 feet.

The 1845 map of the walls prompted an extended archeological investigation of the site back in the early 1970s. This report summarized several interesting theories that had developed over the years concerning the origin of the walls:

*The southern New York State area showing the Hudson Highlands and the western mountain to ridges.*

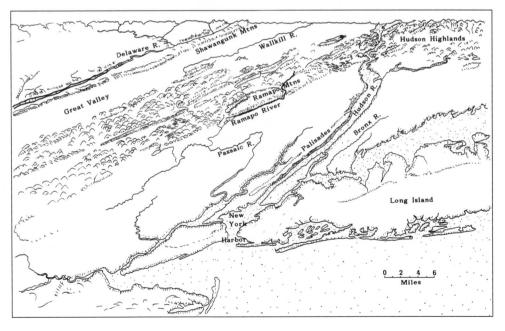

*The Ramapo River cut a natural pathway through the surrounding mountains. Throughout these hills is evidence of ancient activity* (Picturesque America).

- Indians built the stone walls and mounds.
- The site is a fortification built by a colonial militia stationed at Fort Sidman (a Revolutionary War fort under Colonel Hawthorn's regiment, whose responsibility it was to guard the Ramapo Pass to prevent the British from taking the ironworks at the mid Hudson Valley).
- The walls and mounds were built by farmers in the process of clearing the land.
- The walls are property lines, animal enclosures, or corrals.
- The stone walls and mounds were built by an early race of non-Indians as a religious-ceremonial complex.

Four years of documentary analysis, site survey, and archeological excavation produced inconclusive results, although the report's chief scientist felt that the walls and mounds were built by land-clearing farmers. This is a very strange conclusion because if farmers were clearing a field for crops or pasture, why are the piles so carefully constructed? Why not just push them aside? Perhaps someone found great aesthetic pleasure in constructing these mounds.

The site occupies a distinct position on a hilltop overlooking not only the Ramapo Valley but also the Eastern Great Valley as well. The fact that several elliptical stone piles and stone walls lie on an axis of zero degrees due north indicates that some type of astronomical observation may have taken place there. Also, according to the 1845 map and recent surveys, the numerous old roads leading to the site were carefully lined with stones, giving the general impression of an important processional pathway. The conspicuous lack of artifacts at the excavations indicates that whoever built the structures took a lot of care not to deface or despoil the site with debris. The proximity of the other perched rocks, circles, and cairns believed to be ancient in origin strongly suggests that the prehistoric Ramapo walls served some ritualistic hilltop function for a long-gone people.

### Contact Person(s)/Organization

The Historical Society of Rockland County
New City, New York 10956
(914) 634-9629

### Total Magnetic Field/Inclination Angle
There were no strange magnetic aberrations recorded at this site.

### Further Investigations in Area
It would be profitable to explore both the southern and northern Ramapo Mountains—the ridgetops on either side of the Ramapo River. I've received reports of other strange stone piles and balanced rocks in those woods.

About 30 miles north of the Ramapo Pass is the town of Monroe. On private land just off Cedar Cliff Road at the end of Rea Court's cul-de-sac is a strange stone circle that has mystified residents for decades. The circle is approximately 20 feet in diameter, with the stones being around 1 to 2 feet in height. No one knows who constructed this circle or for what reason. But we do know that stone circles were used by many eastern Indian tribes in ceremonial and religious functions.

Just south of Cornwall, New York, about a half a mile north of the United States Military Academy at West Point are over 20 stone piles. This well-preserved cluster of cairns hugs the eastern slope of a hillside and is located near a stream and pond. The easiest way to find these piles is to get the Cornwall, New York, quadrant, 1 : 24,000 series topographic map, which can be purchased at hunting and recreational stores in the area. You can also order individual maps from the U.S. Geological Survey, Washington, D.C. A folder describing topographic maps and symbols is available upon request.

Look in the lower right hand section of the map. Find Bog Meadow Pond. This glacial kettle pond is just north of the West Point boundary. Directly to the west (left) of the Bog Meadow Pond there's a wood trail. The cluster of stone piles are a few yards east off this hilly trail just before it turns to the right.

## ANCIENT CAVE SITE
Florida, New York

### Site Synopsis
On the side of a mountain, in clear view of the once marshy lowlands, is a series of natural limestone caves. There is evidence that people lived and hunted large now-extinct animals here almost 13,000 years ago. On a clear night you can feel the spirit of the ancient ones.

### Location
From New York City take the New York State Thruway (Route 87) north until the Harriman/Route 17 exit. Take Route 17 west until reaching Chester,

New York. At Chester take Route 94 west until the village of Florida, and then go north on Route 17A (Florida Road). Just before reaching Route 6 (Pulaski Highway), you'll see the Dutchess Quarry. The site is on the northwestern side of the mountain.

### Considerations

Seek permission from the Dutchess Quarry Management before venturing down to the cave site. There's an unpaved road that leads up to the base of the site on the northwestern sector of Lookout Mountain. Part way down the path (notice the break, or opening, in the foliage), there's a very steep trail leading to limestone caves. Walk straight up this path, following the archeological debris trail left from years of excavation attempts. As you get closer to the cliff/cave site there's a steep talus slope, dirt removed from the cave during excavation.

Take care to wear good hiking boots and long sleeves and pants. In summer the tick and mosquito problem is prevalent. And watch out for poison ivy!

Hiking to the cave is fairly rigorous. Go slowly. The dry wood around here is perfect tinder for a fire. Carry a water bottle and, remember, take nothing but pictures, leave nothing but footprints.

### History/Background

The cave site overlooks Pine Island, one of the most fertile black-dirt farming areas in the country. But it wasn't always this way. In the early 1900s a shallow lake covered up to 20,000 acres, and the region was called the "drowned lands." The exposed plots of land looked like islands to the first immigrants. Then over the next 100 years, farmers laboriously drained the lake and diverted a local river by digging long ditches. The result of their labor is a large expanse of organically rich land flanked on each side by small hills.

The lake had its origins in the melting of a large, stagnant chunk of ice at the end of the last Ice Age, more than 12,000 years ago. As the temperature warmed, the glacier melted and lush vegetation grew, died, and sank to the bottom of the lake. Over the centuries, the lake became a swamp and deep layers of muck built up. In some parts of Pine Island, the soil is over 13 feet deep.

In the early 1960s, two amateur archeologists, George Walters and William Ehlers, began excavation of a cave on the 660-foot-high limestone Lookout Mountain. The cave is located about 80 feet down—at the 580-foot level—from the top of the mountain peak on its northwestern side.

The cave is about 20 feet wide at the entrance and about 70 feet long. It narrows down to a small crack in the rear of the cave. Ground water percolating from above had caused several masses of flowstone—mineral rich deposits,

*Aerial view of Lookout Mountain, Florida, New York. The cave site is within the*
*tree cover to the left of the quarry. During glacial meltdown, some 12,000 years ago,*
*an ancient lake covered most of the ground in this picture.*

like stalactites—to form on the cave walls. When Walters and Ehlers first began work, the entrance was about 2½ feet wide, having been blocked by thousands of years of rock falls from weathering.

A variety of stone and bone tools were recovered during the dig. Judging
from the type of animal bones Walters and Ehlers suspected that the cave was
occupied only during the warmer summer months—perhaps as a summer
camp between other seasonal hunting sites.

The cave seemed like any other Indian rock shelter that was used in ancient times. That is until they found a Clovis fluted point—a spearhead with a
groove scooped out along its length—next to some caribou bones. The bones
were radiocarbon dated, and the results were astonishing: Someone had killed
and brought a caribou to the cave more than 12,000 years ago! At this time
there were large hunks of glacial ice scattered around most of the northern
parts of America, and people weren't supposed to be occupying this part of
the country. But the evidence was irrefutable. Somehow, an ancient people
well versed in the complicated task of making Clovis points and using them to
hunt big game were mulling about this ancient cave. Where did they come
from? Where did they go? The date for the Clovis point was older by about
1,000 years than the dates for similar points found in the milder southwestern
United States.

It is still possible to visit this ancient hunting spot. As you stroll around the
jagged limestone cliffs, look out upon the black dirt and visualize an enor-

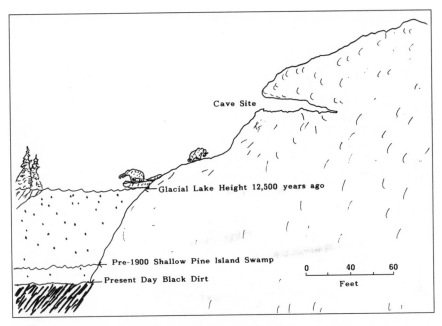

Cave Site

Glacial Lake Height 12,500 years ago

Pre-1900 Shallow Pine Island Swamp

Present Day Black Dirt

0 40 60

Feet

*Ancient cave site, Lookout Mountain, Florida, New York.*

mous lake whose shores were 80 feet below you. Think about the blazing fires that burned here well into the night. Imagine lying down in the cave and falling asleep amidst the primeval sounds of the evening.

### Contact Person(s)/Organization

One of the best reports on the finding and early excavation of this site is *Early Man in Orange County, New York* by former Middletown, New York, resident George R. Walters. Published in the spring of 1974 by the Historical Society of Middletown and the Wallkill Precinct, this twenty-two-page booklet is a gem of firsthand information. Although it is difficult to get a copy, the Historical Society sometimes makes photocopies of its most requested publications.

The Historical Society of Middletown and the Wallkill Precinct
25 East Main Street
Middletown, New York 10940
(914) 342-0941

A good mastodon specimen that was found in the black dirt of southern New York State is on display at:

Orange County Community College
South Street
Middletown, New York 10940

*Looking toward the entranceway to the ancient cave site where people rested and hunted over 12,000 years ago. Sand, dirt, and wind-blown debris filled up most of the entrance when it was discovered in the early 1960s.*

### Total Magnetic Field/Inclination Angle

No significant geomagnetic fluctuations were found at this site.

### Further Investigations in Area

Early Americans hunted large woolly elephants on the postglacial tundra. These ancient creatures came in two distinct types: the woolly mammoth

(*Mammuthus primigenius*) and the mastodon (*Mastodon americanus*). During the last glacial meltdown, these animals flourished and then, mysteriously, they became extinct. The reason for their demise has been a hot topic of debate. Some scientists believe the rapidly changing ecosystem left large numbers of elephants with no food. This, coupled with their suspected slow gestation period of over three years (based on modern elephants), leads these specialists to see a gradual but inevitable extinction.

Other scientists, however, aren't so sure. They believe these creatures were hunted into extinction by skilled Clovis point hunters. They base their suspicions on the extraordinarily rapid decline of these beasts. It was too rapid for an ecosystem disaster. No doubt mammoths and mastodons would have been tempting targets for hungry hunters. You get a lot of meat as the result of one kill.

A large number of fossil mastodon bones have been recovered in the swamps and muck of southern New York State. Near Montgomery and Sugar Loaf, New York, two towns a short distance from the Lookout Mountain cave, road workers in the 1970s found the bones of two mastodons. Could these creatures have been hunted by the same tribes that visited the Lookout Mountain cave? Absolutely.

Also near Sugar Loaf are reports of unusual stone piles topped by flat rocks on a trail between Sugar Loaf Mountain and nearby Mine Hill. The piles reportedly are just off the south side of the trail. The trail begins at the western end of Well Sweep Land, a road coming off Kings Highway (Route 13) just north of Sugar Loaf village. There's a house at the end of the lane, so the trail isn't immediately apparent, but it begins right in back of the residence.

Sugar Loaf Mountain seems to have a lot of strange stone remains scattered around it. I received a report about a stone circle on the southeastern face of the mountain just down slope from where a formation called Giant's Rock or the Old Giant used to be before it fell from the crest of the mountain about 100 years ago.

## UFO SIGHTINGS
Pine Bush, New York

### Site Synopsis
The rural fields around Pine Bush, New York, seem to be the world's UFO capital. An amazing number of strange lights, unusual sightings, and weird noises are reported to occur near this tiny town in the shadow of the Shawangunk Mountains.

### Location
While the best time to watch the sky is nighttime, drive up well before dark or else you may get lost. From the George Washington Bridge on Manhattan's

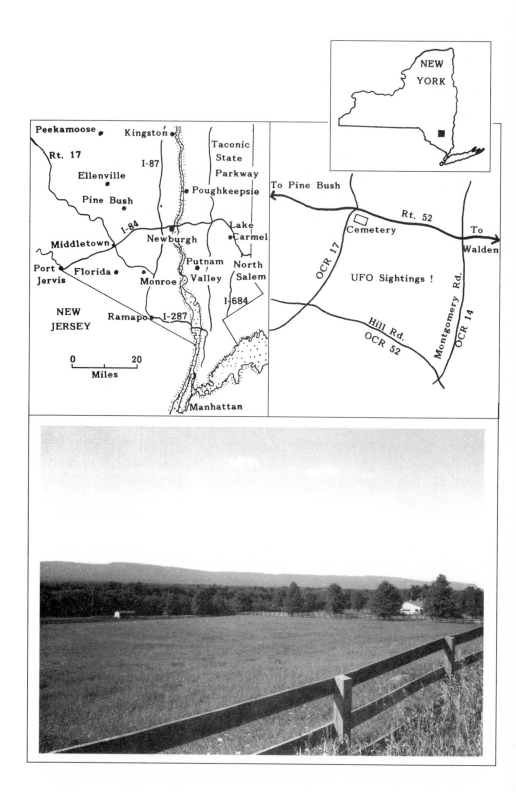

Upper West Side, take the Palisades Parkway north for about 35 miles to exit 18. Take Route 6 going west through Harriman State Park, and at the end of the road exit onto Route 17 going north. Continue for about 23 miles turning off at exit 119. Take Route 302 north for about 10 miles into Pine Bush. Once in Pine Bush center, turn east onto Route 52 (going toward Walden). In 3.5 miles turn right (south) onto Orange County Road 17 (OCR 17). If you pass the Congregation Beth Hillel Cemetery, you've gone too far. The field that's had the most active sightings is the one that borders Route 52 and OCR 17. Continue on OCR 17 for a quarter mile. This is a good spot to stop and watch. If you want a different vantage point continue for about a mile to OCR 52. Turn left (east) here. Drive up about a half a mile, pull out a lawn chair, and enjoy the show.

### Considerations

If you ask the local residents what all the hoopla's about you might get a "boy-are-you-dumb-to-believe-that-crap" look. If you pick the right person, however, and continue to ask questions like, "What do you know about UFOs," you might get a response like, "Where do you want to start?" Prepare yourself for either outcome.

When parking make sure to drive your car or van completely off the road. There's a lot of traffic out here most nights. Do the same with your viewing spot. If you plan on using a chair, set it up well away from the road.

Oh yes . . . if you do make contact with some hideous alien from another galaxy/dimension/space-time warp, please give him (?) my best regards, but don't contact me.

### History/Background

On any evening step out to one of the several fields where many have claimed to see weird, nighttime sky phenomena, and you will see dozens of cars and vans parked on the side of the road. Most of these people have binoculars and Thermos bottles of coffee. Some have experienced a discrepant event in their lives, and they want to relive it. Others come along for the ride. And still others come in search of just a shred of truth to this nighttime ritual.

So many people in this town have seen unusual and inexplicable aerial phenomena—like luminescent discs zigzagging across the horizon—that a support group hot line was established in 1993. The group allows people to call and talk about their experiences without being ridiculed.

So what's up here? I spent many nights out in the fields of Pine Bush, and all I got were "fish stories" of the "you had to be there," variety. And they all sounded the same. But the people talking were all so earnest about their unusual experiences. Should we believe them?

The Pine Bush phenomena are part of a wider set of UFO sightings in the

Hudson Valley of southern New York State. For years, people on both sides of the river have reported extraordinary aerial events. The sightings seem to go in cycles: Some years not much happens, while other years local police stations are overwhelmed with frantic phone calls from frightened residents.

How can we explain these events? It's rather simple, really. Either people have witnessed some unknown type of airborne phenomena, or they haven't. Assuming that they *did* see an unidentified flying object, what exactly, did they see? Perhaps the geology of the Hudson Valley has something to do with the reports.

During the last Ice Age a two-mile-high glacier covered most of southern New York State. This massive ice flow was responsible for scraping Manhattan down to its granite bedrock. It also was responsible for pushing along and depositing millions of tons of dirt into a huge, long pile that we know today as Long Island. When the earth's temperature got hotter, the ice melted and exposed the scars, pits, and grooves caused by the incalculable weight of the glacier.

Some geologists believe that the weight of the glacier depressed the bedrock over 300 feet. While most of the land rose well before modern times, the earth is still moving in this area. Seismic monitors set up around the state testify to the slow uplift of the entire state. Occasionally, the lower Hudson Valley "burps," and low-level earthquake waves spew forth into the surrounding land. Could the luminescent lights and glowing orbs have something to do with the strange geological legacy of the Hudson Valley?

Perhaps the rising granite bedrock, which clearly doesn't happen all in one big block, rubs and crushes and creates unimaginable tectonic tension deep within the earth's crust. Perhaps this pressure and stress bends the rocks as they are forced against each other on their way upwards. Some researchers suggest that this dynamic tension creates a kind of geological static electricity that results in energetic sparks that ionize the local atmosphere. There certainly are enough methane-laden swamps in the lower Hudson Valley that could, in some way, be cofactors in producing weird visual phenomena.

If UFO sightings are not the result of deep geological stress, then my next best guess is that the phenomena are some as yet inexplicable byproduct of our planet. I'm skeptical that UFOs are alien spacecraft, because to date there is no viable evidence to support their existence. We need not go outside the biosphere to witness the unusual. Strange events have been around for as long as life. Only now do we have a level of technology and consciousness that allows us to see and rationally question phenomena that perhaps have always been there.

A part of understanding is knowing what to look for. We've done that with decades of UFO sightings, photographs, and videos, many of which came from the Pine Bush area. The rest of understanding is fitting the inexplicable into some already established mental framework. This has not worked. UFOs behave in seemingly illogical, nonrational, nonhuman ways—globular spheres that suddenly change into cigar-shaped lights; discs that streak across the horizon then suddenly make 90-degree turns, unlike any conceivable flight trajectory. We need to stop scoffing and start looking. Some of us may be missing out on the planet's most spectacular mystery.

### Contact Person(s)/Organization

The definitive source on Hudson Valley UFOs can be found in *Night Siege: The Hudson Valley UFO Sightings* by Allen J. Hynek, Philip J. Imbrogno and Bob Pratt (New York: Ballantine Books, 1987).

### Total Magnetic Field/Inclination Angle

Nothing unusual was detected in these fields.

### Further Investigations in Area

One summer night in 1980, I experienced an unusual event in the Hudson Valley. On a clear, starry, July 4th around 10 P.M., I was driving a friend home. Knowing the area, I took some back-road shortcuts just beyond the boundaries of Middletown, New York. As I was driving south on Route 78 (Rivervale Road), off to my right in a hillside field my friend and I noticed a maple tree that seemed to be pulsating with Christmas tree lights. I turned into the High Barney Road and drove onto a dirt road leading up to the tree. There were swarms of fireflies near every branch and leaf of the maple. Their bioluminescent mating signals flickered off and on.

The Christmas tree light phenomenon was quickly explained. But a few other problems quickly became obvious. Why were the insects clustered only around this tree—there were no signs of other fireflies anywhere else in the field. We then noticed the silence. There were no crickets chirping. There were no dogs barking. All was silent. We got back in the car.

And then it happened. My 1979 Honda Civic started bouncing up and down, almost as if some person or thing was grabbing the front bumper and shaking it. I turned on the headlights. There were neither people nor brown bears moving the car. It occurred to me that this might be an earth tremor. I quickly jotted down the exact time and counted the duration of the car's movement. The bouncing stopped, then started up again in 4 minutes. The successive shakings were 14 seconds, then 16, then 17 seconds. I congratulated myself for thinking so quickly and recording the time sequence—that would be very useful information to pinpoint the epicenter for the next day's phone call to a seismic station in New York. Unfortunately, when it was over, I couldn't start my seven-month-old car and had to roll it down the hill to get it going.

The next day I called the geological station, but they had no record of any earth tremors for the previous night. I insisted that they closely examine their seismic logs. Nothing. I tried another station in Albany. Nothing. Could the devices not have picked up a local tremor? "Impossible," said the supervising engineer. The sensors can detect any level of earth movement all the way to Ohio! "So what happened last night?" I asked. "Damned if I know," was the response. "Were you drinking?" he chuckled.

**Fact:** The Chinese have long been aware that insects and animals act in unusual ways when an earthquake is about to strike. Some animals get restless and agitated while others become ominously silent. Somehow these creatures appear to be sensing impending crustal movement. We heard no nighttime sounds.

**Fact:** The car was shaking up and down. My friend and I were there for the ride. Yet the seismic stations picked up no tremor waves.

**Fact:** After spending an hour trying to figure out my car's trouble, a garage mechanic spotted the problem: a bent metal butterfly valve in the carburetor. "What could cause that?" I asked. "Hitting it with a hammer," he replied.

**Fact:** I didn't hit my butterfly valve with a hammer that night or at any other time.

On a recent sky watch at Pine Bush, while chatting with some of the regulars, I heard a tellingly familiar tale. A couple from Utah told me about a strange light they saw one summer evening while driving across Missouri. They stopped to watch it. They were surprised by the lack of any night sounds: no insect calls, no dogs yapping. After the light zoomed beyond the horizon they tried to start their pickup. It kept stalling. The next day they found out why: the butterfly valve was bent.

Pine Bush is also home to a mysterious array of over 20 circular pits that are about 6 feet in diameter and approximately 4 feet deep. A preliminary search by the property owner nearly 20 years ago exposed flints, stone arrows, and crude pounding implements. The site is about a mile and a half east of the town of Walker Valley. At the intersection of Routes 302 and 52 at Pine Bush, go west on Route 52 for 2.6 miles. Turn right onto Quanicut Road. The pits are out in the fields to your left. Check with the current property owner before entering this private property or you will be trespassing.

## MYSTERIOUS CARVED TUNNELS
Ellenville, New York

### Site Synopsis
On the side of an ancient mountain system is a series of tunnels carved out of the ridge with an ancient form of pick and wedge mining. Local scholars haven't a clue as to who carved these gaping holes.

### Location
From the George Washington Bridge on Manhattan's Upper West Side, take the Palisades Parkway north for about 35 miles to Exit 18. Exit onto Route 6 going west through Harriman State Park. At the end of the road exit onto Route 17 west. Continue for about 32 miles to the Wurtsboro exit. Go north on Route 209 for about 19 miles to Ellenville. Upon entering Ellenville, turn right at the main intersection onto Route 52 (south/southeast). In town this road is called Center Street. Continue on Center Street for a few minutes until you reach Broadhead Street. Turn left and continue past the next intersection (Canal Street) onto Berne Road. Take Berne Road for ⅗oth of a mile past a ball field and turn into the long, paved driveway in front of the red brick factory building with a smokestack. A store presently occupies the site. Park at the extreme left of the large gravel lot. There's a trail at the northeast corner of the lot. Follow it for a few minutes. You'll cross a stream and soon see a concrete-faced opening with water coming out of it. This is the original "mystery" tunnel. The path is hard to follow, so you will probably have to scramble a bit to find it again.

About 75 yards behind this tunnel are large flat slabs. Climb above the small opening in the mountain to the upper tunnel.

### Considerations
Before exploring the tunnels, contact the store owners. Permission is usually given, so be courteous.

Bring along a strong underwater flashlight (in case you drop it in the water) and some hiking shoes that you don't mind getting wet. The lower tunnel's entranceway can be reached rather easily by wading in one to two feet of water. I would not recommend going farther unless you have a partner, extra lights, and are not scared of enclosed spaces. Be careful of your camera gear. It's easy to get wet.

The upper cave seems to be an exploratory tunnel that curves upward. It's an easy climb provided you are agile and have the correct shoes—I would not recommend sandals unless they have good, gripping soles and are *made* for climbing.

## History/Background

The first recorded exploration that carried reports of the northern New World's riches back to Europe was Henry Hudson's in 1609. Within a few days after Hudson entered New York Harbor, he reported that the Indians had "yellow copper." Subsequent expeditions brought settlers up the Delaware River, and reports soon followed of an area rich in ores, including copper, iron, and lead.

Along the east bank of the Delaware River near the Delaware Water Gap, continuing northward along the Kittatinny-Shawangunk Ridge, and ending at the Hudson River port city of Kingston, New York, there once existed a 104-mile dirt path known as the Old Mine Road. The road, long since asphalted and rerouted, is still a major artery of transportation in northwestern New Jersey, and now goes by the name Route 209.

The fame bestowed upon the Old Mine Road stemmed from the dubious fact that it was the oldest trade highway in the nation. Local legend has it that sometime before 1650 the road was built by the Dutch to transport heavy loads of copper ore from mines in Pahaquarry Township, New Jersey, north-ward along the river to Kingston (or Esopus, as it was then known). From there the ore was shipped down the Hudson River for eventual transport to

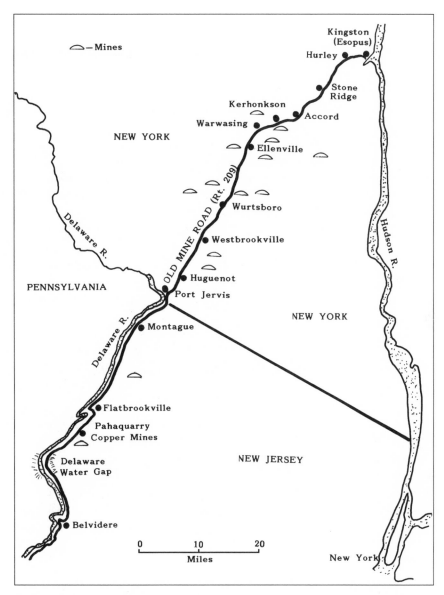

*An old mine road with ancient mines carved into the Shawangunk Mountain ridge*

Holland. Reasons for simply not hauling the ore due east over New Jersey to reach New Amsterdam presumably included the rough terrain, mountain ridges, heavy forest cover, and uncooperative Indians.

Today few scholars accept any Dutch mining activity in the Delaware River Valley much before 1650. But we are nonetheless still faced with the evidence that digging at Pahaquarry has existed for a long time, and that the so-called Old Mine Road is indeed old. In all probability the road originally was an ancient, Native American trail through the dense forest, following the natural contours of the land. This trail surely was used by the people doing the rock exploration.

Perhaps the most impressive evidence for someone coming into the Delaware Valley to search for copper veins are the mines themselves. Along the entire ridge of the Kittatinny and Shawangunk there are numerous cuts and tunnels carved into the base of the mountains. At least seven of these "mines" were worked entirely by hand tools. That is, some people in the dim past simply walked up to the mountain face, took up their hammers, and pounded picks and wedges into base rock.

A few of these tunnels measure 6 feet wide, 4 feet high, and 500 feet deep. The amount of effort and time needed to pry open rock in this manner has been estimated by one local stonemason to be at least ten months for each mine. The detail bestowed upon these exploratory tunnels is unique in comparison to Dutch mineral excavation. The Dutch, and practically everyone who searched for and mined ore during Colonial days, used gunpowder to blast away stone. It was much cheaper and usually the only way for exploratory teams to test the mineral wealth of an area. They couldn't very well spend almost a year hacking away in one place. No trace of gunpowder or the subsequent blasts has been found in the tunnels along the Kittatinny-Shawangunk Ridge.

Near the outer boundaries of the village of Ellenville, at the foot of the Shawangunk Mountains is one of those mysterious tunnels. The tunnel goes straight back into the mountain face for 515 feet. At the end of the tunnel is a water spring.

Further south along the ridge are shafts into lead mines. These shafts are tiny compared to the Ellenville site. They are fully accounted for in maps and documents dating to the 1600s. But not so the Ellenville tunnel. There was no historical mention of it in any documents of the area until 1905 when the tunnel was discovered.

In 1907 a water-bottling company purchased the land leading up to the tunnel. They built the large brick plant and began marketing their "superior water." A small railway was built into the tunnel to satisfy hordes of the curious who ventured up to the mountains. To add to the "charm" of the site, a concrete Roman archway was built near the tunnel's entranceway. Formal gardens also graced the area. Today only the archway remains. The rest is in ruins.

*Contact Person(s)/Organization*

Ellenville Chamber of Commerce
Ellenville, New York 12428
(914) 647-4620

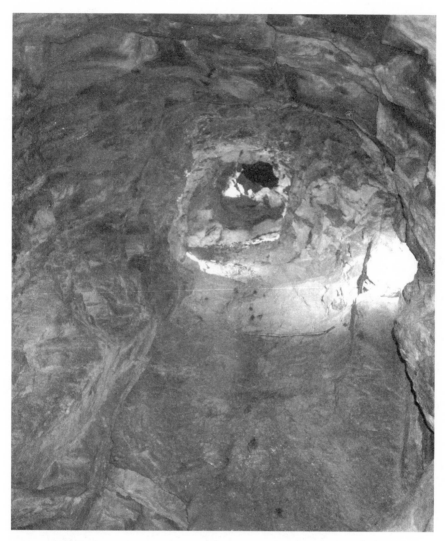

*Interior of the upper carved tunnel, Ellenville, New York. This seems to be an exploratory tunnel—the builders probably were looking for a mineral vein.*

### Total Magnetic Field/Inclination Angle

No geomagnetic deviations were found at this site.

### Further Investigations in Area

Recently, when I climbed down from the tunnels I noticed a variety of rubble stone that had fallen from the upper ridge of the cave. A detailed examination of this debris—as in a professional excavation—should shed light on the origin of the carvers. Also, if you have time, wander both north and south of the main group of tunnels: you may find more than you expected.

## NORTH CENTRAL NEW YORK

The last Ice Age had a tremendous impact on the northern central region of New York, shaping the land and providing the area with good, rich soil. Farmers, fed up with the rocky soil and short growing season of central Vermont and New Hampshire, gave up their farms and moved here to find remnants of previous populations such as large earthworks, embankments, and stone slabs strewn across meadows and hilltops. Most of these ruins were attributed to the Indians, even though many tribes claimed to have no knowledge of their origin. A few of the sites continue to astonish field researchers due to their architectural weirdness.

For years, amateur artifact hunters who wanted to beef up their collections of stone tools would walk up to a long earthen mound just outside of Eagle Bridge New York. The site is about 30 miles northeast of Albany and some five miles west of the Vermont state line. The collectors waited until the summer corn was picked and the vast, flat top of the mound was plowed over. Then they would find stone pestles, arrowheads, scrapers, pounding stones, and other assorted Indian debris. Occasionally, someone found bone remains.

In the early 1980s, a member of an amateur archeology group decided to investigate. The amateur dug into several parts of the mound and found several graves, human skulls, bones, arrowheads, and cremated burials. By using carbon dating on the burned remains, he concluded that a group of people had been burying their dead on this elongated mound of dirt over 5,000 years ago. He announced his findings at a news conference, which then prompted New York State to send a university archeologist to investigate. The team found nothing of importance, only a hearth and some burned-out tree stumps in one section of the mound.

This was good news for a Vermont gravel company that wanted to bulldoze the hilltop to sell off the stone and was waiting for an excavation permit. But the controversy wouldn't die. The amateur archeology group visited the pit the state's archeologist had excavated, dug down another 36 inches, and exposed skulls, bones, stone tools, and evidence of another cremation burial! Another news conference was held. Verbal barbs were traded. The state archeologist accused the amateur group of disturbing and ruining a valuable archeological site. The amateurs claimed that if it weren't for their "illegal" dig no one would have even recognized the importance of the site. Ultimately, the excavation permit was denied, and the mound was left alone.

If anyone had bothered to ask the local Onondaga Indians about the site, all the turmoil could have been avoided. Native Americans in the area had

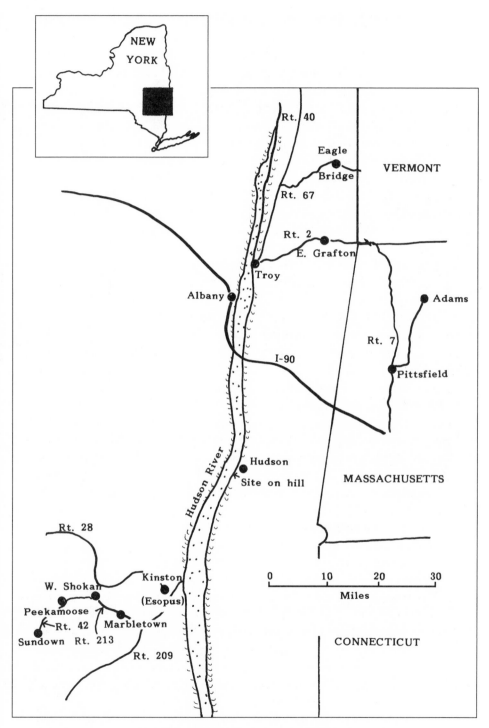

*Mysterious sites along the Hudson River Valley, east-central New York State.*

long considered this site sacred, the mound being a traditional resting place for their ancestors. For the Indians, it was yet another example of how unaware the general population is of Native American culture and traditions. There is no doubt, this mound site is a special place of great power.

In 1824 a geologist writing in the *American Journal of Science*, reported a sacred stone circle on a high hill just south of the town of Hudson, New York. The position of the stones and their remarkable size attracted much attention over the years.[4] I've searched for this stone circle, but to no avail. I suspect it was destroyed by a company putting in some electrical power lines. The general area of the site can be reached by taking Route 9G south out of Hudson. About a half mile out of town, just across South Bay, turn right (northwest) onto Merino Road. Continue on the road, stopping just as it curves around to the west. The stone circle was at the highest point on Mount Merino.

Just off Old Stagecoach Road (also known as Haden Lane) in East Grafton, New York, is a report of a large elliptical stone pile that was in place when the first landowner homesteaded the area back in the early 1700s.

The Dutch set up one of their earliest trading posts near Kingston, New York, because its position on the Hudson River allowed for easy transport of beaver pelts collected from the nearby Catskill Mountains. This area was also home to several Indian tribes who had settlements near the Esopus River. On the cliffs and boulders near where the river empties into the Hudson River, Dutch traders noticed a peculiar petroglyph carved into one of the rocks. (See illustration on following page.) While this was clearly a "modern" petroglyph—one created after white contact brought rifles to the Kingston area Indians—the peculiar headdress and wand in the left hand suggested something very special about the figure. Today, we can only guess what that was, because the carving was demolished by nearby construction in the mid nineteenth century.

I received a report from a scientist who had spent his childhood wandering around the hills in the southern Catskill Mountains. Near the top of a small mountain called Breath Hill—about a one-hour climb—which is adjacent to Peekamoose Mountain, the scientist remembers seeing an unusual stone formation. The stone jutted out from near the top of the hill and was about 10 feet high. The surface was worn fairly smooth, so that in cross-section it was rounded. It supposedly resembled the carved head of a large animal. About 100 yards away on the same ridge, there were two smaller, yet similar formations. The smaller formations consisted of a stone with a larger placed stone on top. The hilltop is privately owned.

*Esopus landing along the Hudson River, mid 1800s. The petroglyph was on the rocks to the left of this illustration* (*Schoolcraft*, History of the American Indians).

*Petroglyph on rock at Esopus, New York. Construction during the mid 1800s destroyed this artifact* (*Schoolcraft*, History of the American Indians).

## SACRED MOUNTAIN
Palmyra, New York

### Site Synopsis

In the early 1800s, on a hill outside of Palmyra, New York, Joseph Smith, Jr., discovered a set of gold-leaf plates marked with strange inscriptions. Smith went on to translate the markings, producing the *Book of Mormon*, which records the history of ancient settlers from Jerusalem to America around 600 B.C. After completing the translations, Smith founded the Church of Jesus Christ of the Latter Day Saints—the Mormon church. What did Smith actually find on this particular hill?

### Location

From Buffalo take the New York State Thruway east for about 80 miles to Manchester. At Manchester take Exit 43 turning north on Rt. 21. In about two miles there's a turnoff on the right (east) to the Angel of Moroni Monument. Park and walk up to this mysterious hill.

### Considerations

Joseph Smith is regarded by people of the Mormon faith as a prophet who had a divine experience here. For them, this is a sacred hill, something to be kept in mind when visiting the site.

### History/Background

Joseph Smith is a controversial and colorful figure in American history. He was born in the central Vermont town of Sharon in 1805. His family moved to the Palmyra region of New York State, near Rochester, when he was ten years old.

Between the ages of fourteen and twenty-five, Smith reported having received a series of divine visions. He said an angel named Moroni had guided him to a hollow cavern atop a hill near the town of Manchester, about three miles south from Palmyra. Inside the chamber he found a set of golden plates marked with strange Egyptianlike hieroglyphic symbols. Buried along with these plates were two transparent, egg-shaped stones through which, Smith wrote, he was able to read and translate the symbols. Each night he labored to decode the markings. Eventually he produced the *Book of Mormon*.

In vivid detail Joseph Smith describes the mysterious plates:

> These records were engraved on plates which had the appearance of gold. Each plate was six inches wide and eight inches long and not quite so thick as common tin. They were filled with engravings in

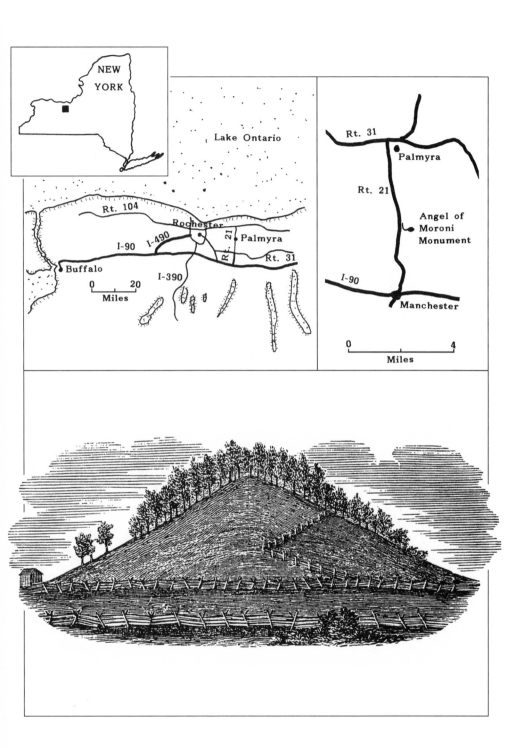

Egyptian characters and bound together in a volume as the leaves of a book with three rings running through the whole. The volume was something near six inches in thickness, a part of which was sealed. The characters in the unsealed part were small and beautifully engraved. The whole book exhibited many marks of antiquity in its construction and much skill in the art of engraving. With the records was found a curious instrument which the ancients called "Urim and Thummim," which consists of two transparent stones set in the rim of a bow fastened to a breastplate.[5]

The actual plates were never shown to the general public. Smith claimed that if they were uncovered for all to see then God would strike them dead. However, there were several men who viewed the plates. Called "witnesses," these eight people wrote about what they saw:

> . . . Joseph Smith, Jr. . . . hath shewed unto us the plates of which hath been spoken, which have the appearance of gold; and as many of the leaves as the said Smith has translated we did handle with our hands, and we also saw the engravings thereof, all of which had the appearance of ancient work and of curious workmanship.[6]

Soon after the decipherment, the plates disappeared. Smith claimed an angel had arrived to reclaim them. This drew much criticism and skepticism from the general public. Smith sent a local farmer, armed with a few drawings of the inscriptions, to New York City to meet with a Professor Anthony. Not only did Anthony pronounce Smith's translation from ancient Egyptian to be correct, but he even identified part of the inscriptions that had not yet been translated as Egyptian, Chaldeac, Assyriac, and Arabic.[7]

*Some of the inscription markings that Joseph Smith copied from the golden plates found at Palmyra.*

When the *Book of Mormon* was first published in 1830, soon after Smith's translation, it received lackluster reviews and even less interest from the Palmyra community. Many of his contemporaries actively tried to debunk his findings, calling it an elaborate hoax.

My suspicion is that Joseph Smith was hunting for treasure or relics around the Manchester area when he came upon something peculiar, unusual, and weird. His treasure-hunting activities around Palmyra were the stuff of local legend. Joseph Smith probably uncovered something from another time, another culture, and it changed him.

The *Book of Mormon* tells the tale of ancient settlers who came from Jerusalem to America. Around 600 B.C., the prophet Lehi led a tribe of Israelites to the New World, where they established an advanced civilization. There were a series of wars and cultural upheavals over the next several generations. In 421 A.D., the Nephites, descendants of the original settlers, were wiped out by the Lamanites, a dark-skinned people who supposedly were ancestors of the American Indians.

This is an astonishing tale that fits in very well with the general outlook in the early 1800s on the American wilderness. As American settlers pushed west into New York State and into the Ohio River Valley, they actually did see evidence of an ancient civilization—although *not* one from Jerusalem. These people saw giant earthworks, massive burial mounds, and stone forts sitting above streams and rivers. These structures, now believed to have been constructed by an early American Indian people collectively called the Mound Builders, were thought to be definitive evidence of an ancient white race.

The general theory of the time was that the *Indians* had killed off this sophisticated white race. The *Book of Mormon* describes this myth in great detail. The point here is that most of the mounds were constructed by American Indians and not by immigrants from Jerusalem—but early settlers and antiquarians didn't know that. Two things spoke of ancient contact: the similarity of the mounds to those in prehistoric Europe, and the "fact" that the contemporary Indians knew nothing about the earthworks.

The purpose here is not to deconstruct the foundations of the Mormon faith but rather to ask a very simple question: What happened to Smith on that hilltop? If Joseph Smith actually was visited by an angel of God, then the following ruminations are pointless. But if he wasn't visited by a heavenly figure, and he wasn't lying, how can we explain his rather unusual experience?

There are several interesting pieces to this story:

- Smith spent his boyhood in a part of central Vermont that's filled with strange lithic remains—from inexplicable stone chambers to boulders etched with curious markings and grooves (see South Royalton, Vermont). Records indicate that the young Smith was quite curious. He supposedly roamed around Vermont's hillsides searching for unusual things, including buried treasure. Given his surroundings, it's impossible that Smith missed all of the weird underground stone rooms found within walking distance of the many places where he lived. By the time the family moved to Palmyra, he was primed to see what others didn't or couldn't.

- Why did Smith find engraved tablets on that particular hill in Palmyra? Angels and visions aside, there's something special about this hillside. Geomagnetic measurements I took there suggest a major aberration as one gets closer to it. Did Smith actually see the Angel Moroni? Hard to say, but you can bet that if the geomagnetic flux was the same in the early 1800s as it is today, Smith could have been influenced by the changes there.
- Did Smith actually find tablets engraved with weird markings in a buried cavern? He probably did. The "buried cavern" he describes sounds suspiciously like an underground stone chamber, typical of those found on hilltops throughout the Northeast. There are dozens of reports over the past two hundred years of farmers finding buried stones with inscriptions. The metal nature of the tablets does leave some concern. While I doubt they were really gold they very well could have been made from polished copper. Were they left by one of the "lost" tribes of Israel? Probably not, but, intriguingly, in other parts of eastern America, some unknown group of people left slabs of stone etched with a script used in ancient Mediterranean countries.

In the early 1800s the time was ripe for religious revival. People were searching for a new and better spiritual way. Smith might have found strange inscriptions on a hilltop where he had experienced a profound physiological change due to the aberrations in areas total magnetic field. His perception of his find, tempered by the region's intense religious atmosphere, could explain all of this.

When you visit this hillside, look beyond the trappings of the modern era and gaze into the past. Perhaps a meditative walk through the grottos will have profound effect on your perception and understanding of life. This is a special place.

### Contact Person(s)/Organization

Joseph Smith Farm
Palmyra, New York 14522
(315) 597-4383

Joseph Smith lived in this restored farmhouse from 1825 to 1827.

## *Total Magnetic Field/Inclination Angle*

As one climbs to the top of this hill, the total magnetic field radically changed from 500 milligauss units to over 900! The angle of incidence also deviated from its baseline reading of 55 degrees to well over 80 degrees.

## *Further Investigations in Area*

It would be intriguing to fully investigate this region, thoroughly, examining the surrounding countryside for unusual artifacts.

In 1938, a newspaper in central New York State reported on a mysterious array of vertical slabs, walls, and other "ancient works" on the 600-foot summit of a promontory known as Bluff Point in Lake Keuka. This aboriginal site, as it was called, was found in the spring of 1880 while a team of geologists were conducting a survey of the region.

The original ruin covered over 14 acres at the time the field geologists interviewed the landowner. The property owner said that when he arrived to homestead the area in the 1830s, "Indians were all about." The man questioned one of the sachems about the origin and use of the ancient ruin and was told that the site was there when the earliest tribesmen first came to the region. No tradition as to its origin had been handed down from the earlier generations of their tribe.

The site, which had mostly disappeared by the 1930s due to farmers hauling away the nicely cut giant slabs of stone for their barns and homes, consisted of walls measuring 8 feet wide and 2 feet high. Vast numbers of large, flat stones had been set in the ground. A number of the rectangular-style compartments were filled with stone slabs, some in circles, some in squares, and some in arcs. At the northwest corner of the bluff was a huge standing stone some 8 feet high and 3½ feet wide. What in the world *was* this site? Who lived there and when?

Today, all the stones have been removed to clear the land and for use in nearby foundations. Some of the larger slabs were taken about 150 years ago for the Wagner House mansion on the south end of the bluff. Nothing remains except two water-filled excavations and a few stones along the edges of the nearby fields. However, there must be a host of artifacts and information just below the ground. This site is begging to be excavated by a professional archeological team.

Interestingly, the 1938 newspaper article mentions *another* site about ten miles north of Bluff Point. Known as "Old Fort," the circular 10-acre enclosure of high-dirt embankments could be clearly seen from Bluff Point.

To visit Bluff Point, from New York City take the New York State Thruway (Route 87) north to the Harriman/Route 17 exit. Take Route 17 west for around 200 miles to Bath. Go north on Route 54 to Hammondsport, then follow Route 54A up the west side of the lake a mile or so beyond

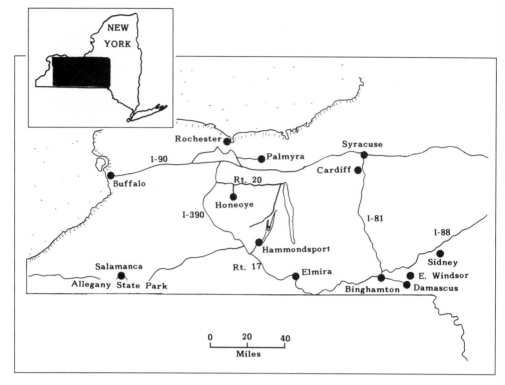

*Mysterious sites found in west-central New York.*

Branchport and then make a right onto the road leading to the Keuka State park. Continue straight south on this road several miles past the park entrance itself to a road to the right called Scott Road. Do not turn here, but go another ⁹⁄₁₀ of a mile and you'll be at the site.

In 1976 an inscribed stone was found at Allegany State Park, near Salamanca, New York. (See illustration on page 248.) Barry Fell claimed to have translated the strange inscriptions as referring to a "King Zari." The stone presently is housed in a warehouse at Allegany State Park. And just across the New York State border from Allegany State Park in northwestern Pennsylvania a corbeled, slab-roofed chamber within a mound was found in the late 1800s.

Near Elmira, New York, an ancient set of earthworks were first reported by Henry Schoolcraft in the mid 1800s. (See illustration on page 248.) Known as Fort Hill, it was located about three miles west of Elmira on the south side of the Chemung River. A small ravine separated Fort Hill from a nearby mountain. As noted in the report:

> The ascent . . . of Fort Hill is very difficult; for some one or two hundred feet it is barely wide enough for one person to ascend, aided by the scattered shrubbery. As you ascend, the path widens, so that two

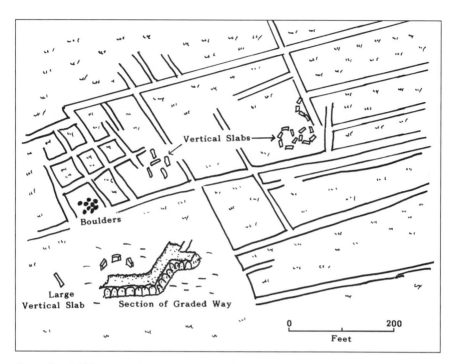

*Part of an 1880 survey of an ancient stone wall complex on Bluff Point,*
*Keuka Lake, New York (redrawn from the Wright survey).*

persons might ascend abreast, though with some difficulty, for the
next two hundred feet. At the top it widens to about ten or twelve feet
and from thence gradually increases in width a distance of seventy to
eighty rods, where the embankment is found. The embankment is
about 270 feet in length . . . from six to nine feet wide at the top, and
from three to four feet high above the surrounding earth. . . . Col.
John Hendy, who settled here in 1788, whose farm is located . . . directly opposite Fort Hill, informed me that when he first saw the embankment, almost seventy years ago, it was "higher than his head." He
was . . . over six feet. He informed me that he had inquired of the oldest Indians about here, but they could give him no account of its origin, or the object of its erection. It commands the river and one person
located at the top of the ascent could keep down any number who
might attempt to ascend, simply by rolling down the stones which are
scattered about in great profusion.[8]

This area of New York has seen an enormous array of people over thousands of years.

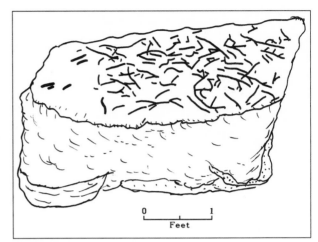

*Inscribed stone, Allegany State Park, Salamanca, New York.*

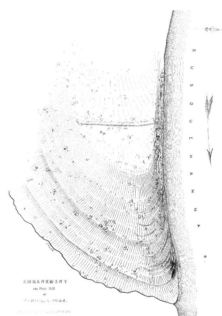

*Earthen embankment on Fort Hill, Elmira, New York* (*Schoolcraft,* History of the American Indians).

About 65 miles east of Elmira in the vicinity of East Windsor and overlooking the banks of the Susquehanna River is Ounquaga Mountain. According to historical records, is was the meeting place of the Chiefs of the Five Nations. The sachems would meet at the top of the mountain at a specific location called Council Rock. Which of the rocks presently there is the real Council Rock is not known. But the place apparently was a sacred site. You can get there by taking Old Route 17 north from Windsor. At East Windsor take a left turn onto Mountain Road, which skirts Ouaquaga Park and climb to the top.

# Pennsylvania/New Jersey

Pennsylvania was one of the original thirteen colonies. People from Sweden were the first European settlers in the area, but by the early 1680s, King Charles II of England signed off the region to William Penn, who in turn provided a colonial safe haven for his fellow Quakers.

Pennsylvania has several different topographies. In the northeastern region, the Delaware River has been a prime area for settlement over the years. In the northern part of the state, two-thousand-foot plateaus define the region. This area is broken down into small, jagged valleys.

In central Pennsylvania the Susquehanna River dominates, meandering north-south through the state and on into Maryland and Chesapeake Bay.

The first white Europeans fought bitter battles with various segments of the Five Nations of the Iroquois. Eventually, most of these tribes were pushed north and west leaving prime agricultural land for Swedish, Dutch, and English settlers.

Pennsylvania has an astonishing number of stone ruins, and a good many of them are located along the banks of the Delaware and Susquehanna rivers. Some are on top of high, isolated hilltops. Mystery surrounds each and every one of these places.

## NORTHEAST PENNSYLVANIA

The Delaware River flows nearly 300 miles from its New York State source to below the city of Wilmington, where it empties into Delaware Bay. It is one of the more ancient rivers of North America in that it travels the same route today that it did some two hundred million years ago. Its course runs between

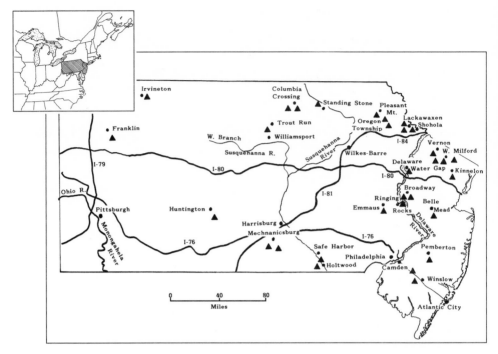

*Mysterious sites in Pennsylvania and New Jersey.*

deeply folded hills of resistant sandstone and conglomerate rock, which are actually the eroded bases of a once mighty range of mountains.

The last Ice Age had greatest impact upon the Delaware River Valley, hol-
lowing out some areas while filling in other regions with soil. Glacial detritus
eventually made for a deep, well-drained soil. Seventeenth-century Dutch,
English, and Swedish settlers made use of the lush flatlands along the narrow
valley of the Delaware River, where the land rises up to the Kittatinny-
Shawangunk Range in New Jersey on the east and folds into the foothills of
Pennsylvania's Pocono Mountains on the west.

The settlers traded with the Delaware Indians, cleared the land of loose
stones, and widened the frontier road along the east bank of the river. There
was fighting as the Indians were forced from their ancestral villages on the islands in the Delaware. But after 1800, major roadways bypassed the area, and
the impact of the nineteenth and early twentieth centuries was slight. Succeeding
generations have peacefully tilled the soil to this day, leaving miniature land-
scapes of the past quite unaltered by modern design. The area's relatively low
population density apparently has preserved many of the intriguing stone
structures of the valley.

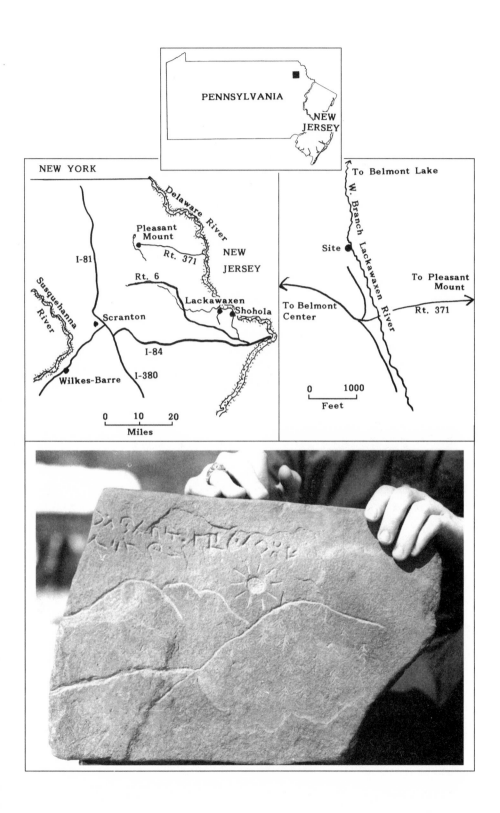

## INSCRIBED STONE
Pleasant Mount, Pennsylvania

### Site Synopsis

During the summer of 1974, a high school student from a rural community in northeastern Pennsylvania found a 40-pound stone in an outcrop of rocks along the west branch of the Lackawaxen near the town of Pleasant Mount. It wasn't just an ordinary stone. The 12-inch-long-by-8-inch-thick sandstone slab had a sketch of mountains, the sun, and trees carved on it; and, most intriguingly, in the upper left hand corner of the slab was a series of unusual markings in some form of script.

### Location

Pleasant Mount is located in the extreme northeastern sector of Pennsylvania, about 17 miles west of the Delaware River following Route 371, and some 20 miles northeast of Scranton.

James Knapp found the stone in a stream bed about 2 miles west of Pleasant Mount. He hiked north off Route 371 along the stream leading up to Belmont Lake. It is the only inscribed slab he has ever found. Twenty years later, Knapp, now married and still interested in all things ancient, displays the stone at the annual Pleasant Mount Historical Day.

### Considerations

If you trek into this part of Pennsylvania, observe all "No Trespassing" signs. Call the land owner for permission to walk any posted land.

### History/Background

James Knapp found the stone when he was in high school. He waited three years before releasing information about the stone, because no one in his small community knew anything about such things. He then forgot about the stone, which remained on the living room floor, until he read an article about mysterious stones in America. Only then did Knapp suspect that he had something important.

The markings on Knapp's stone were thought to written in Iberic script in a style that dates to around 300 to 200 B.C. Supposedly, a rough reading of the script yields the following: "On the appointed day, the sun sets in the notch opposite the House of Worship." Intriguingly, there are many hillsides that afford such a view, and several sites give a grand, westerly view of a mountain "notch." Could the stone be depicting a local scene? And if the translation *is* correct, where's the House of Worship? Was it a stone chamber?

A number of years ago, I poked around these mountains looking for any evidence of this chamber and those viewpoints, and found some possible leads.

## Contact Person(s)/Organization

James Knapp
HC 66 / Box 4
Pleasant Mount, Pennsylvania 18453
(717) 448-2586

## Total Magnetic Field/Inclination Angle
None taken at this site.

## Further Investigations in Area
A thorough investigation of the area around Pleasant Mount no doubt will reveal an assortment of other inscribed stones and other bits of antiquity. Ancient inscriptions do not occur in isolation. Take the time to examine every flat slab in the region.

Ten miles south of Pleasant Mount, off Route 670 near Oregon Township, Wayne County, Pennsylvania, are many curious remnants of ancient activity. I received a report a few years ago about several stone piles located on a hillside area having almost no topsoil. The piles were well constructed on base-rock "platforms." A few yards away was a stone circle having a diameter of over 20 feet. And finally, the property had many elliptical-shaped earthen mounds about 30 feet long, 10 feet wide, and around 3 feet high. (See illustration on following page.) The mounds were composed of soil and stones and were not grown over, dead logs.

About 80 miles due west of Pleasant Mount, near Columbia Crossings Road is an assortment of strange stone piles. On a hillside about a mile from the township, on a slope between Benson's Knob and the road is a cluster of conical stone piles. Near one of these 4- to 5-foot-tall structures is a stone-lined, boxlike enclosure measuring almost 3 feet square. No one in the region seems to know who built these piles or when. It is interesting to note, however, that this site is 18 miles due south of the Elmira, New York, ancient earth embankment (see New York State chapter). The Susquehanna River is 15 miles to the east.

Thirty miles east of Columbia Crossings Road, near the township of Standing Stone, Pennsylvania, along the Susquehanna River is a giant upright rock. Geologists believe a melting glacier plopped the stone along the river bank, but other researchers think it is was cut and placed in position by an ancient people. Over two hundred years ago, soldiers fighting in the War of

*Mysterious 300-foot-long, elliptical-shaped earthen mound, Oregon Township, Wayne County, Pennsylvania. The landowner probed inside one of these mounds, thinking it was simply earth-covered tree roots. It wasn't.*

Independence didn't think much of it. They used it as a target when they camped nearby enroute to Tioga Point. That left it somewhat damaged.

Thirty-five miles south of Columbia Crossings Roads, traveling on Route 14, brings you to Trout Run, Pennsylvania. High on a hill between Trout Run and Williamsport is a stone chamber with an unusually long, laid-stone entranceway. (See illustration on following page.) The site is about 12 miles north of the west branch of the Susquehanna River. Not many people are familiar with this isolated stone ruin. The few that know of it think it was a mine of some sort. It wasn't. If anything, the structure looks like a habitation site. Above the structure there's an opening that looks like chimney, with the stones cleverly laid without mortar.

## SOUTHEAST PENNSYLVANIA

The Susquehanna River is the longest river in the eastern United States that flows into the Atlantic Ocean. It has two main tributaries: the west branch rises in the western slopes of the Alleghenies before looping east-southwest for

*A stone chamber with an elongated entranceway on a hill between Trout Run and Williamsport, Pennsylvania.*

about 250 miles; the east branch originates in New York State before flowing southward for 250 miles. The Susquehanna is formed by the joining of both branches at Northumberland, Pennsylvania. The united stream flows south and southeast for about 150 miles before emptying into the northern end of Chesapeake Bay.

Early settlers moved north from the bay to farm the mineral-rich soil in the lower Susquehanna Valley. By the late-eighteenth century they had pushed into the upper valley, crossing the northeastern folds of the Appalachian Ridge by following the long inland route cut by the river and its tributaries. Rock outcroppings and rapids have always prevented long-distance navigation on the river.

## RINGING ROCKS PARK
Upper Black Eddy, Pennsylvania

### Site Synopsis
In the middle of a large boulder field are rocks that ring when struck with a hammer. Several musical octaves can be produced by striking the right succession of rocks. This field was long a sacred place to tribes who lived here for thousands of years before the first Quakers.

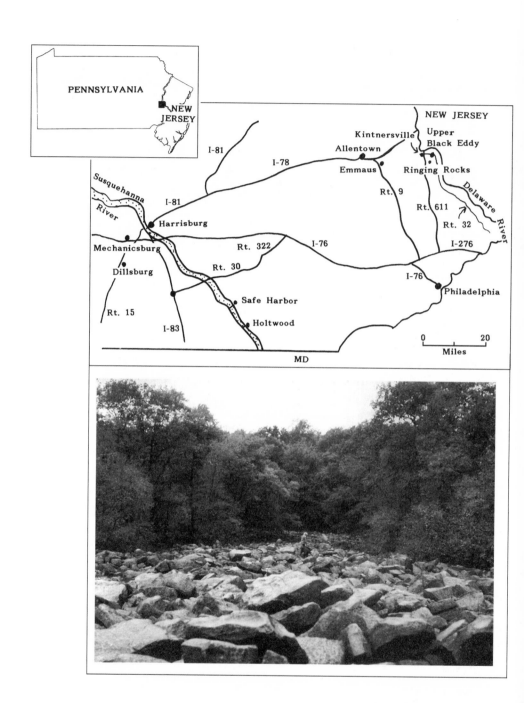

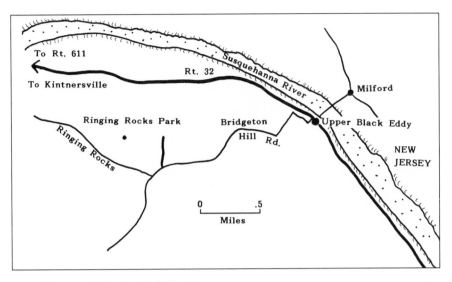

*Detailed map to Ringing Rocks Park.*

### Location

From Philadelphia take Route 611 north for about 32 miles to Kintners-ville. At Kintnersville exit right onto Route 32 and travel for about 5 miles to upper Black Eddy. Turn onto Bridgeton Hill Road. Stay on this road for 2 miles before turning right onto the access road to Ringing Rocks Park.

### Considerations

While the idea of having a souvenir is tempting, please leave these stones in place so that future generations may marvel at them.

### History/Background

The area was originally inhabited by the Unami and Munsee native peo-ple. The descendents of the Unami were the Delaware tribes, so named after the region's first English governor, Lord de la Warr.

To the Unami, the ringing rocks was a sacred place that reflected great harmony with the earth. Their legends tell of the Little People who lived in the woods, who protected the Unami from a Great Horned Serpent. Just why these myths cover this area is unknown. But it was clearly a special place to a people who lived in the eastern Pennsylvania region for thousands of years.

The ringing boulders are situated near an underground stream at the base of a 20-foot bluff. The 180-million-year-old igneous rock boulders, ranging in size from one to 15 feet in diameter, usually have broad, flat surfaces that are stained red by iron oxides. Severe weathering is quite evident throughout this entire region.

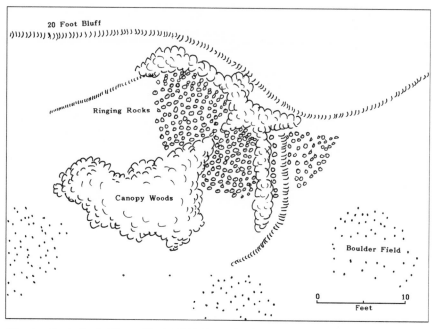

*Ringing Rocks Park, Upper Black Eddy, Pennsylvania.*

So why do they ring? Two researchers who have spent a lot of lab time slicing and dissecting the stones believe it has to do with internal stress. Tensions within the rocks produced by eons of weathering—both chemical and mechanical—allow for different resonant frequencies. The crystalline nature of the rocks produces eerie melodies that add to the sense of mystery in this remarkable place. Those rocks that did not ring had weathered so much that the internal stresses were relieved—they weren't as tightly compacted.

### Contact Person(s)/Organization

Although it has been criticized by those who want to read more into these rocks than is there, the most objective look at the properties of these musical rocks can be found in a report issued by two researchers:

John Gibbons and Steven Schlossman. "Rock Music," *Natural History.* 79. (December 1970): 36.

### Total Magnetic Field/Inclination Angle

There were no significant magnetic deviations at this site.

### Further Investigations in Area

About 20 miles west of the Ringing Rocks, just north of Leibert's Gap near the borough of Emmaus in Lehigh County, Pennsylvania, a geologist

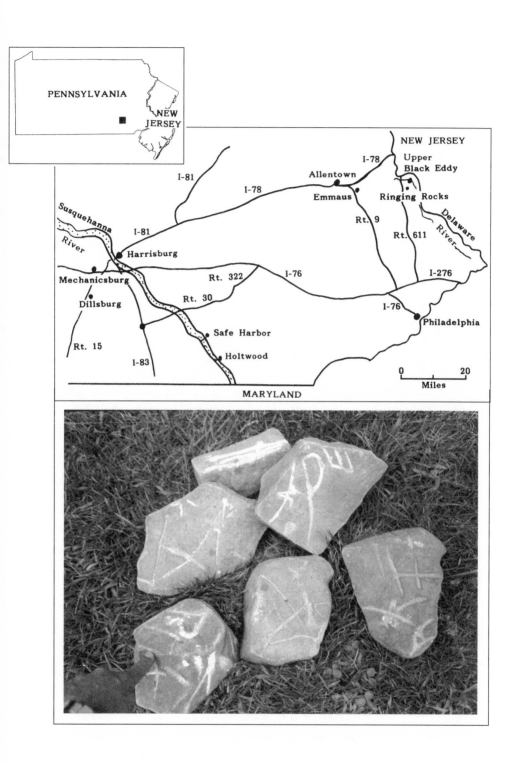

once reported finding a stone formation in the woods that the locals called the Indian Circle. Some people thought it might be an old charcoal burner's pit due to the regularity of the foot-sized stones making up the circle. This prompted the landowner to dig down over 16 inches in the center of the stones. He never found a speck of charcoal.

## INSCRIBED STONES
near Mechanicsburg, Pennsylvania

### Site Synopsis
In the late 1940s hundreds of square-shaped blocks were found in several fields in southeastern Pennsylvania. Interpretation of the grooves and slashes have ranged from plow marks to Phoenician script. More than fifty years later, the stones continue to defy interpretation.

### Location
From Philadelphia, take the Pennsylvania Turnpike (I-76) to Exit 17. The sites are south of Mechanicsburg proper.

The stones were first collected in and around Mechanicsburg. Specifically, the first set of stones was found on the eastern side of the road just off Eppley Road, near the junction of Country Road, south of Mechanicsburg. The next set was found about a half mile south of Diehl Road, also on the eastern side of Williams Grove Road. More were discovered farther south along Williams Grove Road toward Dillsburg.

Just east of Williams Grove, along the northern banks of Yellow Breeches Creek, another pile of these weirdly incised slabs was uncovered. And finally yet another series of marked stones northeast of Dillsburg, along Fishers Run Creek was found.

Today, many of these stones have been moved and can be found in private collections around the country. The Early Sites Research Society in Rowley, Massachusetts, has several specimens.

### Considerations
If you visit these fields, please get permission from the landowners *before* you go stomping over cow manure.

### History/Background
In the 1940s, Dr. William Walker Strong, a professor of physics, collected a number of cubical blocks of stone from a plowed field near Yellow Breeches Creek in the vicinity of Dillsburg, Pennsylvania. Dr. Strong also collected similar stones near his home in Mechanicsburg and from a number of sites scattered along the Cumberland-York County line south of Mechanicsburg.

The stones bore several kinds of grooves and markings which for years

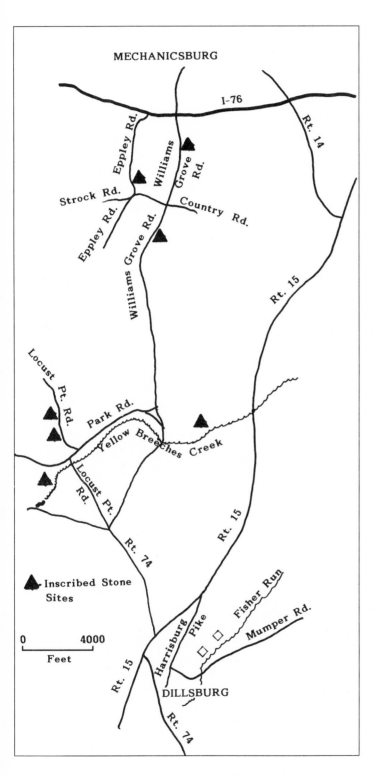

*Sites around Mechanicsburg, Pennsylvania, where Dr. Strong collected "inscribed" stones.*

went unexplained, save for Dr. Strong's insistence that some of the obscure patterns resembled Phoenician letters. He had originally thought the markings were ancient script because many of the stone blocks had grooves that were deep and appeared to be alphabetic in design. Though ridiculed, Dr. Strong believed the inscriptions were made by Phoenicians who voyaged up the Susquehanna River and were stopped by the Conewago Rapids.

The Department of geology at Franklin and Marshall College sent samples of some of the rocks to the Pennsylvania Geological Survey and to the National Bureau of Standards for testing. When the laboratories cut thin sections of the marks and subsequently showed that they followed the natural veins of the rock, Dr. Strong agreed that the grooves were naturally occurring erosion marks.

A remaining group of rocks, however, contained broad, shallow etchings that Dr. Strong maintained were script and not weather markings. These, too, were tested, but he died before this report was issued. At both laboratories it was found that the stones had not been exposed to the elements since the time of the groove cuts; otherwise the pattern of weathering would appear inside the cuts. Furthermore, the laboratories reported that they had found fresh steel dust impacted in the surfaces of the inscriptions. It was therefore concluded that the remaining stones were forgeries that "were foisted upon Dr. Strong by some of his associates who searched for Phoenician inscriptions with him."

It would seem, then, that no further investigation need be made today. However, a number of things must be pointed out concerning the past report. Although it was concluded that the inscriptions on the broad, shallow-grooved stones were fraudulent, it is interesting to note that the authorities originally interpreted these modern-day alphabetic etchings "as chance cuts from agricultural machinery." The very fact that scholars associated with a state museum and a college could not recognize script makes one pause and wonder about some of the other hundreds of untested inscribed stones found by Dr. Strong, not to mention inscriptions found by other people in different parts of the country—stones that have been routinely dismissed as meaningless or cast aside as spurious.

The Mechanicsburg stones lay untouched in a local museum until an archeological group bought up most of them for safekeeping. Close inspection of the stones later revealed that two distinct types of rock were present in the collection. About thirty of the stones were of natural claylike consistency that had scratches the laboratories rightly determined to be the result of weathering. However, about three hundred stones were altogether different, being quite thick and heavy in consistency. These were the ones reputed to be modern forgeries.

It is unlikely that all of the four hundred Pennsylvania field stones were meticulously etched and carefully buried by a misguided colleague of Dr.

Strong. The vast amount of labor and scholarship needed to carry out such a task would preclude someone from performing it without getting caught or without a rumor being spread. Also, the farmer on whose land the stones were found would have been bound to notice sections of his field plowed up every morning, if we assume the forger worked by night. No such accounts were ever reported.

The stones again lay untouched in a New Hampshire barn until 1975, when Harvard professor Barry Fell saw them and claimed they were inscribed with an Iberic script that was related to an ancient language of Portugal. The scientific community at the time went bonkers, for, according to Fell, they appeared to be burial slabs from an Iberian colony on the Susquehanna. Based on writing style, Fell hypothesized a date of 800 to 600 B.C. for the tombstones. The form and content of the deep-grooved stones were supposedly identical to those of similar slabs of that period found in the little-known Tras-os-Montes region of northern Portugal.

Reaction was quick: Fell's theories were almost universally dismissed. Fell eventually claimed that all sorts of people had made it to America before Columbus—all based solely on the interpretation of inscribed stones. Great concept, if true. The trouble was when archeologists looked for the evidence of these people, they found none. This presents a curious problem: If the stones aren't what Fell and others claim, then what are they? Are they merely plow marks? Unlikely. The symbols are too consistent and regular. Are they some unknown script or tally-marking system? Could be. Whatever the marks mean, whoever carved them, there certainly are a lot of these inscribed stones. And the interpretations continue to change, adapt, and generally reflect the sociological mindset of the people looking at them. And therein is the mystery.

The Mechanicsburg Stones are very similar to others found throughout the lower Susquehanna River Valley.

### Contact Person(s)/Organization

Pennsylvania State Historical Commission
3rd & North
Harrisburg, Pennsylvania 17108
(717) 787-2891

The mailing address for the above commission is:

Pennsylvania State Historical Commission
PO Box 1026
Harrisburg, Pennsylvania 17108

Early Sites Research Society
Rowley, Massachusetts 01969

*Total Magnetic Field/Inclination Angle*

No geomagnetic readings were taken at the fields where the stones were found.

*Further Investigations in Area*

About 40 miles southeast of the Mechanicsburg Stones, in the lower Susquehanna Valley, many inscribed boulders were found along the river bank during the 1920s, when the Holtwood and Conowingo hydroelectric dams were being constructed. (See illustration below.) Several newspapers ran fascinating articles about the strange rock markings. An elderly gentleman said his grandfather had questioned the Indians about them. He was told that they were always there. The dam water covered up the boulders.

In the 1930s, during an archeological survey of the lower Susquehanna

*General location of petroglyph rocks, Susquehanna River Valley*

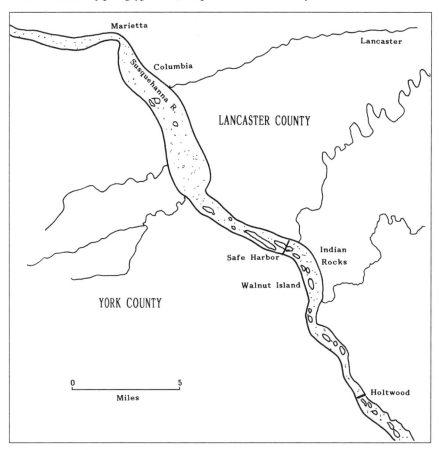

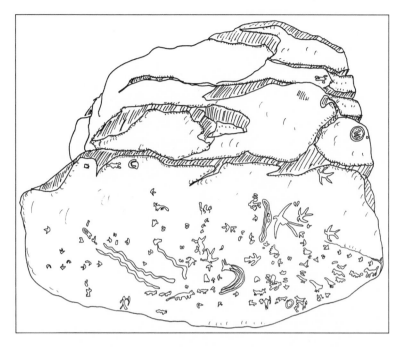

*Petroglyphs on Indian rocks, Safe Harbor, Pennsylvania (after Cadzow).*

River Valley, state archeologists found hundreds of rock carvings. At the site of the future Safe Harbor Dam, a few miles north of the Holtwood dam, a large number of petroglyphs were recorded by the Pennsylvania Historical Commission.

For many years prior to the 1930–32 survey, the rock carvings of the lower Susquehanna were well known to scientists. The first accurate drawing of them was made in 1871. By 1889 many other scientists had sketched and written about the multitude of carvings in this fertile area. Several styles of rock carvings were noted on Walnut Island, about a half mile below the dam site. Some were similar to others found in western Pennsylvania, like a series of petroglyphs found on Indian God Rock in the Allegheny River, south of Franklin, Pennsylvania. (See illustration above.) Others were more exotic: Many of the symbols seemed to be identical to ancient Chinese!

Caution must be observed here, for as the report states, ". . . the Chinese use from 20,000 to 40,000 syllabic characters . . ." [1] With so many characters, the possibility of American Indians stumbling upon the same symbol is very high. Still, the chief archeologist of the report details an astonishing number of these visual analogies. (See illustration on following page.)

The report goes on to explain that a two-year search of the mainland failed

*Petroglyphs found on rock six miles below Franklin, Pennsylvania, on the Allegheny River (Schoolcraft,* History of the American Indians)

to reveal any human occupation sites contemporary with the petroglyphs. But on Walnut Island there was close to eight feet of hard-packed soil separating a known Algonquian campsite from the rock carvings.

> The discovery . . . indicates that a people lived and passed away in Pennsylvania previous to its occupation by known Indians. The early group had reached a state of civilization far in advance of their successors. . . . Who these people were and to what era they belong, we do not know.[2]

Now where have we read *that* before?

## NEW JERSEY

Viovanni da Verrazano sailed by New Jersey in 1524 and commented on the local Indians feasting on fish. Henry Hudson noticed the same thing in 1609. The first white Europeans to take advantage of this major food supply were the English, Dutch, and Swedes.

New Jersey, like many eastern states, has a varied topography. Its 125-mile-long shore, with inlets and barrier islands, provided safe haven for ships over the centuries. The Appalachian Mountains jut across the northwestern section of the state, resulting in steep valleys and high peaks.

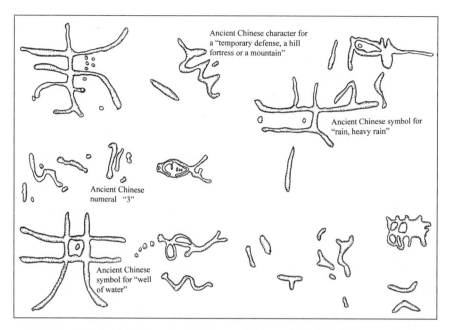

Petroglyphs found on boulders in the Susquehanna River near Safe Harbor, Pennsylvania. Some of these carvings are identical to ancient Chinese symbols (after Cadzow).

## NORTH/CENTRAL NEW JERSEY

From its source in New York, the Delaware River flows some 300 miles, separating New Jersey from Pennsylvania for a portion of its course. Along this valley many inscribed stones have been found.

Near the Delaware Water Gap a hunter found a small highly polished stone with a series of etchings on it. Local archeologists thought it was merely a stone with a series of oddly formed English letters on it. Barry Fell thought differently. He noted that the faint etchings could not have been the idle scribblings of English settlers because they were examples of Iberic script, written in the Andalusian language. The Harvard professor said the stone was a man's amulet for "good luck in love making." Equivalent Andalusian sexual amulets from southern Spain dated back circa 200 B.C. to 100 A.D. Even with Dr. Fell's sometimes dubious theories it is amazing to think that an ancient sexual charm might have been found in northern New Jersey.

I've received all sorts of reports of weird stone formations in the hills and valleys of New Jersey. A good many of these well-meaning letters, notes, and phone calls from interested hikers are pointing out merely the remnants of

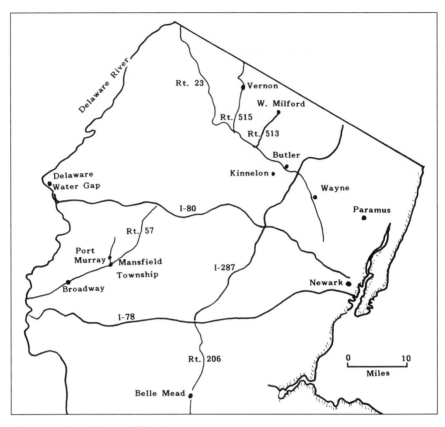

*Site map of north/central New Jersey.*

postglacial meltdown from the last Ice Age—rocks randomly strewn across granite bedrock slabs—or the slashes and gouges of a two-mile-high glacier carving its way across a mass of boulder.

Because I have not spent as much time as I usually do at the following sites, some of the material may be a tad sketchy. But they are definitely worth a look!

Along a series of hilltop ridges in the northern region of New Jersey are an assortment of strange stone remains. The stonework placement suggests this area was used as a sacred site a long time ago.

Within this section are several difficult locations, each requiring a good amount of hiking time and lots of patience. I strongly suggest that you purchase a current topographic map and a regional hiking guide. They will provide detailed information on wooded trails and backpacking routes.

You'll need time, a lot of energy, and a good backpack to see all of these strange hilltop sites. Bring along a compass, some dried food, and lots of wa-

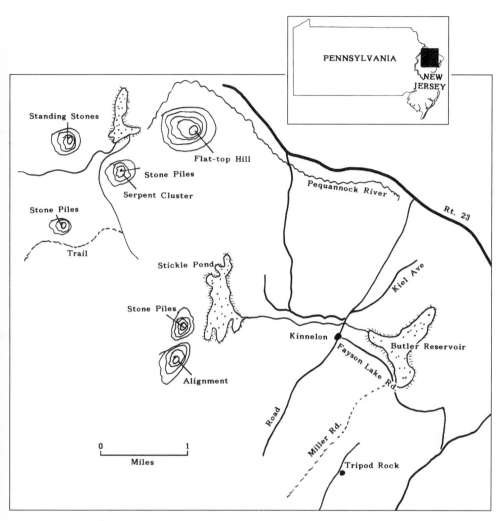

*Site map of mysterious places in northern New Jersey.*

ter. Rattlesnakes often sun themselves on high ridgetops, so make a lot of noise, wear thick leather-top boots, and carry a walking stick.

Running through New Jersey, between the Hudson Highlands and the Kittatinny-Shawangunk ridge, is a fertile, well-drained land that is part of the longest valley in the eastern United States, which extends over a thousand miles from Alabama to Montreal. Since the earliest times the Great Valley, as it is called, as been an important agricultural zone. In modern times, due to its general remoteness, the area never supported great numbers of people. Eons ago the Pequannock River cut a winding path through the Ramapo

Mountains. This river provided a waterway for generations of people traveling into the Great Valley and beyond.

The Kinnelon region of northern New Jersey shows clear evidence of ancient glacial action. Massive boulders are strewn about in a hodgepodge of erratic layouts. Intertwined with this mix of granite and softer rock are man-made examples of stones piled on top of each other. Someone used the high hilltops here for unknown reasons.

Along the northwestern quadrant of the Kinnelon region are several hilltops ranging between 900 and 980 feet. Along a hill near the border of Kinneleon are several stone piles with diameters of up to 10 feet. Around the stone piles is a 200-foot-long cluster of small stones that appears to be in the shape of a serpent.

About a mile south of the Pequannock River, at the peak of a hill in the borough of Kinnelon, near the town of Butler, there's a multiton boulder bal-

*A view of Tripod Rock, Kinnelon, New Jersey.*

anced on top of some smaller stones. Known as Tripod Rock, the stones long have been a source of wonder and amazement for the occasional hiker who wandered by.

The 15 x 8 x 12–foot boulder decked with a peculiar triangular crest running its length is elevated about two feet from the bedrock by three smaller stones. A number of other perched rocks nearby the main boulder suggest either massive glacial action or possibly something man-made.

Intriguingly, the points of contact between the main boulder and its support stones formed an approximate 3-4-5 triangle. Furthermore, the triangular cleavage running across the top of the boulder forms a line of sight that extends due north through two adjacently placed perched rocks. This line of sight seems to pass between a notch formed by two horizon hills about three-quarters of a mile away.

It's possible that what started out as a glacial erratic was manipulated and adjusted for some unknown ceremonial purpose. But by whom?

In nearby West Milford is a large boulder locally known as Spook Rock. The Ramapo Mountains here are loaded with high-quality iron that was relatively easy to extract, which has made them the heart of a heavily mined area since the Revolutionary War. Spook Rock is located about half a mile west of where the railroad tracks cross Ringwood Avenue in West Milford. Local lore has it that early-nineteenth-century miners were spooked by weird sounds that rushed from the rock as wind passed through a huge crack in its side. Frankly,

*A view of the so-called Indian Oven stone chamber, West Milford, New Jersey.*

I find this a bit difficult to believe. Miners of the period had more frightening things to worry about—like a shaft collapsing on their heads. I suspect there were two reasons for fearing this rock: There were (and still are) countless reports of eerie lights emanating from the rock—balls of fire or plasma of some type; and the legend of the Ramapo Mountain witch, Black Mag—who made this site her home. This place is definitely weird.

West Milford, New Jersey is also the location of a tiny stone chamber. Some residents call it an "Indian Oven."

## SOUTHERN NEW JERSEY

The southern part of New Jersey is quite different from the rugged country to the north. In the south hill hills are lower and more gentle. The central plain is mixed with glacial loam. This gives way to the sandy beaches and barrier islands of the eastern coast.

### DEADLY SLEEP ZONE
Atlantic City Expressway, westbound, Camden County, New Jersey

#### Site Synopsis
Along a stretch of highway west of Winslow, New Jersey, drivers have mysteriously dozed off, resulting in a series of fatal accidents.

#### Location
The "sleep zone" section of the Atlantic City Expressway is a five-and-a-half mile stretch west of Winslow Township, approximately equidistant along the Expressway between Atlantic City and Camden.

#### Considerations
If you plan on driving over this site, then watch out! While this phenomenon obviously doesn't happen to everyone along this route, I highly recommend that anyone driving here take precautions: Bring along a talkative friend, drink several cups of espresso, and turn on the stereo to music you hate.

#### History/Background
In the 1970s, Atlantic City was a shabby boardwalk community that had seen its glory days half a century earlier. By 1978, when the first gambling casino opened, the city began to see more tourists and traffic. Today, millions of people from the Philadelphia region and communities along the southern section of the state use the 65-mile-long Atlantic City Expressway to get to their dreams.

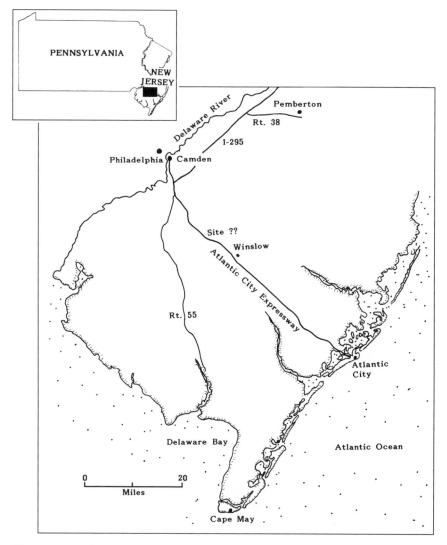

*Site map to southern New Jersey's mysterious sites.*

According to the police who monitor accidents, the crashes occur only to motorists going *west* on the highway near Winslow. They happen in daylight, during good weather, and on a section of the highway not burdened with construction or traffic obstacles. In other words, the highway variables run contrary to those that generally cause crashes. In 1987 alone, there were ten fatal accidents and twelve deaths—all confined to one stretch!

State Police officials speculate that drivers, weary from their experiences at the casinos, stay awake for the first 30 miles west on the expressway because of construction, a toll plaza, and the sole restaurant/gas station along those miles.

Thereafter, they suspect that drivers relax and doze off. The evidence for this sleeping behavior is the absence of tire skid marks and the accounts of surviving drivers. Drivers who were stopped by police due to their weaving on and off the road shoulder proved negative for alcohol consumption and positive for drowsiness.

Could there be another explanation? Perhaps this section of New Jersey has some weird geomagnetic aberration. Could the admittedly few people out of the millions who drive this stretch each year be more susceptible to changing magnetic fields? Unfortunately, I have not yet fully tested this stretch of road. I keep getting sleepy right around Winslow. . . .

Whatever the reason, be it exhaustion from a day at the beach or the casinos, or something more mysterious, caution is advised here.

### Contact Person (s)/Organization

New Jersey State Police Troop A Headquarters
PO Box 270
Hammonton, New Jersey 08037
(609) 561-1800

### Total Magnetic Field/Inclination Angle

I have not yet completed baseline readings along this entire stretch of road. But stay tuned.

### Further Investigations in Area

It would be interesting to check at local libraries and historical associations west of Winslow to see if any of the earliest settlers in the region ever experienced unusual behaviors. Perhaps there are local southern New Jersey legends that need rethinking in light of this place.

Pemberton, New Jersey, is about 15 miles east of the Delaware River, just north of Camden along the Rancocas Creek. In 1859 Dr. J. W. C. Evans addressed a letter to the officers and members of the American Ethnological Society, stating that his neighbor in Pemberton had found a 6-by-4-inch sandstone ax with ten characters inscribed on it. Dr. Evans's letter and an illustration of the stone were published in the *American Ethnological Proceedings* in 1861. The report went unnoticed until James Whittal, archeologist for the Early Sites Research Society of New England, came across it in a Boston library. Whittall subsequently published part of the report and Barry Fell's interpretation of the markings in the society's *Bulletin*.

The markings on the stone were thought to be in a language called Iberic.

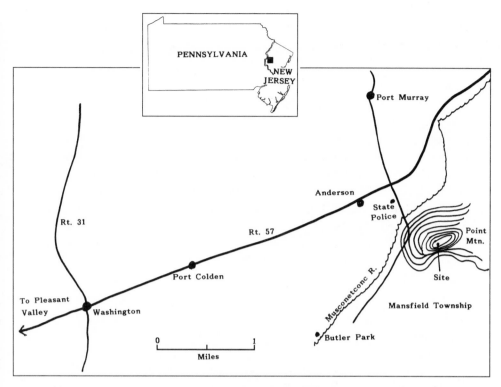

*Site map to stone altar atop Point Mountain, Mansfield Township, New Jersey.*

In fact, Fell offered up a translation: "STAND FIRM, ON GUARD, PARRY, CLOSE IN AND STRIKE."

Perhaps a good guess for a battle ax.

I've received rather vague reports from residents of the area that other strangely inscribed stones exist in this region. A walk along the Rancocas Creek would be a wise and profitable venture.

### STONE ALTAR
Mansfield Township, New Jersey

#### *Site Synopsis*
A large rock atop a local mountain was the site of great gatherings of Indian tribes.

#### *Location*
This site is located on the mountain behind the State Police building off Route 57. Go about 4 miles east of Washington center. The building is on the south side (right) of the road just past the old armory.

### Considerations

Do get permission to walk up the mountain from the State Police on Route 57.

### History/Background

Among the many oral legends in this part of New Jersey is the story about the Great Spirit Rock. On a nearby mountain was a house-sized flat rock in the center of which, according to a local historian, was a stone altar. There were also twelve "seats" carved out of the granite slab.

Legend has it that during the autumn, Indians from all over northwestern New Jersey walked up the trail to this rock to settle their tribal differences, because this was neutral territory. After arbitration, they would burn some of their harvest as an offering to the Great Spirit. Sometimes they would also burn the bones of their loved ones at this spot to appease the spirit of their warriors.

Early in this century, this mountain definitely had several Indian mounds, as was reported by early researches. At present there is a large rock at the top of the mountain, but I couldn't find the altar or the carved seats. No doubt that within this legend are the seeds of an ancient tradition.

### Contact Person(s)/Organization

State Police Building
Route 57
Mansfield Township, New Jersey 07882
(908) 689-3100

The mailing address of the above building is:
State Police
Box 137
Port Murray, New Jersey 07865

### Total Magnetic Field/Inclination Angle

No magnetic readings were taken here. (I know I should have but I didn't!)

### Further Investigations in Area

In Broadway, New Jersey, a few miles down the road from Washington and just off the south side of Route 57, is a stone cellar about 400 feet west of the Broadway Post Office. Some of the residents believe this is an old lime kiln. Directly north of the site is Montana Mountain, reputed hilltop site of an ancient Indian village. Hundreds of stone tools have been found in the ravines leading up to the hilltop.

*Stone cellar, Broadway, New Jersey. Is this an old lime kiln? Montana mountain seen on the horizon in this photograph, is the locale of an ancient Indian village.*

Northwest of Washington just south of the Delaware Water Gap, 150 yards ashore of the river bank is an unexplained stone enclosure. The site is far from any known habitation, and there never were any homes in the vicinity. The laid stones rise up around 6 feet. The enclosure is approximately 20 by 20 feet square. Many years ago a New Jersey agency placed a tablet beside the construction that reads, "Walpack Fort, 1775." If this was a fort, it certainly offered no protection from attack on any side. Perhaps this was a blockhouse. Go take a look.

# ELEVEN

# District of Columbia/ Maryland

The city of Washington, built upon a tidal water swamp, was chosen by President George Washington because of the navigability of the Potomac River there. Washington then appointed Pierre L'Enfant to design a grand city plan within a 10-mile-square area along the Virginia-Maryland border. The District of Columbia was established in 1800 as a federal seat of national government.

During the decades-long construction of this federal city, thousands of Indian artifacts were uncovered along the banks of the Potomac and Anacostia rivers. Most people had no interest in these "aboriginal" remains, but Thomas Jefferson was the exception. He reveled in the stories that old bones and stones could tell, and in fact, attempted one of the first scientific excavations of a small burial mound near his Monticello home. His comments were recorded in his *Notes on the State of Virginia* in 1785. However, it wasn't until the late nineteenth century that serious study of the Potomac valley began—long after many of the Indian sites were covered over.

King Charles I granted the territory of what is now Maryland and Delaware to George Calvert in 1632. Eventually a colony was founded based on religious tolerance for all.

Maryland is geographically diverse. The eastern shore's flat terrain and shallow bays flow into the huge Chesapeake Bay. To the west are the Appalachians and the Blue Ridge Mountains.

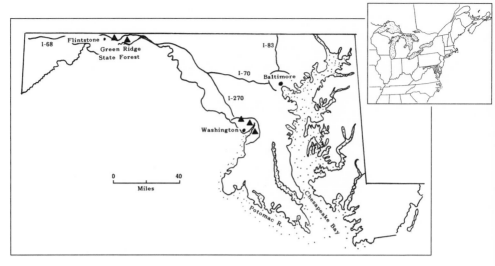

*Mysterious sites in the District of Columbia and Maryland*


## ANCIENT INDIAN VILLAGES
Washington, D.C.

### Site Synopsis
Long before anyone ever conceived of the nation's capital, dozens of Indian villages were thriving in the tidewater basin of the Potomac River.

### Location
All of these ancient villages were paved over by the ever-expanding Washington. However, by examining old maps of the region, we can generally locate them today. A glance at the illustration on the following page will show the astonishing number of villages lining the Anacostia River. In the northern quadrant of the city near Rock Creek Park are examples of native quarry sites. Stone tool material was chipped from these ledges.

### Considerations
While many of the sites have long been covered over, a few curiosities crop up each year. In the 1970s when the presidential pool was being built, many stone tool artifacts were uncovered. A Park Service curator conducted a salvage operation. Security measures, as well as general apathy, prevented any type of full-scale archeological dig. Another set of excavations in President's Park behind the White House in 1976 revealed a series of Indian artifacts.

All of these sites are on private or government property. Get permission to walk the grounds of any of these places.

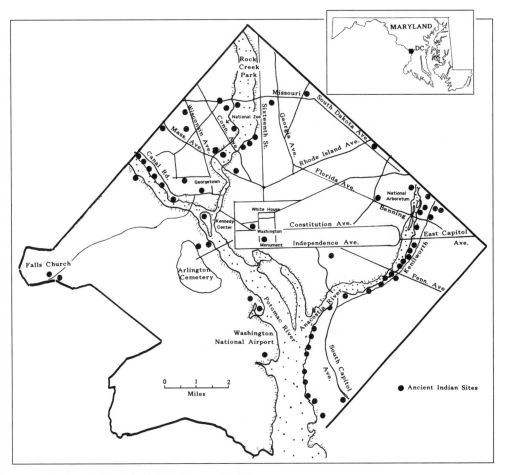

*Ancient Indian sites in Washington, D.C.*

### History/Background

Early white settlers drove off the natives in the Potomac Valley, so that by the 1800s all that remained were occupation sites and shell heaps (shell heaps were garbage piles of cracked oysters, fish bones, and other refuse that accumulated after years of camping in a particular spot).

A quick glance at an early map of the Potomac shell heaps indicates a remarkable number of village sites. The reason had to do with the abundance of food: The tidewaters around Washington were teeming with shad, herring, and sturgeon, and wild game were attracted to the naturally growing grains of the region.

Archeologists believe that Native Americans were probably living in the Potomac Valley for close to 10,000 years. The shadowy history of this ancient population is still buried below modern Washington today. Perhaps thousands of years from now future archeologists will descend upon this site and marvel at the continued occupation of this impressive area!

### Contact Person(s)/Organization

The best sources for this type of search are the writings of early Potomac archeologists:

Otis T. Mason. "The Archeology of the Potomac Tide-Water Region," *Proceedings of the United States National Museum,* Vol. XIII. No. 776, Washington, D.C.: Smithsonian Institution, United States National Museum, 1889.

### Total Magnetic Field/Inclination Angle

None taken at these sites.

### Further Investigations in Area

Spend time in the National Museum and the Smithsonian to get a fine perspective of early Washington, D.C. Also, a springtime trip down the Potomac to Mount Vernon will quickly reveal the wealth of trees gracing the river bank. It's easy to imagine tiny villages dotting the landscape.

## RINGS OF STONE

Green Ridge State Forest, near Flintstone, Maryland.

### Site Synopsis

Hidden amid poison ivy and rotting leaves, 200 circles of sandstone rocks grace the western slope of Polish Mountain in Green Ridge State Forest in western Maryland. No one knows who put them there or why.

### Location

From Baltimore take Interstate 70 west for about 100 miles to Hancock. At Hancock pick up Route 40 and travel west for about 20 miles, to the Green Ridge State Forest. Park at the ranger station and ask for directions to this strange site.

### Considerations

Lather up with a skin barrier. This place is teeming with poison ivy. Try to go during the fall season when the temperature is bearable and it's easier to find these enigmatic ruins.

### History/Background

For more than twenty years close to 200 circles of stones along the western slope of Polish Mountain in western Maryland's Green Ridge State Forest

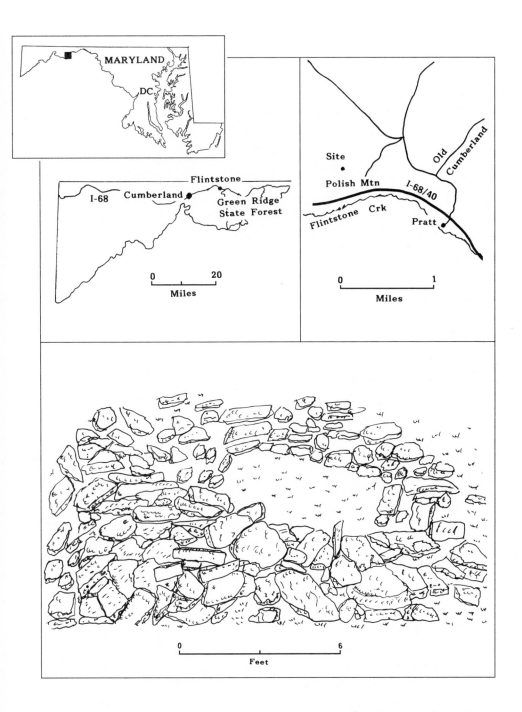

have baffled hikers, researchers, and archeologists. During this time a host of weird theories has been proposed to explain these strange rock rings. Some people claimed they were Indian sweat lodges, while others said they were Civil War foxholes or moonshine pits.

The circles are around 20-feet in diameter with a 6-foot center depression

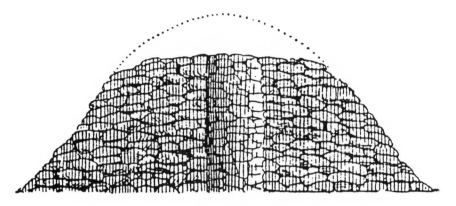

*Stone pile with a 3-foot-wide vertical shaft from Fayette County, West Virginia. Called "well-holes" by unknowing pioneers, these were ancient Indian burial tombs. The Smithsonian Institution reported in 1894 that decayed bones were found within the layers of the pile with the skull pointing towards the shaft. These piles are very similar to the Maryland rings of stone* (10th Annual Report).

that drops down 2 to 3 feet. Each ring is made up of hundreds of flat sandstone slabs that have been carefully laid one over the other.

While local residents were fully aware of these ruins for decades, park rangers first took notice of them in the early 1970s. An archeological dig several years later uncovered nothing: no artifacts, no disturbed soil, nothing to help explain these enigmatic rings of stone. Because of the negative results, no future digs were planned.

Around the ranger station, the going theory is that the rings once encircled fruit trees. A station manager guessed that turn of the century immigrant workers, who couldn't understand English, were told to clear the ridge rocks to plant apple trees. Supposedly these workers wanted to please their employers so much that they moved and placed hundreds of rocks around 200 future trees.

Early pioneers in other eastern states saw many of these ruins. They were in place well before the first whites began clearing ridgetops for hardwood trees. The Smithsonian Institution even studied these curious structures in the late 1800s.

Perhaps the words *circle* or *ring* are a bit misleading, since the width of the ring is around 14 feet. If anything, they are *platforms* of stone mounds with a circular depression at the center.

So what are these enigmatic ruins? No one knows for sure. But if the work of James Mavor and Byron Dix holds true, such "non-functional" stone piles, mounds, embankments, and the like were part of the cosmology of early Native Americans. These structures were built to encapsulate some ritualistic ideal or some spiritual belief. They were sacred spaces that had no secular, or everyday use.

*Contact Person(s)/Organization*

Green Ridge State Forest
7 miles east of Flintstone, Maryland 21530
(301) 478-3124

For more information on this state park contact:

Department of Natural Resources
State Forest and Park Service
Tawes State Office Building—E3
589 Taylor Avenue
Annapolis, Maryland 21401
(410) 974-3771

*Total Magnetic Field/Inclination Angle:*
    None taken at this site.

*Further Investigations in Area:*
    Details about similar stone platforms can be found in:

John Wesley Powell. *Twelfth Annual Report of the Bureau of Ethnology to the Secretary of the Smithsonian Institution.* Washington, DC: Government Printing Office, 1894.

# TWELVE

# West Virginia/Virginia/ North Carolina

## WEST VIRGINIA

West Virginia, originally part of Virginia, broke away during the Civil War when the eastern part of the state sided with the Confederacy. By the nineteenth century, coal mining was king here.

Most of the state is comprised of folded sedimentary rocks that form deep ravines and jagged mountain peaks. The ruggedness of the region and the poor soil prevented large-scale agriculture. These factors allowed many of the state's prehistoric mysteries to remain intact.

### PREHISTORIC WALL
on Mount Carbon, West Virginia

#### Site Synopsis
High above the confluence of two rivers, near the top of a precipitous mountain, are the remains of a 10-mile-long wall. No one knows who built this mysterious construction or for what reason. Radiocarbon dates indicate it was a ruin when the first Indians entered the valley.

#### Location
From Charleston take Route 60 southeast for around 25 miles to Montgomery. Cross the river and get on Route 61. Travel for another 3 miles toward Mount Carbon. Just before the train stop at Mount Carbon turn right (south) onto County Route (CRT) 61/24 going toward Kimberly. At Kimberly the road forks. Take the *left* road, which skirts Mount Carbon. In about half a

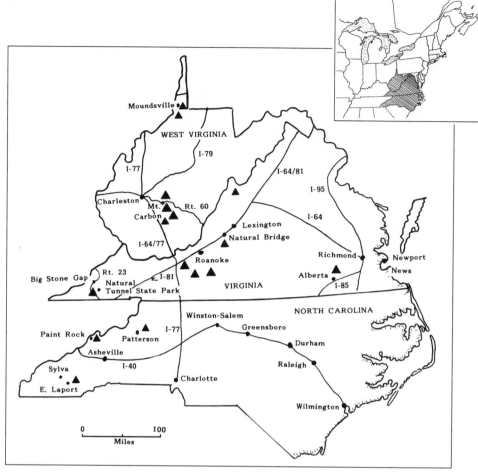

*Mysterious sites in West Virginia, Virginia, and North Carolina.*

mile park well off the road and walk up the mountain. Be prepared to imagine what once was.

### Considerations

Today, this site is very difficult to see, especially in the summer when leaves obscure everything. It is best to wait for the thinning leaf cover of autumn.

When you climb to the top of Armstrong Ridge, you need to focus on odd assortments of stone. Look for mounds of stacked rock. Once you see the long pattern of the wall and are able to distinguish it from random rocks and boulders, follow its contour. Very little remains of this former glorious construction.

### History/Background

The cliffs rising up out of the Kanawha River Valley are majestic: Small brooks have sliced through the hills, creating an idyllic locale. Generations of

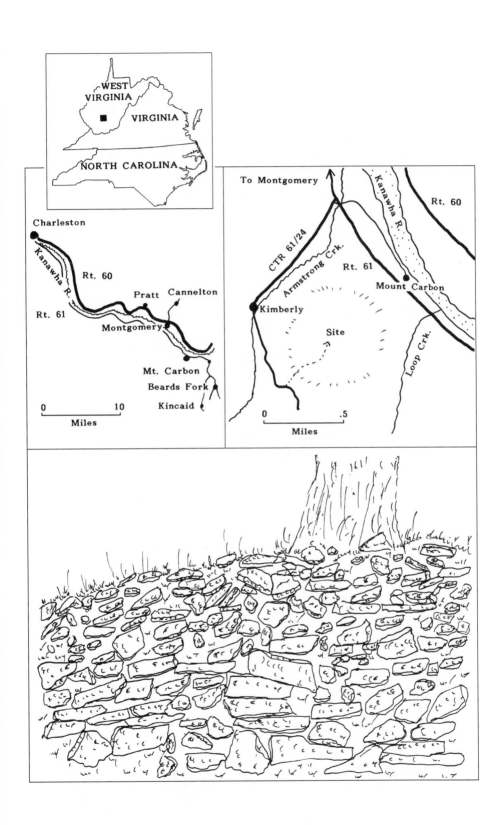

Native Americans made this their home before moving on to other lands. When the first Europeans entered this southern part of West Virginia, the Cherokees claimed a good portion of the territory as their hunting grounds. Since there were no Cherokee villages here, and no portion of the forest was cleared for farming, it seemed to white settlers that they were entering virgin land. That is, until they discovered earthworks, burial mounds, and artifacts that had nothing to do with the Cherokee.

Near the summit of a mountain separating the Loop and Armstrong creeks near Beards Fork, the first pioneers noticed a strange wall. A historian interviewed residents in 1877 about the mountaintop ruin. He spoke to the first white settler who was by then a very old man.

> He remembered talking to the Indian "medicine men" in his boy-hood, as they frequently passed up the river, and discussed this wall and the numerous relics of bones, stone implements, and pottery found all over the surrounding bottom lands. . . . the Indians knew of these monuments [the wall], but claimed no part in them. One of their legends sets forth . . . that the Kanawha valley had been occupied by a fierce race of white warriors, who successfully resisted the approach of the "red man" from the west for a long time, but had finally succumbed and passed away in death. The Indians claimed never to have occupied the valley, except for hunting expeditions; that they found these relics old when they first entered; and that their origin was beyond their records.[1]

Variations of this story—of Indians wandering into a valley and stumbling across ancient ruins that were supposedly built by an "ancient white race"—are ones we've heard before, from Nova Scotia to West Virginia to Mexico. Could there be something to this? Or it is just a bastardized myth that somehow diffused through the native population after contact with Columbus?

The wall was a marvel of careful engineering. Its foundation width of 8 feet tapered up to a height of 6 feet. The wall was constructed about 300 feet below several high ridgetops. It followed the weathered contours and ravines of the ridge slope, forming a vast enclosure that faced out toward the river below. Many of the blocks of black flint making up the wall came from an outcrop much lower down on the slope, meaning that the builders had to carry tons of rock *uphill*. Two large stone piles, perhaps towers of some sort, measuring 20 feet in diameter by 20 feet high were also found inside the walled enclosure.

The wall has fallen along the steepest slopes and can be traced only by looking at the tumbled debris. Curiously, whenever the builders encountered a cliff along the slope contour, they placed their stones at the base rather than at the top. This would suggest keeping something from *entering* the enclosure rather than keeping something inside it, like animals.

Nearby on the prominent bluffs, spurs, and high points in this range, pioneers also came across heaps of angular stones. These stone piles were unlike the loose arrangement of stones found elsewhere in the country. Each was systematically constructed with a well-like space in the middle. These heaps of stone were from 10 to 50 feet in overall diameter, with the central space about 3 feet in diameter. Slabs of stone, some measuring 4 to 6 feet in length, were carefully placed around the center. Layers of stone were added to the circle until a height of 4 to 8 feet was attained.

The stones used to construct these enigmatic heaps were quarried from cliffs almost half a mile away. Early excavations revealed that charred human remains were often found *between* the stone layers. Other stone piles were found in the Mount Carbon area.

On the flatlands at the base of the ridge in front of the wall portion facing the Kanawha River Valley was an extensive burial ground. A late nineteenth-century railway cut across this ground, exposing scores of burials. The bodies were found in sitting position facing the rising sun.

### Contact Person(s)/Organization

Geological and Economic Survey
White Hall/PO Box 879
West Virginia University
Morgantown, West Virginia 26505
(304) 293-0111

### Total Magnetic Field/Inclination Angle

No magnetic aberrations were detected at this ridgetop.

### Further Investigations in Area

Across the Kanawha River from Mount Carbon, in Fayette County, West Virginia, early researchers found a circular earthen enclosure measuring about 430 feet in diameter and 4 feet in height. Rock "etchings" were reported near the riverbank.

On a high mountain facing the river just above Paint Creek, 10 miles below the mouth of Armstrong Creek on the Kanawha River, nineteenth-century archeologists found a wall site almost identical to the Beard's Fork site. A similar burial site was also located at the base of the mountain. The village of Pratt, West Virginia, was built on top of this sacred resting place.

In the late 1920s, hunters discovered a walled-up entrance to a cave on a mountain near Cannelton, West Virginia. Once they breeched the wall they found a cave burial filled with human remains, flint, fabric, and berries.

A number of years ago *Wonderful West Virginia Magazine* published an amazing article on an inscribed rock-shelter wall site that had been known for years. The cave is located near Beards Fork, West Virginia, near the prehistoric wall site. The site is known locally as "Lettered" or "Chiseled" Rocks. Along one stretch of stone are a number of vertical grooves (see illustration below) that until the magazine article puzzled most historians. And then Dr. Barry Fell stepped in. He emphatically claimed that the markings were written in ogam, an ancient European writing system defined by vertical and horizontal slashes.

Reaction was swift. Archeologists in the area asked to see the proof of ancient contact with West Virginia. Where were the habitation sites, the burials, the artifacts? The controversy is still raging. Some researchers think these markings are a tally system of some sort, perhaps to keep track of important hunting events. Whatever they are, the same sort of vertical grooves and slashes are found in many states west of here, including Oklahoma, Colorado, and Utah.

*Close-up of inscribed rock-shelter wall. For years, scholars have wondered about these strange slashes that are found throughout America from New England to Utah. Some researchers believe they are a prehistoric Indian tally-mark system—perhaps for keeping count of some ancient ritual. Others believe the incised grooves are markings of ancient Celtic peoples from western Europe.*

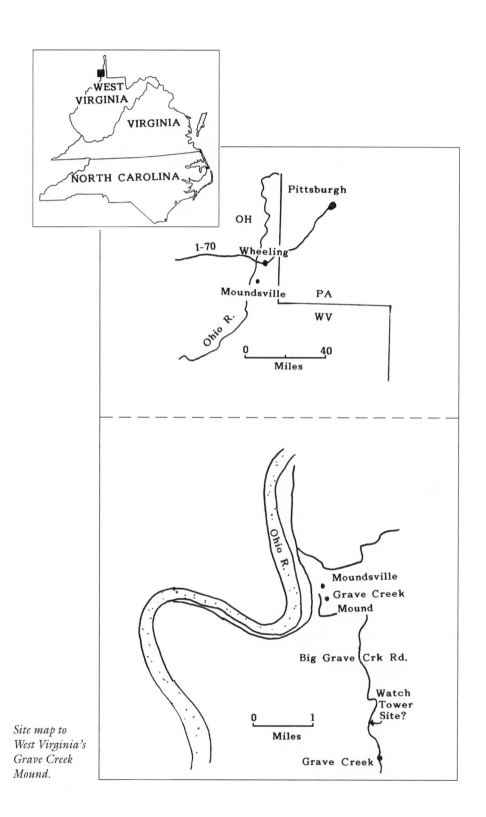

*Site map to
West Virginia's
Grave Creek
Mound.*

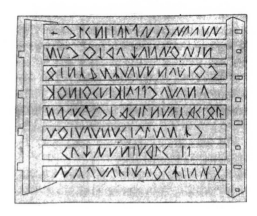

*Metal plate with inscriptions found in the Great Mound at Grave Creek, West Virginia. Some scholars believe these symbols represent an ancient European writing system. This artifact vanished a few years after it was found (Schoolcraft, History of the Indian Tribes of the United States.)*

In 1838 a large burial mound was opened at Grave Creek Mound (Moundsville) in West Virginia. Two of the artifacts—a small stone and a metallic sheet—uncovered near a skeleton were etched with strange inscriptions. (See Illustration above.) Professor Carl Christian Rafn (see Rhode Island's Newport Tower) was convinced the markings were ancient Celt-Iberic writing.

On a nearby hilltop at Parr's Point, Grave Creek Flats, West Virginia, settlers also found the stone ruins of a watchtower. Local Indians were not able to explain its origin.

---

# VIRGINIA

---

One of the first English colonies in the New World was established at Jamestown. The early establishment of this community allowed for a major British presence in the developing country.

Virginia's eastern coastal plain rises into a series of mountain ranges as one heads west. The Great Valley, which is made up of several river valleys, including the Shenandoah, continues on up into New York State.

## NATURAL BRIDGE
Natural Bridge, Virginia

### Site Synopsis
Since the mid 1700s, generations of people have traveled to this arched stone curiosity rising 215 feet above a river to experience the sublime power of nature.

### Location
The Natural Bridge is about 14 miles southwest of Lexington, Virginia. To reach it from Richmond, take Interstate 64 west for about 95 miles to

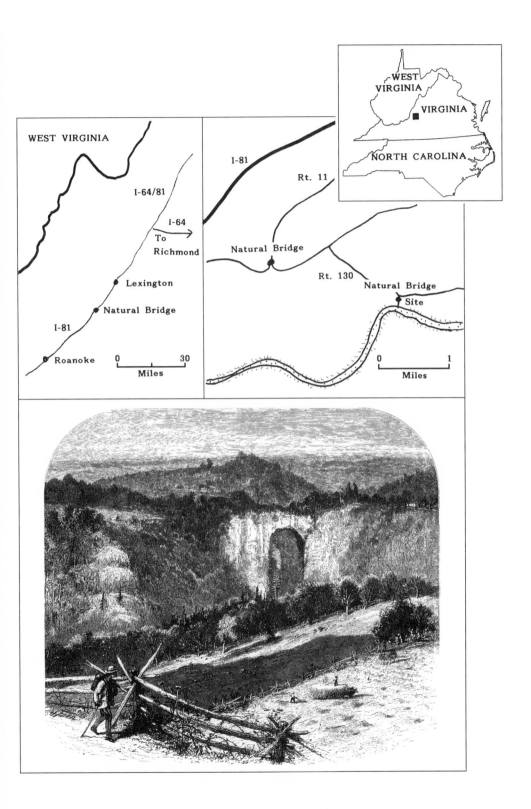

Interstate 64/81. Continue south on I-64/81 for about 45 miles to Natural Bridge, Virginia. Follow the signs to the Natural Bridge.

### Considerations

Regardless of your climbing abilities, do not scale the rock walls here. It is easy to get hurt, and the local authorities frown upon it.

### History/Background

Natural Bridge rises 215 feet above Cedar Creek. The arch is composed of limestone covered with earthy clay, and trees cover its top. The bridge was once described having the proportions of art: It was "constructed" on the very spot where a bridge would have been built.

Most people who look at Natural Bridge ask, "How did that happen?" While not as romantic a notion as a giant poking his foot through the rock, the answer is river erosion, wind, and time. Thousands of years of frost/thaw action combined with the flowing river and storm gales have enlarged and eroded away the weakest parts in the once solid mass of rock. The resulting arch is a geological phenomenon that is pretty common given the right combination of forces.

This site was quite popular among antiquarians and travelers from Europe who, when visiting western Virginia, made the obligatory stop here. Natural Bridge is intriguing because it was one of the first natural arches discovered in early America. As the country moved west, more of these fanciful geological wonders became well known. Natural Bridge, Virginia, nonetheless, is impressive for its span, height, and spectacular setting.

### Contact Person(s)/Organization

Natural Bridge
Natural Bridge, Virginia 24578
(703) 291-2121

Natural Tunnel State Park
11 miles south of Big Stone Gap, Virginia 24219
(703) 940-2674

### Total Magnetic Field/Inclination Angle

No geomagnetic readings were taken here.

### Further Investigations in Area

Early historians wrote of the multitude of Indian Monuments, or piles or small stones located on many mountains in this area, including Salling's, Blue

*Inside the Natural Tunnel, Virginia.* (Picturesque America.)

Ridge, and the North Mountains. White trailblazers noted that they occur at the gaps of mountains where the "Indians were accustomed to cross."[2]

Another geological curiosity is Natural Tunnel at the Natural Tunnel State Park situated upon Stock Creek, about 11 miles south of Big Stone Gap, Virginia. This site is in the southwestern part of the state near the Tennessee border. Over hundreds of thousands of years, a stream carved its way 450 feet through a mountain. No doubt the early natives knew of this place.

Just off Route 3, about 5 miles east of Alberta, Virginia, on a granite outcropping overlooking a small stream, are several carvings. They've been known for close to a hundred years, although the carver of these weird, gridlike symbols is unknown. The petroglyphs are located at the junction of Horse Creek and Trace Branch and necessitate a walk from the main road. Permission must be secured from the current landowner.

---

# NORTH CAROLINA

---

One of the earliest mysteries in this state is still unsolved. In 1587 John White led 121 settlers to Roanoke Island to form an English colony. He went to England for supplies only to return in 1590 to a vanished colony. Not a soul was left. Speculation as to what happened to the settlers has raged for centuries. An early guess was that an Indian tribe killed or carried off the group. If so, why were there no signs of struggle? Famine or disease was another possibility. But where were the bodies? Recently, some have suggested that the entire colony was abducted by space aliens! After four hundred years, we still have no idea what happened to the colonists on Roanoke Island.

Eastern North Carolina was an ancient seabed of sand, gravel, and clay. Today the flat plains greet the spectacular beaches of the Atlantic Ocean. In the west is the Piedmont Plateau, which rises into the Great Smoky Mountains within the Blue Ridge Mountain system.

## HUNTING-GOD ROCK, (JUDACULLA ROCK)
East Laport, North Carolina

### Site Synopsis
At the end of a narrow trail is a 15-foot-long, 10-foot-wide steatite boulder that's etched with dozens of strange markings. The Cherokee Indians who greeted the first white settlers more than two hundred years ago claimed they were carved by Judaculla, the God of the Hunt.

### Location
From Asheville in western North Carolina, take Interstate 40 west for 17 miles, bear left onto Route 23, and continue for another 20 miles to Sylva.

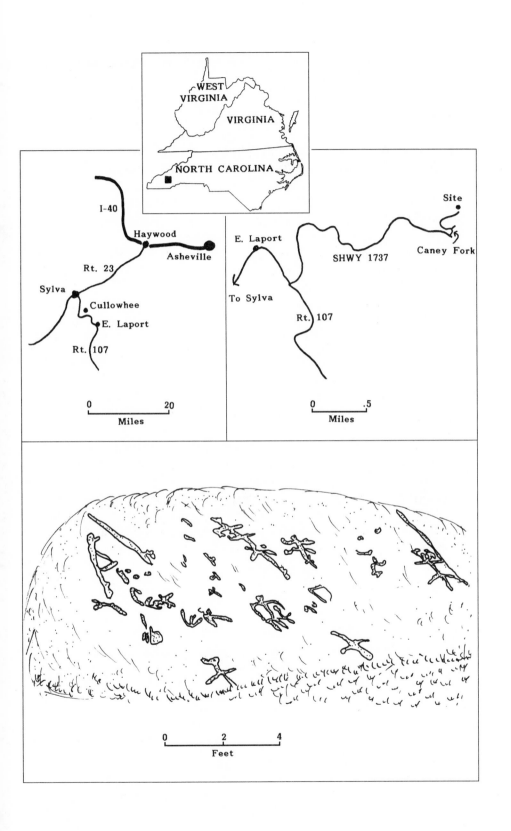

From Sylva take Route 107 south for 7 miles, passing through Cullowhee to East Laport. Turn east onto State Highway 1737 and stay on it almost two miles before turning north onto Caney Fork Road. The road ends at a pasture. On your right is a trail leading down to the site.

### Considerations

This inscribed rock is located under a wooden shelter. It's open all year round.

### History/Background

The Cherokee Indians occupied most of the Carolinas before they were forced west by early white settlers. Before the Cherokee left, they regaled the pioneers with strange stories about their past and about the weird things strewn across mountaintops and valleys.

Within the Caney Fork Valley of western North Carolina, a slant-eyed giant named Judaculla angrily jumped down from a nearby mountain, fuming over someone hunting his lands without permission. He then scratched out a warning on a large boulder. That is the Cherokee explanation of the mysterious rock.

No one really knows anything about these symbols. While they bear some similarity to markings found elsewhere in the valley, those symbols remain unexplained as well. Over the years, various scholars have tried to interpret the stone. Some claimed they were made by the Cherokee, denoting the site as a sacred place. Others believed the symbols represent an earlier aboriginal culture that inhabited the valley over 5,000 years ago. And still others said the markings were the result of a pre-Columbian exploration by ancient Europeans.

The bottom line is that we don't know. My instruments picked up nothing unusual about this place. The meaning of this site and the markings vanished with the people who carved them at some time in the dim past.

### Contact Person(s)/Organization

Western Carolina University
Mountain Heritage Center/Administration Building
Cullowhee, North Carolina 28723
(704) 227-7129
(704) 227-7211

Jackson County Chamber of Commerce
PO Box 245
Sylva, North Carolina 28779
(704) 586-2155
(704) 586-2336

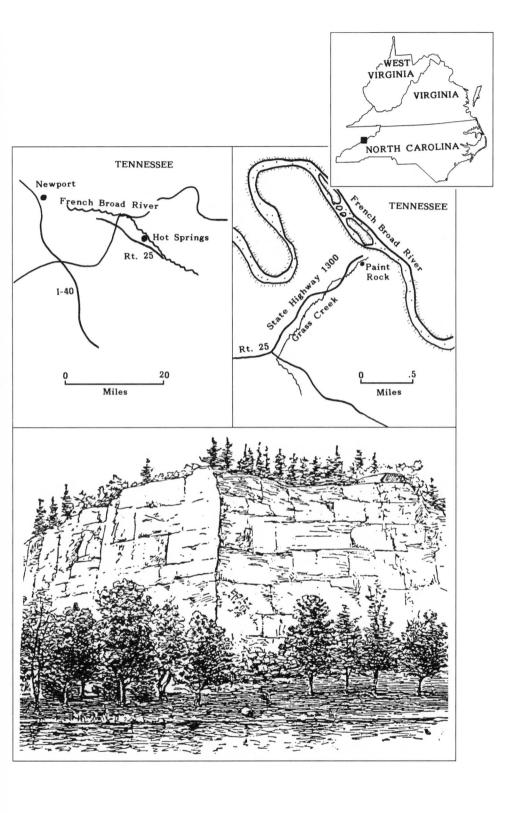

*Ancient stone-pile burials found near Patterson, North Carolina. A team from the Smithsonian Institute excavated these tombs in the late 1880s* (12th Annual Report).

### Total Magnetic Field/Inclination Angle

No magnetic anomalies were detected here.

### Further Investigations in Area

Details about other curious, more traditional archeological sites in the state can be found at:

The Archeology Branch
Division of Archives and History
109 E. Jones Street
Raleigh, North Carolina 27611
(919) 733-7305

About 60 miles northeast of East Laport is a colored-petroglyph site that was first reported in the literature in 1886. Known locally as Paint Rock, the site is situated on the east bank of the French Broad River near the North Carolina/Tennessee border. Partway up the rock face of a 100-foot limestone cliff is a series of painted short, straight lines. White families who settled this region in the early 1800s could not learn anything from the local Cherokee

Indians who still inhabited the area. No one knew anything about these weird, angular symbols. Today we still have no idea who put them there or for what purpose, although their prominent position on the cliff face next to a waterway suggests a sign or message of some sort.

In the 1890s, about two miles southeast of Patterson, North Carolina, on the farm of the Reverend T. F. Nelson, a team from the Smithsonian Institution excavated an earthen mound and uncovered the unexpected. They found ten stone piles and six skeletons at the base of this 38-foot-diameter mound. (See illustration on page 302.) The beehive-shaped piles of stone were built *around* the bodies of Indians. Many of the stones had been burned.

Clearly, the western part of North Carolina was home to many ancient tribes who worked in mysterious ways.

# THIRTEEN

# Mysterious Finale

The results of the search for strange and unusual sites of the East took a long time to compile. Many miles were covered hiking up and down mountains, valleys, and coastal waterways investigating rumors, heresay, and centuries-old documents. Untold hours were spent chatting with archeologists, farmers, sailors, and plenty of other people. But the most precious times, the best moments, were those at the end of a trail—when a ruin finally came into view. Those magical moments of discovery always left me pulsating with energy, regardless of the mosquitoes, the heat, and exhausted laptop computer batteries.

Throughout this book I have alluded to mysterious peoples who constructed some of the strange tunnels, chambers, stone piles, and the like. The Native American tribes that met the Spanish, the Dutch, and the English were relative newcomers to the land. They were following an ancient practice of movement dictated, most likely, by ecological overuse of a region. These early groups moved on to "virgin" territory that had been abandoned by earlier groups centuries, if not thousands, of years, before.

The oral legends of the Native Americans speak loudly of such ancient ones. The archeology of the twentieth century has confirmed this to some extent—many of the mound embankments of the Ohio River Valley indeed were abandoned many years before white settlers and the Native Americans met by these settlers moved into the region. And there were probably *earlier* groups of people who passed through in search of food, shelter, and life's mysteries.

Unfortunately, there is no continuous record of the earliest archaic hunters from 12,000 years ago to the 1600s. We know very little about their sense of place in the world and nothing about their relationship with the forest, the animals they hunted, the stones they piled. But this is nothing new. We've never devoted enough resources to investigating our past. America is a country that looks to the future.

The words of the nineteenth-century American archeologist Warren K. Moorehead speak to our neglectful attitude toward ruins in this country:

> The English people take a sort of national pride in the protection of [their] ancient remains. . . . These peoples are concerned for the safety of all that links them with ancient civilizations; they do not believe in snapping the bonds which bind together successive generations. . . . We Americans do. Not content with having almost entirely extermi-nated the natives of this continent; unsatisfied with the tremendous fact that we have violated covenant engagements and treaty pledges with the Indians a hundred times over, we seem to be intent on eras-ing the last vestige of aboriginal occupation of our land.[1]

And so the meaning of these ruins has been lost. Perhaps we will never fully understand their purpose.

This second book on mysterious places is part of a continuing series dedi-cated to finding, examining, measuring, and reporting on peculiar spots that will force you to reconsider some long-held beliefs. The intent has been to see our world in a fresh, new, exciting way. There are many strange places on the planet that defy explanation. Stay tuned for more reports about the unusual, the weird, and how to get there!

# Notes

## Introduction

1. Winifred Gallagher, *The Power of Place* (New York: HarperPerennial, 1994), p. 83.
2. Ibid., pp. 84–85.
3. Robert Becker and Gary Selden, *The Body Electric* (New York: William Morrow, 1985), p. 249.
4. Jiri Malek, J. Gleich, and V. Maly, "Characteristics of the Daily Rhythm of Menstruation and Labor," *Annals of the New York Academy of Sciences 98* (1962), p. 1042.
5. Gay Luce, ed., *Biological Rhythms in Psychiatry and Medicine* (Washington, D.C.: United States Government Printing Office, 1970), p. 14.
6. Howard Friedman, Robert O. Becker, and Charles H. Bachman, "Geomagnetic Parameters and Psychiatric Hospital Admissions," *Nature* 200 (1963), p. 626.
7. Ibid, pp. 626–628.
8. Howard Friedman and Robert O. Becker, "Psychiatric Ward Behavior and Geophysical Parameters," *Nature* 205 (1965), pp. 1050–1052.
9. Ibid, p. 253.
10. Ibid, p. 255.
11. Gallagher, *The Power of Place*, p. 83.

## 2. Mysterious Places: Overview

1. Total magnetic field (TMF) can be calculated by the following formula:

$$TMF = \sqrt{H^2 + V^2}$$

where $H$ = horizontal vector
and $V$ = vertical vector
Inclination Angle (IA) = Arctan (V/H)

2. James Adair, *History of the American Indians* (London, 1775). Reprint edited by Samuel Cole Williams (New York: Promontory Press, 1930), p. 194.

3. Dennis N. Bertland, Patricia M. Valence, and Russel J. Woodling, *The Minisink* (Monroe and Pike Counties, PA.; Sussex and Warren Counties, N.J.: Four County Task force on the Tocks-Island Dam Project, March, 1975), pp. 67–68.

4. Cornelia Horsford, *An Inscribed Stone* (Cambridge, MA: Private Printing, 1895), p. 6.

## 3.  Nova Scotia/Quebec/Ontario

1. K. G. T. Webster, "The Fletcher Stone," *Transactions of the Nova Scotia Institute of Science*, Vol. 17 (January 11, 1892), p. 209.

2. Robert B. Blauveldt, "America's First White Settlement," *Maclean's Magazine* (March 1, 1935), p. 24.

3. Marion Robertson, *Rock Drawings of the Mismac Indians* (Halifax, Nova Scotia: The Nova Scotia Museum, 1973).

4. Staneley T. Spicer, *Glooscap Legends* (Hantsport, Nova Scotia: Lancelot Press, 1994), p. 9.

5. Frederick Pohl, *Prince Henry Sinclair* (New York: Clarkson N. Potter, 1974).

6. Michael Bradley, *Holy Grail Across the Atlantic* (Willowdale, Ontario: Hounslow Press, 1993), p. 137.

7. Ibid., p. 154.

## 4.  Maine

1. John Wesley Powell, *Tenth Annual Report of the Bureau of Ethnology to the Secretary of the Smithsonian Institution*, 1888–1889 (Washington, DC: Government Printing Office, 1893), p. 82.

2. Ibid., p. 83.

3. John R. Wiggins, "Archaeological Riddle," *The Ellsworth American* (August 3, 1989): 1, 3.

4. "Did the Vikings Arrive First?" *Time* (December 11, 1978): 72.

## 5.  New Hampshire/Vermont

1, Junius Bird, "Excavation Report: North Salem, New Hampshire," *Early Sites Research Society Work Report* 3, no. 27 (1997).

2. Ibid.

3. E. G. Squier, "Aboriginal Monuments of the State of New York," *Smithsonian Contributions to Knowledge*, Vol. 2 (1849), p. 89.

4. Ibid., pp. 87–88.

5. James P. Whittall, "Roman Coins Found in New England," *Bulletin of the Early Sites Research Society,* Vol. 11, No. 1. (December, 1984), pp. 53–54.

## 6. Massachusetts

1. The following elements were detected in very high amounts and in the same proportions in the red paint: aluminum, iron, silicon, and sodium. The specimen list was as follows:

| | |
|---|---|
| Morrill's Point, Salisbury, MA | 6,290 years BP (before the present) |
| Wapanochet, Middleboro, MA | 5,000 year BP |
| Mansion Inn, Wayland, MA | 4,000 years BP |
| Atlantic Point, Nova Scotia | 2,000 years BP |
| Moorehead Complex, Eddington Bend, ME | 4,000 years BP |
| Cremation burial, Eagle Bridge, NY | 4,000 years BP |
| Cremation burial, red soil, Eagle Bridge, NY | 4,000 years BP |
| Cremation burial, brown soil, Eagle Bridge, NY | 4,000 years BP |

2. Robert Ellis Cahill, *New England's Ancient Mysteries* (Salem, MA: Old Saltbox Publishing House, 1993), p. 3.
3. ———, *The Horror of Salem's Witch Dungeon* (Peabody, MA: Chandler-Smith Publishing House, 1986), p. 47.
4. Ibid., p. 45.
5. Donald Blake Johnson, *Upton's Heritage* (Canaan, NH: Phoenix Publishing, 1984), pp. 41–43.
6. Pratt Pond, Jr. (Daniel Fiske), "Upton Traditions: A Deserted Haunt of Unknown Origin." Carbon of original manuscript dated April 20, 1893. First published: *Milford Journal.* (April 26, 1893), pp. 1–3.
7. James P. Whittall, "A Report on the Pearson Stone Chamber, Upton, Massachusetts," *Bulletin of the Early Sites Research Society,* Vol. 1, No. 2 (1973), pp. 35–38.
8. Pond, p. 1.
9. Barry Fell, *America BC* (New York: Quadrangle, 1976), p. 91.
10. Quoted in David W. Crocket, Archaeological Anomalies (Decorah, IA: Anundsen Publishing Company, 1994), pp. 111–12.
11. James Mavor, Jr. and Byron E. Dix, "New England Stone Mounds as Ritual Architecture," *Bulletin of the Early Sites Research Society* Vol. 10, No. 2 (December 1983), p. 10.
12. Ibid.

## 7. Rhode Island

1. James P. Whittall II, *Ground Penetrating Radar Survey: Newport Tower Site, Touro Park, Newport, Rhode Island* (Rowley, MA: Early Sites Research Society, 1994), p. 3.
2. Philip Ainsworth Means, *Newport Tower* (New York: Henry Holt and Company, 1942).

3. Robert Ellis Cahill, *New England's Ancient Mysteries* (Salem, MA: Old Saltbox Publishing House, 1993), p. 86.

## 8. Connecticut

1. James P. Whittall II, "The Quinebaug River 'Tholos' Chamber Site," *Early Sites Research Society Bulletin,* Vol. 18, No. 1 (October 1991): pp. 3–5.
2. Quoted in James P. Whittall II, "The Gungywamp Complex, Groton, Connecticut," *Early Sites Research Society Bulletin,* Vol. 4, No. 1 (May 1976), p. 18.

## 9. New York

1. John Finch, "On the Celtic Antiquities of America," *American Journal of Science* 7 (1824).
2. Ibid.
3. Quoted in John Wesley Powell, *Twelfth Annual Report of the Bureau of Ethnology to the Secretary of the Smithsonian Institution* (Washington, DC: Government Printing Office, 1894), p. 691.
4. Finch, "On the Celtic Antiquities of America."
5. Thomas Gregg, *The Prophet of Palmyra Mormonism* (New York: John H. Alden, 1890), pp. 19–20.
6. Ibid., p. 14.
7. Ibid. p. 23.
8. Henry Rowe Schoolcraft, *History of the Indian Tribes of the United States* (Philadelphia: J. B. Lippincott, 1857), p. 666.

## 10. Pennsylvania/New Jersey

1. Donald A. Cadzow, "Petroglyphs (Rock Carvings) in the Susquehanna River near Safe Harbor, Pennsylvania," *Safe Harbor Report* No. 1, Volume III. (Harrisburg, Pennsylvania: Pennsylvania Historical Commission, 1934), p. 18.
2. Ibid., p. 45.

## 12. West Virginia/Virginia/North Carolina

1. J. T. Peters and H. B. Carden, *History of Fayette County, West Virginia* (Charleston, WV: Fayette County Historical Society, 1926), pp. 14–15.
2. Henry Howe, *Historical Collections of Virginia* (Charleston, SC: Babcock, 1845), p. 456.

## 13. Mysterious Finale

1. Warren K. Moorehead, *Fort Ancient* (Cincinnati, OH: Robert Clarke & Co., 1890), p. 107.

# Bibliography

Adair, James. *History of the American Indians*. London, 1775. Reprint edited by Samuel Cole Williams. New York: Promontory Press, 1930.

Aristotle. *Minor Works*. Edited by W. S. Hett. Cambridge: Harvard University Press, 1955.

Baldwin, James D. *Ancient America in Notes on American Archaeology*. New York: Harper and Bros., 1872.

Barber, John, and Henry Howe. *Historical Collections of the State of New York*. New York: S. Tuttle, 1842.

Baring-Gould, S. *The Deserts of Southern France*. New York: Dodd, Mead and Company, 1894.

Barron, David P., and Sharon Mason. *The Greater Gungywamp: A Guidebook*. Noank, Connecticut: The Gungywamp Society, 1994.

Beck, Lewis C. *Natural History of New York. Mineralogy of New York,* Vol. 3. Albany: W. A. White and J. Visscher, 1842.

Becker, R. O., and Gary Selden. *The Body Electric*. New York: William Morrow, 1985.

Bertland, Dennis N., Patricia M. Valence, and Russell J. Woodling. *The Minisink*. Monroe and Pike Counties, Pa.; Sussex and Warren Counties, N.J.: Four County Task Force on the Tocks-Island Dam Project, March, 1975.

Bird, Junius. "Excavation Report: North Salem, New Hampshire," *Early Sites Research Society Work Report* 3, no. 27 (1977).

Blauveldt, Robert B. "America's First White Settlement." *Maclean's Magazine* (March 1, 1935): 24, 41.

Boyle, David. "Mounds." *Annual Archeological Report*. Ontario: Royal Ontario Museum, pp. 14–57.

Bradley, Michael. *Holy Grail Across the Atlantic*. Willowdale, Ontario, Canada: Hounslow Press, 1993.

Brown, Robert, ed. *Science for All,* Vol 1–5. London: Cassell, Petter, Galpin & Co., n.d. (possibly late 1870s, 1878, or 1879).

Bryant, William Cullen, ed. *Picturesque America,* Volumes I & II. New York: D. Appleton and Company, 1874.

Butler, Eva L. "The Brush or Stone Heaps of Southern New England." *Archaeological Society of Connecticut Bulletin,* no. 19 (1946): 2–12.

Cadzow, Donald A. "Petroglyphs (Rock Carvings) in the Susquehanna River near Safe Harbor, Pennsylvania." *Safe Harbor Report* No. 1, Volume III. Harrisburg, Pennsylvania: Pennsylvania Historical Commission, 1934.

Cahill, Robert Ellis. *The Horrors of Salem's Witch Dungeon.* Peabody, Massachusetts: Chandler-Smith Publishing House, 1986.

———. *New England's Ancient Mysteries.* Salem, Massachusetts: Old Saltbox Publishing House, 1993.

"The Cardiff Giant." *Harper's Weekly* (December 4, 1869): 776.

*Chamber's Encyclopedia.* Philadelphia: J. B. Lippincott and Company, 1867.

Coffin, Charles Carleton. *Old Times in the Colonies.* New York: Harper and Brothers, 1880.

Crocket, W. David. *Archaeological Anomalies.* Decorah, IA: Anundsen Publishing Company, 1994.

Crooker, William S. *Oak Island Gold.* Halifax, Nova Scotia: Nimbus Publishing Ltd., 1993.

Dana, Henry Swan. *History of Woodstock, Vermont.* Boston: Houghton Mifflin, 1889.

Dana, James D. *The Geological Story.* New York: Ivison, Blakeman, Taylor and Company, 1875.

De Nadaillac, Marquis. *Manners and Monuments of Prehistoric Peoples.* New York: G. P. Putnam's Sons, 1892.

———. *Pre-Historic America.* New York: G. P. Putnam's Sons, 1901.

"Did the Vikings Arrive First?" *Time* (December 11, 1978): 72.

Diodorus of Sicily. *Library of History.* Vol 3. Edited by C. H. Oldfather. Cambridge: Harvard University Press, 1952.

Du Chaillu, Paul B. *The Viking Age.* New York: Charles Scribner's Sons, 1889.

Erdman, David V., ed. *The Poetry and Prose of William Blake.* Garden City, N.Y.: Doubleday & Co., 1970.

Fairbanks, Edward T. *The Town of St. Johnsbury, Vermont.* St. Johnsbury, Vermont: The Cowles Press, 1914.

Fell, Barry. *America BC.* New York: Quadrangle, 1976.

Fenn, Waldemar. *Grafica Prehistorica de Espana y El Origen de la Cultura Europea.* Menorca: M. Sintes Rotger, 1950.

Fergusson, James. *Rude Stone Monuments.* London: John Murray, 1872.

Finch, John. "On the Celtic Antiquities of America." *American Journal of Science* 7 (1824): 149–161.

Fleming, Stewart. *Authenticity in Art.* New York: Crane, Russack and Company, 1975.

Fowke, Gerard. "Antiquities of Central and Southeastern Missouri," *Smithsonian Institution Bureau of American Ethnology, Bulletin 37.* Washington: Government Printing Office, 1910.

Friedman, Howard, and Robert O. Becker. "Psychiatric Ward Behavior and Geophysical Parameters." *Nature,* 205 (1965): 1050–1052.

Friedman, Howard, Robert O. Becker, and Charles H. Bachman. "Effect of Magnetic Fields on Reaction Time Performance." *Nature,* 213 (1967): 949–950.

———. "Geomagnetic Parameters and Psychiatric Hospital Admissions." *Nature,* 200 (1963): 626–628.

Galante, Anna-Maria. "Stone's Markings Spur Theories of Ancient Irish Visit," *The Chronicle-Herald and the Mail-Star,* Halifax, Nova Scotia (January 24, 1992).

Gallagher, Winifred. *The Power of Place.* New York: HarperPerennial, 1994.

Geller, L. D. *Sea Serpents of Coastal New England.* Plymouth, Massachusetts: Cape Cod Publications, 1992.

Glanvill, Joseph. *Saducismus Triumphatus: or, a Full and Plain Evidence, Concerning Witches and Apparitions.* London, 1681.

Glynn, Frank. "The Effigy Mound, A Covered Cairn Burial Site." *NEARA Journal* 4, no. 4 (December 1969): 75–79.

———. "Excavation of the Pilot Point Stone Heaps." *The Archaeological Society of Connecticut Bulletin* no. 38 (August 1973): 77–89.

Godfrey, Leland H. "The Goshen Stone Mystery." *Yankee Magazine* 35, no. 11 (November 1971): 218–223.

Goodwin, William B. *The Remains of Greater Ireland in New England.* Boston: Meader, 1946.

Gordon, Cyrus H. *Before Columbus: Links Between the Old World and Ancient America.* New York: Crown, 1971.

Gramly, Richard Michael. "Witchcraft Pictographs from Near Salem, Massachusetts." *Historical Archaeology,* vol. 15, no. 1 (1981): 113–116.

Green, Eugene, and William Sachse. *Names of the Land.* Chester, Connecticut: The Globe Pequot Press, 1983.

Gregg, Thomas. *The Prophet of Palmyra Mormonism.* New York: John H. Alden, 1890.

Hansen, Chadwick. *Witchcraft at Salem.* New York: New American Library, 1969.

*Harper's New Monthly Magazine,* Volume 54. (December, 1876–May, 1877). New York: Harper & Brothers, 1877.

*Harper's New Monthly Magazine,* Volume 63. (June–November, 1881). New York: Harper & Brothers, 1881.

*Harper's New Monthly Magazine,* Volume 65. (June–November, 1882). New York: Harper & Brothers, 1882.

Hayden, Dorothy L. "The Lost City." *Institute Newsletter,* nos. 11, 12 (November–December, 1989): 7–15.

Herodotus. *History,* Vol. 4. Translated by A. D. Godley. Cambridge: Harvard University Press, 1963.

Hertzberg, Ruth, Beatrice Vaughan, and Janet Greene. *Putting Food By.* Brattleboro, Vt.: Stephen Greene Press, 1974.

Higginson, Thomas Wentworth. "The Visit of the Vikings." Originally in *Harper's New Monthly Magazine,* no. 388, vol. 65. (September, 1882): 515–527.

Hines, Donald M. *Magic in the Mountains, The Yakima Shaman: Power and Practice.* Issaquah, Washington: Great Eagle Publishing, 1993.

Horsford, Cornelia. *An Inscribed Stone.* Cambridge, Mass.: private printing, 1895.

Howe, Henry. *Historical Collections of Virginia.* Charleston, South Carolina: Babcock, 1845.

————. *Ohio: Its History and Antiquities.* Cincinnati, Ohio: Derby, Bradley & Co., 1847.

Humphrey, Robert L., and Mary Elizabeth Chambers. *Ancient Washington,* No. 6. Washington, DC: George Washington Studies, n.d.

Hynek, J. Allen, Philip J. Imbrogno, and Bob Pratt. *Night Siege: The Hudson Valley UFO Sightings.* New York: Ballantine Books, 1987.

Johnson, Donald Blake. *Upton's Heritage.* Canaan, New Hampshire: Phoenix Publishing, 1984.

Johnson, Richard B. "The Archeology of the Serpent Mounds Site." *Ontario Art and Archeology Occasional Paper* 10 (1968). Ontario: Royal Ontario Museum.

Joseph, Frank. *The Lost Pyramids of Rock Lake.* St. Paul, Minnesota: Galde Press, 1992.

Leslie, Vernon. *Faces in Clay.* Middletown, New York: T. E. Henderson, 1973.

*Lief Eriksen Drive.* Document Number YMS 13 F27, Yarmouth, Nova Scotia: Yarmouth County Historical Museum, n.d.

Lossing, Benson J. *The Hudson: From the Wilderness to the Sea.* New York: Virtue and Yorston, 1866.

Luce, Gay G., ed. *Biological Rhythms in Psychiatry and Medicine* (Public Health Service Publication #2088). Washington, D.C.: United States Government Printing Office, 1970.

Madariaga, Salvador de. *Christopher Columbus: Being the Life of the Very Magnificent Lord, Don Cristobal Colon.* New York: Ungar, 1967.

Malek, Jiri', J. Gleich and V. Maly. "Characteristics of the Daily Rhythm of Menstruation and Labor." *Annals of the New York Academy of Sciences.* 98 (1962): 1042–1055.

Mallery, Garrick. *Picture-Writing of the American Indians.* 2 vols. Reprint. New York: Dover, 1972.

Mason, Otis T. "The Archeology of the Potomac Tide-Water Region." *Proceedings of the United States National Museum,* Vol. XII. Washington, DC: Smithsonian Institution, United States National Museum, 1889.

Mavor, James J., and Byron E. Dix. "New England Stone Mounds as Ritual Architecture." *Early Sites Research Society Bulletin,* vol. 10, no. 2 (December 1983): 2–11.

Means, Philip Ainsworth. *Newport Tower.* New York; Henry Holt and Company, 1942.

*Memory: A Souvenir.* New York: Leavitt and Allen, 1854.

Mertz, Henriette. *Atlantis: Dwelling Place of the Gods.* Chicago: Private printing, 1976.

————. *The Wine Dark Sea.* Chicago: Private printing, 1964.

"A Monstrous Sea Serpent," *Salem Gazette* (August 1817).

Montelius, Oscar. *The Civilization of Sweden in Heathen Times.* London: Macmillan and Company, 1888.

Moorehead, Warren K. *Fort Ancient.* Cincinnati, Ohio: Robert Clarke & Co., 1890.

Morison, Samuel Eliot. *Admiral of the Ocean Sea: A Life of Christopher Columbus.* Vol. 1. Boston: Oxford University Press, 1942.

————. *Christopher Columbus, Mariner.* New York: Mentor Books, 1956.

"New Radiocarbon Dating Indicates an Even Greater Antiquity for North Salem Megalithic Site." *NEARA Newsletter* 6, no. 2 (June 1971): 40.

*Oak Island Special Bi-Centennial, 1795–1995 Edition*. Private Printing, Oak Island, Nova Scotia: Oak Island Tours, Inc., 1995.

Olson, Julius E., and Edward Gaylord Bourne, eds. *The Northern, Columbus and Cabot, Nine Eighty Five to Fifteen Three*. 1906. Reprint, New York: Barnes and Noble, 1959.

"Operation Bull Moose," *Early Sites Research Society Newsletter*. Rowley, Massachusetts: Early Sites Research Society (September, 1984).

Peet, Stephen D. *Ancient Monuments and Ruined Cities*. Chicago: Office of the American Antiquarian, 1904.

———. *The Mound Builders*. Chicago: Office of the American Antiquarian, 1892.

Peet, T. Eric. *Rough Stone Monuments and Their Builders*. London: Harper & Brothers, 1912.

Perryman, Margaret. "Sculptured Monoliths of Georgia." *Tennessee Archaeologist*. Vol. XVII, No. 1 (Spring 1961): 1–9.

Peters, J. T., and H. B. Carden. *History of Fayette County, West Virginia*. Charleston, West Virginia: Fayette County Historical Society, 1926.

Phelan, Nick. "Stone Tower Myth Crumbles." *The Newport (RI) Daily News* (September 23, 1993): A1 + A10.

Phillips, Henry. "On a Supposed Runic Inscription at Yarmouth, Nova Scotia," *Proceedings of the American Philosophical Society* (May 2, 1884).

Phillips, William A. "See-Quo-Yah." *Harper's New Monthly Magazine,* no. 244, vol. 41: 542–548. n.d.

Plato. *Dialogues*. Translated by H. Rackham. Cambridge: Harvard University Press, 1938–63.

*Plutarch's Moralia*. Vol. 10. Translated by Harold North Fowler. Cambridge: Harvard University Press, 1960.

Pohl, Frederick. *Prince Henry Sinclair*. New York: Clarkson N. Potter, 1974.

Pond, Pratt Jr. (Daniel Fiske). "Upton Traditions: A Deserted Haunt of Unknown Origin," Typescript copy of original manuscript dated April 20, 1893. First published: *Milford Journal* (April 26, 1893).

Powell, John Wesley. *Fifth Annual Report of the Bureau of Ethnology to the Secretary of the Smithsonian Institution*. Washington, DC: Government Printing Office, 1880.

———. *Tenth Annual Report of the Bureau of Ethnology to the Secretary of the Smithsonian Institution, 1888–1889*. Washington, DC: Government Printing Office, 1893.

———. *Twelfth Annual Report of the Bureau of Ethnology to the Secretary of the Smithsonian Institution*. Washington, DC: Government Printing Office, 1894.

Rafn, Carl Christian. *Antiquitates Americanae*. Hafniae: Typis Officinae Schultzianae, 1837.

Robertson, Marion. *Rock Drawings of the Micmac Indians*. Halifax, Nova Scotia: The Nova Scotia Museum, 1973.

Ruttenber, E. M., and L. H. Clark. *History of Orange County, New York*. Philadelphia: Everts and Peck, 1881.

*Scribner's Monthly*. Vol. IX. (November 1874–April 1875). New York: Scribner & Company, 1875.

Schiller, A. Arthur. *Ten Coptic Legal Texts*. New York: Metropolitan Museum of Art, 1932.

Schoolcraft, Henry Rowe. *History of the Indian Tribes of the United States*. Philadelphia: J. B. Lippincott, 1857.

Smith, Philip H. *Legends of the Shawangunk*. Pawling, New York: Smith and Company, 1877.

Sodders, Betty. *Michigan Prehistory Mysteries*. Marquette, Michigan: Avery Color Studios, 1990.

Spicer, Stanley T. *Glooscap Legends*. Hantsport, Nova Scotia, Canada: Lancelot Press, 1994.

Squier, E. G. "Aboriginal Monuments of the State of New York." *Smithsonian Contributions to Knowledge*, Vol. 2. 1849.

Squier, E. G., and E. H. Davis. "Ancient Monuments of the Mississippi Valley." *Smithsonian Contributions to Knowledge*. Vol. 1, No. 1, 1848.

Stapler, W. Mead. "A Pre-Colonial Wall in Manhattan?" *NEARA Newsletter* 9, no. 2 (Summer 1974): 40.

Stewart, Henry. *The Shepherd's Manual*. New York: Orange Judd Company, 1879.

Stiles, Ezra. *Extracts from the Itineraries and Other Miscellanies of Ezra Stiles. 1755–1794, with a Selection from His Correspondence*. New Haven: Yale University Press, 1916.

Stone, Robert E. "The Mechanicsburg Stones—Two Distinct Types." *NEARA Newsletter 5, no. 3* (September 1970): 53.

Stone, William L. *Life of Joseph Brant-Thayendanega*. New York: Alexander Blake, 1838.

Strandwold, Olaf. Document No. F21 YMS13 (Photo of original site of Yarmouth Stone). Yarmouth, Nova Scotia: Yarmouth County Historical Museum, October, 1934.

Swan, Marshall W. S. "The Bedevilment of Cape Ann (1692)." *Essex Institute Historical Collections*, vol. 117, no. 3 (July 1981): 153–177.

Tacitus. *Dialogs, Agricola, and Germania*. Translated by W. Hamilton Fyfe. New York: Oxford University Press, 1908.

Tarbell, Arthur Wilson. *Cape Cod Ahoy!* Boston: A. T. Ramsay & Company, 1932.

Thucydides. *History of the Peloponnesian War*. Edited by Benjamin Jowett. New York: Oxford University Press, 1900.

Tuck, James A., and Robert J. McGhee. "An Archaic Indian Burial Mound." *Scientific American* 235, no. 5 (November 1976): 121–129.

Twain, Mark. *The Innocents Abroad*. Hartford, Connecticut: American Publishing Company, 1873.

United States Department of Agriculture. "Home Freezers, Their Selection and Use." *Home and Garden Bulletin* No. 48. Washington, DC: Government Printing Office, 1973.

———. "Storing Vegetables and Fruits in Basements, Cellars, Outbuildings and Pits." *Home and Garden Bulletin* No. 48. Washington, DC: Government Printing Office, 1973.

Vastokas, Joan and Ron. *Sacred Art of the Algonkians.* Peterborough, Ontario: Mansard Press, 1973.

Vega, Garcilaso de la. *The Florida of the Inca.* Edited by John Varner and Jeanette Varner. Austin: University of Texas Press, 1951.

Vermont History. *The Proceedings of the Vermont Historical Society,* vol. 47, no. 2 (Spring 1979): 73–168.

Walters, George R. *Early Man in Orange County, New York.* Middletown, New York: The Historical Society of Middletown and the Wallkill Precinct, 1973.

Webster, K. G. T. "The Fletcher Stone." *Transactions of the Nova Scotia Institute of Science,* Vol. 17, Nova Scotia Historical Society Collections (January 11, 1892): 208–214.

Whittall, James P. II. "An Inscribed Stone from Comassakumkanit (Bourne Stone)." *Occasional Publications of the Epigraphic Society 2,* no. 44 (May 1975): 1–3.

———. "Copper Tin Projectile, Monhegan, Maine." *Early Sites Research Society Bulletin 5,* no. 1 (February 1977): 7–9.

———. *Ground Penetrating Radar Survey: Newport Tower Site, Touro Park, Newport, Rhode Island.* Rowley, Massachusetts: Early Sites Research Society, 1994.

———. "The Gungswamp Complex, Groton, Connecticut," *Early Sites Research Society Bulletin,* 4, no. 1 (May 1976): 15–27.

———. "A Report on the Pearson Stone Chamber, Upton, Massachusetts." *Early Sites Research Society Bulletin,* vol. 1, no. 1 (1973).

———. "Roman Coins Found in New England." *Bulletin of the Early Sites Research Society,* no. 1 (December 1984): 53–54.

Wiggins, John R. "Archaeological Riddle," *The Ellsworth American.* Ellsworth, Maine (August 3, 1989): 1, 3.

Wilson, Daniel. *Prehistoric Annals of Scotland.* 2 vols. London: Macmillan, 1863.

Wilson, Ian. *The Columbus Myth.* New York: Simon & Schuster, 1991.

Yaggy, L. W., and T. L. Haines. *Museum of Antiquity.* New York: Standard Publishing House, 1882.

Zarzynski, Joseph W. *Champ: Beyond the Legend.* Wilton, New York: M–Z Information, 1988.

# Index